D0962102

SONIC
BOOM

SONIC BOOM

The History of Northwest Rock, from "Louie Louie" to "Smells Like Teen Spirit"

Peter Blecha

Backbeat
Books

An Imprint of Hal Leonard Corporation
New York

Published in 2009 by Backbeat Books
An Imprint of Hal Leonard Corporation
7777 West Bluemound Road
Milwaukee, WI 53213

Trade Book Division Editorial Offices
19 West 21st Street, New York, NY 10010

Printed in the United States of America

All memorabilia and photos in this book are from the author's collection unless otherwise noted.

Book design by Publishers' Design and Production Services, Inc.

Library of Congress Cataloging-in-Publication Data
Blecha, Peter.
    Sonic boom the history of Northwest rock, from "Louie Louie" to "Smells like teen spirit" / by Peter Blecha.
        p. cm.
    ISBN 978-0-87930-946-6 (pbk.)
    1. Rock music—Northwest, Pacific—History and criticism.   I. Title.
ML3534.3.B54 2009
781.6609795—dc22

                                                            2008051529

www.backbeatbooks.com

To my lovely girlfriend-turned-wife, Kate

Contents

Contents

Get Lost!

The Fabulous Wailers. The Ventures. The Sonics. The Kingsmen. Paul Revere and the Raiders. Little Bill and the Bluenotes. The Frantics. Sherree Scott and Her Melody Rockers. Clayton Watson and the Silhouettes. The Playboys. The Regents. The M-G Trio. Joe Boot and the Fabulous Winds. The Amazing Aztecs. The Teen Kings. The Velvetones. Bobby Wayne and the Warriors. Leon Smith. Vinny's Rhythmaires. Jim Valley and the Chain Gang. The Dynamics. Don and the Goodtimes. George Washington and the Cherry Bombs. The Viceroys. The Versatiles. Mr. Lucky and the Gamblers. The Rocking Kings. Paul Bearer and the Hearsemen. The Beachcombers. The El Caminos. The Chambermen. The Counts. The Agents. The Swags. Thomas and His Tomcats. The Boss Five. The Continentals. Mr. Clean and the Cleansers. The Imperials. The Checkers. The Downbeats. The Casuals. The Titans. The Impacts. The Pulsations. The Nitecaps. The Adventurers. The Searchers. The Solitudes. The Thunderbirds. The Statics. The Vibrators. The Blue Comets. The Keynotes. The Turnabouts. The Soul Searchers. The Royals. The Phantoms. The Galaxies. The Checkmates. The Mark V. The Raymarks. The Dimensions. The Squires. The Courtmen. Thee Unusuals. The Bootmen . . .

A short list, it is, a very short list indeed, a modest dip into the roiling boil of rock 'n' roll that emerged from the Pacific Northwest over a fifty year span. A fraction of the many active bands there would break out to national and international fame, but most would hit, git, and split on their home turf, the lucky ones leaving recorded evidence on some small neighborhood record label before vanishing like a hitchhiking runaway on a foggy mountainside road.

Every city in America with any kind of population erupted with its own homegrown rock 'n' roll sensations when the big beat started—finally, at last, and officially—stomping the sap out of mannerly music. Rock 'n' roll was freedom, and at its best continues to be, the unblurred line in the sand between Us and Them. The Hep and the Jive Turkeys. The Tough and the Cream Puffs.

Everybody wanted in on the racket. Local pop, jazz, and country-and-western musicians fell into the fray with the new breed of war-baby noise-makers hell-bent on mayhem, filling the immediate need brought on by beat-crazed teenagers who had seen the light and heard the word and who demanded regular access to in-person combos to beat and blast and boil any given night. This national obsession, this boogie disease, swallowed cities big and small across the country, and most every burg and its hapless hamlets within a reasonable radius reverberated with a local accent, flavor, and sound.

Recognizable regional sound is evident in blues, rhythm and blues, and country—all the feeders that created the big, bad bang. But once the whole mess peaked and held steady for a short spot in time, certain geographic locales were actually ablaze with their own version of the way it was supposed to be.

For sheer loud-ass, teenage bad attitude, get-lost arrogance, no geographical area of the US serves up such a readily identifiable heap of teenage blast better, faster, or louder than the Pacific Northwest.

The blues, shout, thump, and howl initiated by touring rhythm and blues combos who traveled north up the coast from Los Angeles and San Francisco to the many dance halls, social clubs, and nighteries throughout Washington State, Oregon, and bordering state lines manifested their credos on the locals, and as the author of this tome, Peter Blecha, indicates, it was just one such R&B blast that proved pivotal for the region.

As we learn in *Sonic Boom*, in 1957, an unheralded opening act on a Junior Parker/Bobby "Blue" Bland bill would wail a self-penned ditty with an infectious beat that would so forever jar the entire top left corner of the country that the song would instantly become a required staple in every working combo's repertoire. Peter Blecha adds Elvis Presley's first area appearances a few weeks earlier to the formula, and the fuse it lit. Those late summer nights in 1957 sparked fifty years of unstoppable, deliciously loud, and frantic rock 'n' roll that is all firmly rooted in the first-run ballyhoo brew of rhythm and blues, howl, and hillbilly grease.

Blecha serves up all the politics, the pressures, and the players on the local scene—the disc jockeys, the label owners, the recording studio engineers, the agents, the club owners and dance hall bookers and, oh, yes, the bands—hundreds of superb combos all bearing the signature of the first-run local chart toppers—the Ventures, the Fabulous Wailers, Paul Revere and the Raiders, the Frantics, and this girl's top faves, the Sonics, who managed, in my estimation, to perfectly combine words, music, and psychological savagery to convey a singular message: Take it and like it—or get out of the way.

All of the bands, all of the bizwigs, all of the players, relay the rant with their own inflection, and with the big, big beat of the Pacific Northwest, that brand of pummel that has never been replicated on any other terrain. It may be the water, or the weather, or some oath made under a full moon to a sound track of "Werewolf," but whatever the reason, it will remain a hushed secret until day is done. In the meanwhile, strap in for a rare peek behind the scenes of fifty-some years of insanely fantabulous, and uniquely Northwest, rock 'n' roll.

—Miriam Linna, Norton Records

Lost and Found

I t was a backhanded challenge, served up in 2008 by the almost-universally esteemed *Encyclopœdia Britannica*, that provided the ulti-mate motivation to finally put two decades' worth of research behind me and get on with the *writing* of this book. I had been enjoying (perhaps a bit too much) the actual gathering of information, especially the interviews I was conducting with hundreds of Pacific Northwest musicians—an effort that had been ongoing ever since I'd realized that the rich saga of rock 'n' roll from this area was consistently getting short shrift in history books.

For example, 1976's *Rolling Stone Illustrated History of Rock & Roll* allotted all of *a half dozen sentences* (amongst its robust 382 pages) to the Northwest's contributions (setting aside Paul Revere and the Raiders, whose two dozen hits presumably earned them their very own paragraph). The following year, Harmony Books' 256-page *Illustrated Encyclopedia of Rock* devoted far *less* space to the topic. It was almost as if the Ventures, Kingsmen, Wailers, Raiders, Frantics, and Sonics had never happened. Meanwhile, the likes of Jan and Dean and the 1910 Fruitgum Company were being elevated to icon status.

And thus began my quest to document this "lost" history. But the pleas-ures of shaping a manuscript allowed years to pass—and even more time could have slipped by before I ever got around to finding an enthusiastic publisher. The tipping point finally came last year when I happened across the aforementioned *Encyclopœdia Britannica* and its authoritative assertion about Northwest rock:

> "The Seattle of the 1980s, in which Nirvana came to life, was a rainy city of lakes, rusty bridges, and more than a few disaffected . . . teenagers. . . . Jimi Hendrix had grown up in the city in the 1950s but had to go to

London to get noticed, and *not much happened of note musically in Seattle* until Nirvana formed in 1987. . . ." (emphasis added)

That misinformation, so carelessly inaccurate and inept, drove me to complete the manuscript. It seemed that I had no choice. Luckily, my spirited Backbeat editor—legendary wild man Mike Edison—took an instantaneous interest in *Sonic Boom* and spurred me on, and for that I thank him. In addition, I wish to convey my gratitude to Backbeat's whole team, especially my project editor, Marybeth Keating, who worked diligently to guide the book through its final production stages. Then, too, I should acknowledge the inspiration, camaraderie, and help provided over the decades by the small coterie of my fellow superfans and/or early archivists of Northwest rock 'n' roll history, Jeff Miller, Greg Shaw (RIP), Billy Miller, Miriam Linna, Bruce Smith, Don Rogers, Pat Lee, Lou Holscher, Rich Strauss, and Bob Jeniker (RIP). The greatest supporter of my work on this topic, however, has been my wife, Kate, who graciously endured many years of my maniacal foraging for rare artifacts and information–an activity which was interspersed by occasional periods of un-exceeded sloth: Thank you, sweetie. Lastly, I offer heartfelt appreciation to those many, many individuals—some being my own musical heroes—who lent their voices to the project. Thank you for trusting me with your stories.

SONIC BOOM

CHAPTER 1

The "Gonest" Sounds

On the late-summer evening of September 21, 1957, an eager crowd gathered outside of the old Eagles Auditorium at 700 Union Street in downtown Seattle. It was a Saturday—one of those rare special nights when a genuine rhythm and blues revue passed through town while on tour and electrified local fans with their gutbucket dance music.

Few in attendance could ever have guessed that they were about to witness an epochal event—a historic moment that sparked the Pacific Northwest's very own rock 'n' roll traditions. And that's because the odds are *that* most of the young couples showed up at the hall on that particular night to see and hear the two Southern headlining blues stars—Little Junior Parker and Bobby "Blue" Bland—both of whom were popular repeat visitors to the area.

But an auspicious surprise awaited everyone just inside the hall. Although the gig had been advertised in local newspapers as a "Battle of the Blues," Parker and Bland's audience would first be treated to a performance by the show's opening act—an unfamiliar black singer from Los Angeles named Richard Berry. And when he mounted the stage and counted off his new single, "Louie Louie," the crowd went wild on the teeming wooden dance floor. This odd tune was no blues, but rather, a pioneering example of West Coast rock 'n' roll—and one that would prove to have an enduring impact across the region.

It is possible that a few of that dance's attendees might have already been aware of the magical power of "Louie Louie"—but *only* if they happened to be among the loyal listeners of *Cool Breezes*, a weekly radio show broadcast on Tacoma's KTAC. Hosted by the area's pioneering black disc

jockey, Bob "Bop" Summerise, the program always delivered on its promise to bring music fans "The Gonest Sounds in the Puget Sound."

Still, hearing a tune on the airwaves is one thing—*feeling* the same
song pounded out by a live band is quite another—and when Berry kicked
into "Louie Louie" the dancers instantly picked up on the fact that the tune's
exotic dropped-beat rhythms were perfect for doing the then-popular cha-
cha-cha dance step. Meanwhile, the local musicians eyeing the band mar-
veled over the tune's minimal two-and-a-half-chord structure and hypnotic
pulse.

That subtle little ditty was actually an easy one to underestimate: Even
Berry's own record company, Flip Records, initially overlooked its mojo,

placing it as the sacrificial throwaway B-side on his new single. In fact, it took the will of the people to make the song a hit. In the Northwest, marketplace demand for that B-side caused the 45 to be added to just about every jukebox in every tavern that catered to Seattle's black community. And because the region's 1950s R&B "circuit" also included stops at old roadhouses like Olympia's Evergreen Ballroom—which welcomed the military personnel from the giant Fort Lewis Army and McChord Air Force bases outside of Tacoma—numerous black-oriented taverns around Tacoma also prized the record. Soon the Flip 45 was also selling like crazy out of Tacoma's Broadway Record Shop, and Summerise's store, the World of Music Record Shop, up in Seattle—to the extent that by the week of November 12, "Louie Louie" entered the Top 40 charts at Seattle's pop station, KOL, casting its spell even over listeners of mainstream AM radio.

The upshot is that once imbedded, this improbable tune would quickly take root regionally, flower into the Northwest's very own signature rock 'n' roll song—and ultimately develop into a rich and complex legend of its own.

Of course, that Eagles hall dance was not the only—or the best-publicized—music event that occurred in Seattle that season. Exactly three weeks prior to the Berry show, Elvis Presley and his trio had swept through the region while out on their first West Coast road tour. This new hillbilly rock—or "rockabilly"—band wowed crowds at Spokane's Memorial Stadium; Vancouver, B.C.'s Empire Stadium; Lincoln High School's Lincoln Bowl in Tacoma, where they played an afternoon show; Seattle's fabled old outdoor ballpark, Sick's Stadium, where they played an evening show; and Portland's Multnomah Stadium. In addition, an Oregon-based promoter named Pat Mason had been bringing great early rockabilly stars like Bill Haley and His Comets, Gene Vincent and His Blue Caps, Jerry Lee Lewis, and many seminal R&B acts to small-town dancehalls across the region since the middle of the decade.

But Mason didn't work the Seattle market. The old showbiz veteran had been stung in the past—getting caught up in endless layers of governmental red tape and losing money whenever he'd tried bringing bands to the larger cosmopolitan centers—so Mason preferred to build his circuit where his efforts were appreciated and he could make a decent buck. Which meant that other daring entrepreneurs would have to step up to the task if they wanted to see any of the top stars Mason handled play in Seattle. But that was a largely hit-or-miss prospect, and local teenagers often missed out: For example, while several other Northwest towns enjoyed concerts by

September 1957 newspaper ad.

Ritchie Valens—the East L.A. Chicano teen who was riding high with "Donna" and "La Bamba"—no promoter bothered to book him a Seattle date.

But thanks to the efforts of a few local black businessmen like Billy Tolles and Leonard Russell, Seattle's music-loving *adults* did get the chance

4

Richard Berrys Seattle debut, September 21, 1957.

to witness incredible shows at the Eagles Auditorium by seminal rockin' blues and R&B artists including T-Bone Walker, Muddy Waters, Howlin' Wolf, Little Milton, Fats Domino, Bo Diddley, Bill Doggett, Little Richard, James Brown, Earl Bostic, the 5 Royales, Little Willie John, and Hank Ballard and the Midnighters.

But even *more* credit must be given to Tolles and Russell: Beyond creating entertainment opportunities for older fans, their real genius was to realize that perhaps a few additional bucks could be generated by producing a series of matinee events by those same acts, geared for under-age minors. And *that's* how an entire generation of Seattle's rock 'n' roll musicians (including a fifteen-year-old kid named Jimmy Hendrix who'd plucked out the chords to "Louie Louie" when he got his first guitar in that fall of '57) was initially exposed to the music that would drive the area's teen scene throughout its formative years, despite the fact that music in the Northwest was still very much dominated by the orthodox tastes of a majority populace of predominantly Scandinavian descent—not your ideal demographic for the sprouting of an indigenous, African-American-inspired, musical aesthetic.

Yet that's *exactly* what happened. And all it took was the embedding of a subversively addictive song—arguably the ultimate "can't get it out of my head" tune, "Louie Louie"—that inspired young people (both black and white) to take up musical instruments, form bands, and eventually create a distinct homegrown sub-strain of R&B that would come to be known as the original "Northwest Sound."

CHAPTER 2

What'd I Say

The Pacific Northwest region has—despite its reputation as a placid refuge from the mean old world—still always had its share of tensions boiling just below the surface. Even polite-to-a-fault Seattle has suffered from long-term sociocultural battles. Soon after this place transitioned from its origins as a native encampment and into a settler's hamlet around 1851, disagreements arose within the new community over issues related to nightlife activities—a philosophical clash that has directly impacted the establishment of a robust music "scene" here ever since.

Local busybodies, fire-and-brimstone-spewing preachers, and opportunistic authorities have seemingly *always* tried to keep their thumbs on the town's nightlife action: This goal simultaneously stunted the growth of a healthy music biz and led to ruinous political corruption scandals erupting in more than one era. Although many prim Seattleites would likely prefer that it weren't so, the town's Wild West past is not only its prelude but remains an enduring thread in our regional character. In Washington, the tussle over alcohol and nightlife got under way quite early on—local temperance groups successfully brought alcohol prohibition to the state in 1916 (several years *prior* to the ban going national)—and the commingling of drinks and loud music remains an active point of contention today.

A second sore issue that was even more central to the music scene's woes is that of racial disharmony. After many years of being shunned by the all-white Seattle Musicians Union, (American Federation of Musicians) Local 76, the area's African-American players were finally compelled to form their own Negro Musicians Union, (AFM) Local 493, in 1913. But by then, Local 76 had solidified their position of power by controlling Seattle's downtown core, which made all those lucrative gigs in the major hotel ballrooms, nightclubs, and theaters *their* turf. And they defended it vigorously for the next four decades. So the membership of Local 493 were forced to make do with whatever gigs popped up within their own community, at the sketchy rooms on the town's southern perimeter, perhaps picking up a few measly scraps leftover after the members of 76 were all happily booked up. This, then, was the sorry standoff that existed in Seattle—and other towns like Tacoma and Portland, Oregon, were even worse.

Among the negative effects that that inequitable balance of power fostered was a willful blindness to what was *really* happening musically in the area. This cultural ignorance ultimately helped create the great lost secret of Northwest music history: that Seattle was, in fact, the home of one of the nation's hottest "underground" jazz scenes—one that would eventually produce such national treasures as Ray Charles, Ernestine Anderson, Robert A. "Bumps" Blackwell, and Quincy Jones. So while the town's typical white citizen gravitated to musical happenings like performances by the Seattle Symphony (after 1903), the Seattle Ladies Musical Club, church choirs, hillbilly string bands, and *innumerable* Scandinavian accordion trios . . . they were, as a group, perfectly clueless that just across town there was an entire alternate universe of hot music swirling around every night of the week.

Certainly the area's newspapers and radio stations were of no help, providing just about zero recognition of *any* activities on the largely black jazz scene. And that void of validation helped render Seattle jazz invisible to a vast majority of the town's residents. That *unseen* scene was mainly based in scores of nightclubs in the old Skid Road area of the town's Pioneer Square area and eastward along Jackson Street and Yesler Way and into the black business zone that stretched into the Central District (or "C.D."), where the black community had been allowed to settle. And while many newly arrived blacks found the racial atmosphere in the Northwest to be preferable to that of their former hometowns in the deep South, the fact was that some serious social inequities remained.

Consider what were then euphemistically called Seattle's "Sunset Laws"—a set of rules that allowed police officers to stop and question any black citizens found to be in any neighborhoods (other than the C.D.) after dark. The family of black bandleader, distinguished pianist, and founding father of Northwest jazz, Oscar Holden Sr.—the New Orleans–reared musician who originally rolled into town with jazz pioneer "Jelly Roll" Morton (who recorded his famous boogie-woogie tune "Seattle Hunch" after playing here around 1919 or 1920)—has recalled the time returning home from a late-night gig at a room like the Clover Club or Doc Hamilton's Barbecue

Pit he was beaten and bloodied from an assault sustained at the hands of racist policemen who'd found him walking home and applied their traditional deterrent.

With the huge influx of black workers (and their families) immigrating here to take advantage of the wartime shipyard defense jobs in the 1940s—and then the return of many proud black veterans after World War II—some of these abhorrent practices were moderated. But the injustices took many forms, one being the purposeful stifling of entertainment opportunities for the newcomers. Not allowed into many downtown theaters and ballrooms, various black entrepreneurs had tried to establish nightclubs—or "cabarets," as they were then called—only to be frustrated by the red tape they encountered. In point of fact, the Seattle city government had for years played a central and willing role in this ugly game by consistently rejecting any black's applications for business licenses to open venues anywhere near the "borders" of the C.D. The blacks had been fairly effectively boxed in, and the powers-that-be didn't want the newcomers' physical presence—or cultural influence—to creep into white turf.

But political pressure from the black community swelled to the point that finally, on February 19, 1946, the *Seattle Times* reported this momentous bit of news: "An unwritten but rigid policy of the city council, forbidding cabarets east of Eighth Avenue in the central portion of the city, was relaxed yesterday, to give Seattle's Negro community a dine-and-dance establishment at the Savoy Ballroom, 2203 E. Madison St., operators of which were granted a cafe-dance license." And so, with this announcement that the city had approved a license for a neighborhood billiard hall owner, Lemeul Honeysuckle, to go ahead and open his planned Savoy Ballroom, history took a momentous stride forward—one that would have lasting repercussions that nobody (well, except for opponents of the policy shift) could have ever imagined.

In hindsight, it was the specific *location* of the Savoy—situated on the border between the C.D. and the rather more affluent and homogeneous (i.e., nearly all white) neighborhoods of North Seattle, East Capitol Hill, and Madison Park—that would, in time, prove to make the place so significant to the town's musical richness. And so, because of its geographic accessibility, white music fans eventually found their way to the ballroom, and with that social intermingling, a new sense of racial tolerance began to grow. People of varying means and circumstances found common ground listening and dancing till the wee hours to music played by some of the greatest jazz (and later, R&B) musicians around.

It was in 1947 that Seattle bandleader Bumps Blackwell discovered and began managing a young black band led by saxophonist Charlie Taylor that also included Quincy Jones (the teenage trumpeter whose family had just moved over to Seattle from segregated housing in the naval shipyard town of Bremerton) and two of the musically gifted offspring of Seattle jazz legend Oscar Holden Sr.—Oscar Jr. (saxophone) and his sister, Grace (piano). Blackwell quickly proved his worth by getting them high-profile gigs playing opposite Cab "Hi-De-Ho" Calloway at the prestigious Civic Auditorium downtown, and then backing up jazz diva Billie Holiday at the Eagles Auditorium. Inspired by the group's abilities, Blackwell then convinced Honeysuckle to hire the band at the Savoy for a series of weekly dances. Those dances went well, and in time Blackwell began tweaking the band's lineup by bringing in new members, including a sweet-voiced teenage jazz and blues singer named Ernestine Anderson.

But it was in 1948 that Blackwell would make his greatest discovery to date, when he stumbled across a blind seventeen-year-old pianist named Ray Charles Robinson performing at the Old Rocking Chair club at 1301 E. Yesler Way. This was another venue that had fully earned its status as a legend in the town's musical lore—it was where *everybody* in the know went to check out the action: The joint boasted a full liquor bar downstairs, an illicit gambling room upstairs, and music that attracted traveling musicians who loved to hang out after hours.

It was in March that Robinson had rolled into town on a bus direct from his gig in Tampa, Florida, and luckily landed smack-dab in the middle of Seattle's Jackson Street jazz scene. The very night of his arrival he was tipped off to the possibilities of a meal and jam session over at the Rocking Chair. At first denied entry because of his youthfulness, he pleaded successfully with the bouncer at the door, and was finally let in. When his turn onstage came up, the pianist played two blues numbers, and within minutes he was approached by a fellow who complimented his playing and asked if he thought he could pull a trio together quickly and take on a regular gig at the blacks' Elks Club. After picking up a couple players at the AFM 493 union office—Milt Garred (bass) and Gosady McKee (guitar)— he began the Elks gig

The three musicians devised a name for their ensemble by conflating the surnames of McKee and Robinson—the McSon Trio, which soon was altered to the Maxin Trio, while along the way Robinson simplified his stage name to the catchier-sounding Ray Charles. A beautiful career was now under way. After getting their act together at the Elks, the trio was offered a highly prized

RAY CHARLES

Exclusive Management
BEN WALLER'S ENTERPRISES
223 W. Second St., Suite 201 • Michigan 9681
Los Angeles 12, California

Promotional photo, circa 1950.

nightly after-hours gig—from 1 to 5 A.M.—back at the Rocking Chair, and then they scored a radio gig on KRSC that they used as a way to advertise themselves. Soon after the Maxin Trio proved themselves at the radio station, KRSC expanded to television. KRSC-TV debuted in November, and the trio began hosting their own regular weekly live show on the air. Charles began making a few extra bucks writing arrangements for local groups—including the Bumps Blackwell Band. He also spent his off nights jamming at various black rooms, including the Savoy Ballroom.

It was February of '49 when Jack Lauderdale—the man behind one of the very first black-owned independent labels, Downbeat Records, arrived from Los Angeles on business. He was here to give a pep talk to his distributor. Although Downbeat had in its first year and a half of activity already issued strong R&B and blues sellers by fine artists, including Lowell Fulson and Joe Turner, winning airtime in Seattle's anemically whitebread radio market was still an enormous struggle. So after a long day, Lauderdale sought out a bit of relaxation, and, after asking around, he basically got the same advice that Ray Charles Robinson had received one year prior: Head over to the Rocking Chair for some friendly gambling, stiff drinks, and great live music. The story goes that while shooting dice upstairs at that joint, the record exec really began digging the tunes that were wafting up from downstairs. As Charles recalled: "He approached me and told me that he had a record label." Wow! Just the *thought* of getting the chance to record was a thrill: "A record! Man, that was the ultimate! I had been listening to records my whole life . . . and here I was actually about to make one. Yes, we'll cut a record, Mr. Lauderdale. Good God Almighty! Just show us the way, Papa. Nothing I want to do more." The "way" that Lauderdale showed the Maxin Trio was straight over to Western Studios (in the Northern Life Tower building), where they quickly cut two tunes—"Confession Blues" and "I Love You, I Love You." Lauderdale was satisfied with the session's results and upon his return home the songs were issued as the latest Downbeat 78-rpm disc.

Though the record was not the smash hit Downbeat had hoped for, it did enjoy some retail action up and down the West Coast—but the more significant point is the fact that what they'd created that night was no less than the soon-to-be-great Ray Charles' debut recording, and simultaneously, the very first R&B record ever produced in the Northwest. Lauderdale was just getting started, though: He persuaded Charles to come down to California and record again—solo this time. Charles showed up—but with his full trio in tow—and recorded a couple new songs, "Rocking Chair Blues" and "Alone in the City," both of which hinted more than a little at the members' apparent homesickness for Seattle. The guys returned to Seattle and started up their club gigs again, but when Charles was called back by Lauderdale once more, both Garred and McKee opted to stay—and the next thing anyone knew, Charles was out traveling on a big national tour, opening for the popular bluesman Lowell Fulson.

Longtime local jazzers have testified plenty that Ray Charles' impact during his time here from 1948 into 1950 was profound. Within a remarkably brief period, and on the strength of his rootsy sound, Charles had gone from upstart newcomer to king of the scene. With his departure, the Northwest's loss was the world's gain: Before long, Ray Charles would earn the well-deserved nickname "The Genius of Soul" with world-shaking 1950s hits like "I Got a Woman" and "What'd I Say." But before those gems, Brother Ray's indelibly blue influence had played a key role in the eventual rise of an original Northwest Sound.

CHAPTER 3

Doin' the Birdland

It was in 1955 that Seattle's Savoy Ballroom changed hands and another black entrepreneur named Wilmer Morgan decided to cast it as the Birdland Supper Club. Renamed in honor of the bebop jazz sax icon, Charlie "Bird" Parker, the room reopened in mid-August with a show by the Dizzy Gillespie big band's popular former saxophonist, James Moody, who now had his own group, the Bop Men. And, for a Monday night, the large turnout was encouraging. It seems the locals had been hungry for a room that could regularly present first-tier acts.

Morgan set out to remedy that situation by booking more great jazz names into the Birdland, along with some of the finest national R&B stars, including Big Jay McNeely, T-Bone Walker, Hank Ballard and the Midnighters, Percy Mayfield, Amos Milburn, Solomon Burke, and James Brown. The Birdland became a welcome addition to a small but growing string of rooms that was beginning to serve as the Northwest's version of the Deep South's "chitlin' circuit."

Two other Seattle rooms that were now open to booking gritty jazz and/or rockin' R&B music were the Mardi Gras Grill, which Morgan also owned, and Ayer's Café, owned by Myrt Francois. In 1956 the newly formed Billy Tolles Trio—with keyboardist Dave Holden (another son of Oscar) and Seattle's father of funk drumming, Tommy Adams, aboard—began attracting crowds to gigs at both these rooms. And the R&B music that the trio was blasting out was so novel that word spread fast, and soon white students from up at the University of Washington started showing up in droves, and it became evident that the rock 'n' roll trend was growing.

But with the Tolles Trio now in high demand and booked solid playing adult rooms, a huge void was created on the local teen scene: one that another young talent named Dave Lewis stepped right into. The footprint

Lewis would go on to make in Northwest music was a big one: Indeed, not only was his the first teen band to adopt and further popularize Richard Berry's "Louie Louie," but Lewis would also go on to shape the aesthetics behind Seattle's teen R&B sound more than any other individual.

Lewis was a member of yet another family—like their former neighbors, Quincy Jones' family—who had relocated to a home in Seattle from the navy shipyard town of Bremerton at war's end. As a kid who was attracted to music early on, he found his C.D. neighborhood's black business districts quite an irresistible lure: "Birdland was in my neighborhood," recalled Lewis. "It had started when I first moved into the area. It was a legitimate nightclub, and they booked in some major black artists. When Birdland first opened, I couldn't get in, because they had liquor and everything. But I could go around to the stage door and they would let me sneak in the back wing, you know, and stand and just listen. So, you know, I got to know the proprietor, Wilmer Morgan, and he'd say, 'David! Whatchoo doin' here? Get out of here!' [laughter] And so I got to *know* what was happening."

Inspired, Lewis also knew that he wanted to make music. His first group was an Edmund Meany Jr. High School–based doo-wop quintet called the Five Checks—which included singers Ronnie Height, Hank Rollins, Larry Lombard, and a another kid who'd moved to town directly from the great American music capitol of New Orleans—George Griffin. Formed in 1955, the Five Checks debuted—with their eye-popping matching threads: boldly checkered dress shirts—at the school's seasonal talent show, and they evidently made a *big* impression. After that first show, they were invited to perform at other pep rallies and assemblies, first at Meany and then at other public schools all across Seattle—in the process giving a lot of white kids their very first exposure to live doo-wop singing.

Then, in 1956—when the guys moved on to Garfield High School—it was decided that they'd form a genuine band with instruments. A few members dropped out, and because of Lewis's superior grasp of musical theory, he became the band's leader. Lewis played piano, Griffin contributed his deadly New Orleans–steeped drumming, and the new recruits were Jack Grey, thumpin' on his doghouse bass; Barney Hilliard and J.B. Allen, rippin' on their dueling saxes; and Al Aquino (and later Bud Brown), on electric guitar. The Dave Lewis Combo started building up their repertoire and got a few modest early gigs playing for teenage sock hops at the C.D.'s East Madison YMCA. Then—with the Local 76 union's stranglehold on downtown gigs beginning to slip a bit—the combo got their first big-time gigs performing at a series of R&B matinee shows at the old Trianon Ballroom and the Palomar Theater. They wowed the teenage crowds, opening for national recording stars including Sugar Chile Robinson, Horace Henderson, Nellie Lutcher, and the pioneering R&B organist "Wild" Bill Davis.

Then, as May 1956 came around, the combo's daring drummer, George Griffin, had the crazy idea of trying to host his own event, which would feature various local acts all in one show. It was a fine notion, and the only really "crazy" part about it was that the venue he had in mind for the gig was Parker's Ballroom—the preeminent 1930s roadhouse dancehall in the lily-white north end of Seattle—but it was a room whose success had been founded upon music from another era. Dick Parker had built his Highway Pavilion just north of the city limits at 170th Street out on the "New Seattle-Everett Highway" back in 1930. For its first quarter century of its existence, the room had drawn crowds who appreciated popular Local 76 acts (including Putt Anderson & his Dixieland Band, and orchestras led by Frankie Roth and Jackie Souders) as well as the occasional touring stars like Tommy Dorsey and Guy Lombardo and their orchestras.

In short, it was *not* known as a haven for black music or Local 493 players. Still, if you don't dream big and take chances, nothing ever happens. And so it was on the evening of May 11, 1956, that the management at Parker's decided to defy their longtime "understanding" with Local 76 and book Griff's Dance and Jam Session, a spectacular that featured both the Five Checks and the Dave Lewis Combo, *and* a white ensemble called the Ted Simon Octet (whose desires to be hip were undercut by their stiffness and the sheet music they stared at on their old-school music stands).

The date was so successful that Parker later agreed to allow Tacoma's KTNT-TV to broadcast a new teen-dance show, *Rock 'n Roll Party*, from the hall—replete with Seattle's black rockin' R&B pioneer, Billy Tolles, as the host. Not only that, but among the local bands that Tolles wanted to feature on occasion (besides his own new group, the Vibrators) was the Dave Lewis Combo. And so while the turnout for Griffin's dance was excellent for business, the fallout of Parker's decision to allow blacks in was met with blustery resistance by Local 76 officials. As a matter of fact, Lewis himself once recalled how after some sort of union clash had occurred he personally witnessed Parker management arguing over the telephone with those union bosses—in short, telling them that if they protested the presence of Tolles and Lewis (and their crowd) in "their" hall, that would be the end of any further 76 gigs there. Ever.

The *Rock 'n Roll Party* events were such a hit with the younger set— both black and white—that even the region's most active concert and dance promoter, Pat Mason, took notice. And because he couldn't find a single local white band to serve as the opening act on the Northwest leg of the 1956 summer tour by Bill Haley and His Comets, he took a chance and hired Seattle's black upstart band, the Dave Lewis Combo (and audaciously billed them as the "Northwest's Greatest Rock N' Roll Band").

So it was that on the night of June 28, 1956, the Comets opened their summerlong Rock N' Roll Jamboree tour with a show at Olympia's Evergreen Ballroom—which was located at 9121 Pacific Avenue S.E. on the "old Tacoma and Olympia Highway"—and the good news was that the crowds loved it all, the two bands got along great, and Mason booked them together around the region into the fall season. And from there Mason's Far West Amusements, Inc. simply built upon that success by bringing in all of the other major rockabilly stars of the day, including Gene Vincent, Jerry Lee Lewis, Carl Perkins, Johnny Cash, Eddie Cochran, Buddy Holly, Johnny Burnette, Jimmy Bowen, Buddy Knox, Duane Eddy, and Roy Orbison—and Mason also started working with black talents like Little Richard, Little Willie John, Fats Domino, the Coasters, the Drifters, and Richard Berry.

Perhaps Mason's greatest trailblazing achievement—aside from discovering and encouraging the region's first-generation rockabilly bands like Albany's Sherree Scott and Her Melody Rockers, Vancouver's Vinny Duman and the Rhythmaires, Yakima's Jerry Merritt and the Pacers, and Centralia's Clayton Watson and the Silhouettes (who were billed as "The First Rock 'n' Roll Band in Washington State")—was the daunting task of carving out sensible tour routes. Mason made a discovery that would have a profound impact on the future course of Northwest rock 'n' roll, and that was that the many National Guard armories spread across the region were available for rent on weekends. And even though the old brick buildings offered criminal acoustic properties, their mere existence made them a key link in the eventual rise of a Northwest teen scene.

But the rockabilly music of those early bands would soon begin sounding dated, and though the public's musical tastes moved on, that music undeniably served the critical role of attracting a lot of white folk to big-beat music. However, as fresh local groups began emerging, rather than displaying any sort of stylistic connection to that seminal form of country-derived rock music, they almost all instead were exploring a particular aesthetic that would ultimately come to be recognized as the original Northwest Sound— a "school" of rock 'n' roll that could be characterized by its reliance on core elements of jazz-tinged *rhythm and blues*.

Meanwhile, as the summer of 1957 approached, Wilmer Morgan faced some tough choices at the Birdland. He had been growing weary of all the hassles one faced in running a full restaurant, and he realized that simply operating a dancehall-nightclub instead would make everything easier. Such a change promised far less paperwork and fewer inspections by the various city departments including fire, health, and police. But as far as Northwest music history goes, Morgan's breakthrough move was a policy shift that opened the joint up to early shows for the younger set. Once established, this new policy gave minors a chance to enter the premises, sip soda pop, and dance from 8 P.M. until 11 P.M. Then, from 11:30 P.M. until about 4 A.M., it was adults only.

And along the way, the Birdland effectively evolved into a de facto "bottle club," where the patrons brought their own brown-bagged liquor bottles (which they checked in with the bartender upon entry) and then the house simply charged them for glasses, mixers, and ice cubes. With this new regime in place, the Birdland was on the fast track to earning its reputation as the hottest damn after-hours dancehall in Seattle. And then, in May 1957, Morgan made *another* of his finest business decisions: He offered to hire the Dave Lewis Combo as the Birdland's new weekend house band. And over time the draw of the combo—and of the doo-wop groups like Tacoma's Barons and Four Pearls, and Seattle's Gallahads and Joe Boot & the Fabulous Winds (who recorded Seattle's first rock 45, "Rock and Roll Radio," for Celestial Records in 1958) that often joined them—helped the Birdland become a catalytic force on the scene, and the ethnically mixed clientele it attracted made the room a model of social tolerance as well as the town's best music room.

That fall saw the Dave Lewis Combo take leave from their perch at the Birdland to begin a long string of dates around Washington, Oregon, and Vancouver B.C., opening for shows headlined by hip stars such as Ray Charles, Little Richard, Ike and Tina Turner, and the Platters—as well as other gigs for mostly all-white audiences (like those they'd already done with the Comets) in rural dancehalls with rockabilly boppers Gene Vincent and His Blue Caps.

In Lewis's absence, Morgan brought in a string of touring bands. One artist he booked was Watts-based sax honker with a well-deserved reputation for riotous live shows—the one and only Big Jay McNeely, who'd cut many great tunes for seminal R&B labels, including Imperial and Aladdin Records. While in town for that gig, McNeely decided that he wanted his band to cut a new single—but the question was, where? At that time, Seattle could boast of a mere three capable studios—Chet Noland's Dimensional Sound (and Celestial Records), Lyle Thompson's Commercial Recorders, and Joe Boles' Custom Recorders—luckily, the last of these was run by a hobbyist sound engineer from his home basement in West Seattle. Boles was really beginning to get some fine sounds on tape. After settling into their weeklong gig at the Birdland—but before the band ever made to Boles' place—another recording engineer wannabe named Fred Rasmussen set his own gear up at the club and managed to tape them in full glory on a cold night with a very hot crowd. The Birdland crowd's enthusiastic vocal interaction with McNeely's singer, Little Sonny Warner, on songs like Ray Charles' "I Got a Woman" is a wondrous thing to hear—and ever since that tape finally surfaced, some three decades after the fact, as McNeely's *Live at Birdland* CD, it stands as one of the finest aural documents of a 1950s black nightclub in existence.

Then, right around New Year's Day 1958, McNeely's combo entered Boles' studio for sessions that yielded a number of tunes—including "There Is Something on Your Mind," which McNeely offered to let Boles and his associate, Tom Ogilvy (who owned the local pop label Seafair Records), release, but the pair declined due to concerns that Seattle's whitebread radio would never support it. So when McNeely's Birdland gig was over, he headed back to Los Angeles and cut a deal with Swingin' Records. "There Is Something on Your Mind" quickly shot up to the No. 5 slot on *Billboard*'s R&B charts—more significantly, it also "crossed over" to *Billboard*'s pop charts, peaking at No. 44, and after four continuous months of charting, it proved to be one of the top-selling R&B songs of 1959.

It must have been a bittersweet thing for Boles and Ogilvy to watch their production become such a huge hit—the first ever out of Seattle—when they could have tried marketing it themselves. But they also knew that had it been issued on the Seafair label the disc would almost certainly have sunk into oblivion. The upsides to the situation were that McNeely was grateful (he'd scored the biggest pop hit that he ever would), the producer and engineer had renewed faith in their ears and abilities, and a song had been created which would come to be a cornerstone of the nascent Northwest teen R&B scene over the next half-dozen years, attaining such popularity in the Northwest that scores of local teen bands would adopt it. In fact, Seattle's soon-to-be-famous guitar player, Jimmy Hendrix, would choose to cut it during one of his first sessions upon arrival in New York City in 1965.

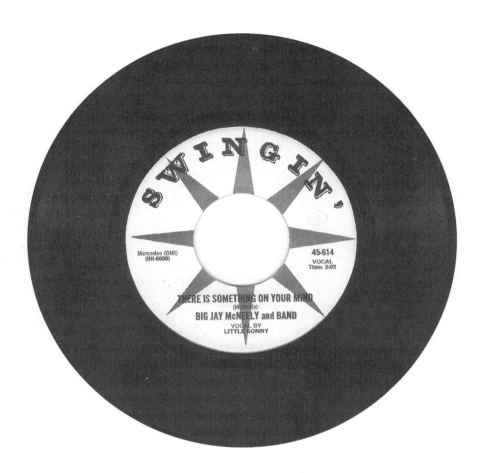

CHAPTER 4

Posse on Broadway

I t was on the momentous day of January 14, 1958, that the entire musical landscape in Seattle suddenly shifted, when the two racially segregated musicians' unions—AFM Local 76 and Local 493—finally joined together. The old turf lines were formally erased—although in practice the black players would still face a long road of getting some venue owners to actually welcome their presence. But the live entertainment venues in the Northwest were now poised to offer better music than ever. As they happened, however, the ensuing changes were important cumulatively: In 1958 the Frank Roberts Combo became the first all-black band to ever get booked at the Magic Inn, where they worked steadily supporting touring R&B stars; Billy Tolles and the Vibrators scored an extended engagement at Dave's Fifth Avenue; and then, in 1959, a black bandleader named Little Willie Bell and his white band, the Thunderbirds, got a booking at another downtown room, the Roll Inn Tavern.

Between the years of 1957 and 1958, a whole new batch of young musicians came of age and began forming the next generation of Northwest rock 'n' roll and/or rhythm and blues bands. In Seattle, the two most significant ones would prove to be the Central District neighborhood's multiracial group the Playboys and the north end's all-white combo, the Frantics. In Tacoma, there were two white groups: One, the Blue Notes, fancied itself a full-on R&B band; the other, the Wailers, would eventually dominate the regional teen dance scene for nearly a decade.

The Playboys were an ensemble that got its start when a drummer named Andy Duvall and a pianist named Bob Risley hooked up with Carlos Ward (sax), who played with Garfield High's pep band. Ward brought along the school's football star, Rolen "Ron" Holden (yet another son of Oscar Holden Sr.) as their singer, and he brought along a sax-playing neighborhood buddy, Johnny O'Francia, and the Playboys began to gel. Having grown up in the 'hood, these guys had been provided with a very accessible model of musical excellence to emulate: "When I first started getting into the musical scene," recalled Holden, "we had to *sneak* into places like Birdland. *That's* where the music was happening. They would let me in the back door. The Dave Lewis Combo was the hottest thing happening. He was *it.* They had a saxophone duo—it seemed like it was the hottest sax duo anywhere in the world! Yeah, those twin horns, they were just *monsters.* That combo *owned* this city. They were the hottest rhythm and blues band. Well, it was rhythm and blues—but [laughter] they *called* it 'rock 'n' roll'!"

And because the Playboys were a young, untested band, the earliest dances that they got to play—modest, nonpaying, gigs held under marginal circumstances, at oddball locations—were not exactly as exciting as the vibe over at the Birdland. "What *we* did was *tea* parties," chuckled Holden. "House parties. And our first gig was an intermission at a record hop/sock hop at the University Presbyterian Church." As the Playboys refined their act, they quickly began earning a reputation as the town's best new teen R&B combo—but at just about that same time, another hot band began making waves. As Holden recalled it, "The Playboys' first recognizable competition came from the Frantics."

Promotional photo of the Dave Lewis Combo, circa 1957. (Courtesy Dave Lewis.)

The Four Frantics had actually begun in about 1955 when the Hi-Fi's—a duo consisting of Ron Peterson (guitar) and Chuck Schoning (sax)—added a bassist and drummer. According to Peterson, "When we were sophomores or juniors, we played these assemblies at various schools and at one at Lincoln High, and there was a vice principal and he didn't want the kids too riled up. So after the first assembly he said, 'You play "Honky Tonk" one more time and yer outta school!' And so we went back and did the second assembly, and we played it [laughter] and got kicked out of school!"

After performing at a few other school talent fests, the Four Frantics won first prize at the West Seattle neighborhood's annual Hi-Yu summer fair amateur talent show in 1956—and that same season they and even got

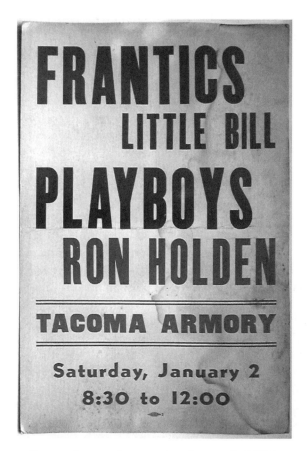

Tacoma Armory dance poster, January 2, 1960.

a couple chances to open for Billy Tolles and the Vibrators up at Parker's Ballroom. That era's biggest youth-oriented music events were the seasonal All-City PTA dances, which typically featured an old-school big-band orchestra that played boring mainstream tunes for standard ballroom-style dancing. But then the Four Frantics came up with the brilliant idea of volunteering to play a few numbers during the headliner's intermission breaks. This plan was all going well—and earned the Four Frantics some enthusiastic new fans—but it also eventually put them in the crosshairs of Local 76 union boss Chet Ramage.

It was at one particular dance—held at the old Civic Auditorium—where Ramage first took note of the young combo, realized they were not union, and reacted decisively by cutting the power supply to their amps and barking in their faces that "you guys aren't gonna play another job in this town until you join the union." In no great hurry to follow his commands, the Four Frantics were about to learn yet another hard lesson about the ways of the music biz: After performing well in the local runoffs for the *Ted Mack Amateur Hour* TV show's national talent search, they were (thanks to Ramage's intervention) disqualified—thus clearing the way for the Dave Lewis Combo's easy win. Finally convinced, the Four Frantics joined Local 76, and they were now poised to become the town's first-call rock 'n' roll band—and in time Seattle's first to score international hit records. But all that was still a few years off.

In the meantime, the playing field had yet to be sorted out, "and there were definite lines drawn," recalled Ron Holden. "There were boundaries: The Frantics more or less played the north end, and we more or less played the south end. The Wailers played Tacoma, and Little Bill and the Blue Notes played the South [Puget] Sound area. And we kind of kept it like that for a while, and then pretty soon someone had the idea to start these Battles of the Bands. And then we would meet at like the Spanish Castle or the Encore Ballroom, the Tacoma Armory or the Evergreen Ballroom or Parker's, and all these bands would get together and battle. Then the cultures meshed. They started overlapping."

At that time, back in the 1950s, the racial divide in Tacoma was fairly stark—and the lines were drawn right through one of the town's main downtown streets. The shopping district known as Upper Broadway was, of course, the domain of Tacoma's majority white population, while Lower Broadway—or at least its pool halls, rib joints, and dives like the Blue Note, Congo Café, the Grill, the Sea-Port Tavern, the Casino, the El Paso, and the Tiki—had been allotted to the black community.

And situated down there in the middle of all, at 1325 Broadway, was the Broadway Record Shop—a fixture that originally served the needs of the black community, but which eventually began to attract curious and somewhat daring white kids who had no other source for buying the R&B records they were hearing on Bob Summerise's *Cool Breezes* radio show. But there was a risk inherent in journeying into Tacoma's black neighborhoods: The cops would pick up straying white kids and either drive them home (if they cooperated) or to the juvenile authorities (if they rebelled). The cops tried to keep an eye on the action—the Broadway Record Shop was a self-contained center of commercial activity. A combination barber shop/record store, it was a crossroads for numerous other activities. Until it was eventually raided by lawmen, the Broadway Record Shop was *the* place in Tacoma where customers could come away with a new hairdo, a couple new jazz or R&B platters, and a matchbox full of reefer or a handful of various pills.

It was also a sort of social hub where music fans could hang out and discover all the latest sounds. And this was important for black kids as well as the very few white misfits like budding musician "Little Bill" Engelhart, who found a sanctuary amidst the bulging racks of hot discs at the store. Engelhart was a rather unlikely candidate for pop stardom. As a guitar-playing child living in Chelan, Washington, he'd contracted polio, which resulted in the necessity of crutches, and his enrollment in the cruelly named Crippled Children's School. Later, after his family moved to Tacoma, Engelhart's guitar skills and singing improved to the point that his father bought him a better instrument at Bart's Music shop, and at age twelve he paired up with a fiddle-playing Tumwater kid named Donny Ulrich. As a duo, they played country tunes at a gig or two for patients at the nearby Indian Hospital and for the enlisted men's club at Fort Lewis.

Although the odds of ever finding any other young white guys in Tacoma who'd ever be caught dead playing in a rockin' R&B combo in the 1950s were steep, Engelhart began entertaining far-fetched dreams of meeting exactly such comrades. One day in 1955 he took the first step. "When I was fifteen or sixteen, I was going to a vocational school in Tacoma, and one day there was a notice up on a bulletin board that said they were going to have a dance in the lunchroom, and anyone who played an instrument could show up and audition," recalled Engelhart. Long story short, only three people showed up to audition: the crutch-bound guitarist, Engelhart; a one-legged trumpeter; and a black drummer named Jimmy Green. Needless to say, the dynamic threesome got the gig,

27

and Green promised to bring along a few more friends to round out the "band."

"So he brought these black guys and we did this dance," Engelhart continued. "And afterwards they asked me if I wanted to go down to the George Washington Carver American Legion Hall, which was an after-hours black club, a bottle club, on Tacoma Avenue. So I said, 'Sure, I'll go *anywhere* with musicians.' He was impressed by this young white guitar kid: He took me down to these guys and they hired me. The name of that band was the Blue Notes." That group of much older black cats were apparently charmed by this odd teenage white kid who'd come with his electric guitar in tow, and tickled by his enthusiastic, if green, talent. Suddenly, Little Bill was a member of an R&B band that performed every Friday and Saturday night at that Hilltop neighborhood hall. Over the next few months a few different players drifted in and out of the group, and in time the Blue Notes dissolved. But in the meantime, Engelhart had struck up a friendship with a white sax player named Frank Dutra, and they began plotting how to round up enough other guys to put together a steady band. Initial efforts to find other potential players at the nearby Stadium High School met with no luck. But then one early summer evening in '57, Engelhart and Dutra— and pretty much every other kid who was taken by all this new rock 'n' roll stuff—attended the Friday night premier of *Rock Around the Clock*, the new flick that featured the music of Bill Haley and His Comets.

And so it was that Engelhart and Dutra crossed paths in the lobby of the Sunset Theater with a couple of eighth-graders named John "Buck" Ormsby and Lasse Aanes, who were also hanging out. They got to talking rock, and Aanes blurted out that he had a drum set, while Ormsby said he owned an electric lap steel guitar that was strung with only four strings so he could play bass lines on it. They had already been jamming together, and the foursome quickly agreed to meet up the very next day at Engelhart's parents' garage. It took just a couple of jam sessions to convince the guys that they could be a band—but first, they needed a name. And since the Blue Notes had broken up, they agreed to adopt that moniker for their new R&B band. The guys practiced, built up a repertoire, and soon got a chance to compete at an amateur talent contest at a downtown hall, the Crescent Ballroom. After they won the trophy, it was announced that there was another "special prize" (probably one that the promoter thought of right on the spot as he saw how many teens were packing the joint): a weekly gig every Saturday night. After a couple weeks, that expanded to both Friday and Saturday nights.

The Blue Notes' next fortuitous moment came in September 1957, when the band ran into a kid named Lawrence "Rockin' Robin" Roberts, who, as it turned out, was a major R&B fan and a regular visitor to the Broadway Record Shop. Of course no one knew it then, but in time "Rockin' Robin" would also become a major Northwest legend—and one who died tragically young.

"We met him at the Puyallup Fair," said Engelhart. "Buck and I went to the fair and we were walking around and we saw a bunch of people around this bench, and there was this guy up on top of it. And we thought he was *talking*, so we got a little closer and realized he was *singing*. It was Robin Roberts. We were just *amazed* that anybody would just stand up there in the middle of all these people and sing. It was like an early street singer! That had never been done around Tacoma that I knew of. And so we asked him if he'd like to be in a band and he said, 'Sure.'"

Roberts was an odd bird: an ultrabrainy honor roll type who served in school as a PTA representative, Science Club secretary, German Club vice president, and Red Cross representative, but who was also—as his band mates soon discovered—the rock 'n' roll version of Clark Kent. Although somewhat nerdy in appearance, when fronting the Blue Notes he transformed into a high-voltage and charismatic R&B singer whose wild abandon would soon inspire a generation of local musicians. In turn, Roberts and the rest of the boys were now being directly inspired by the hot discs they found at the Broadway Record Shop—not to mention their latest discovery: the fact that they could gain access to live shows by those very same R&B artists, who were now beginning to get booked for Sunday shows at Olympia's Evergreen Ballroom. And as firsthand witnesses to so many fantastic shows, they began getting direct lessons in playing R&B from the masters of the form.

By then the Evergreen had been presenting live music (mostly big-band orchestras and country bands) for over twenty-five years—but in 1954, when the owner, Irving Sholund, realized that he could get great deals by booking various touring R&B revues on their off nights, he gave it a go. And the response from the mainly black crowds that showed up soon positioned the hall as the newest tour stop on the West Coast's chitlin' circuit. Best of all, Sholund instituted the innovative idea of sending a free bus out to a number of locations to pick up people for a direct lift right to the Evergreen—and the Broadway Record Shop served as one of these pickup spots. "We used to go to the Evergreen Ballroom and watch the road shows that would come through on Sunday nights, people like Little Willie John, and Ike and

29

Tina Turner," enthused Engelhart. "It was the greatest school there was for young musicians. We used to just *haunt* that place."

No Eisenhower-era white teen was ever likely to forget a genuine gut-bucket R&B revue, with its smoky payday party atmosphere, where the audience was as loose as the music was tight, the dance floor as sweaty and packed with fun lovers as any Southern Delta juke-joint fish-fry shack, or ghetto blues or jazz dive. "We were underage," recalled Ormsby, "but we got in all the places. I don't know *how*—I just hung with Bill. He'd say, 'Come on I wanna show you somethin.' And I went out there to the Evergreen Ballroom and I went, 'Whoa . . . let's not miss *one* night of this!' And it was *all* black. Bill and I used to stand in a sea of all black people. And Bill knew a lot of 'em from his previous band. So he knew all these people and they knew him and I just hung close. And they liked him and were real encouraging and supportive and the musicians were real nice. Real good people."

If the older audience was charmed at all by the presence of these young white boys, the black music stars were downright helpful to them. "There were so many of them—the Ray Charles band, Bobby "Blue" Bland, Junior Parker—it didn't matter: We'd be there. I think we went every Sunday for about two or three years. We never missed one. We used to hang out afterwards and talk to all of 'em. Little Richard, Bobby Bland . . . *God*, it was great! We used to go back in their dressing rooms and they'd remember us because they'd be up there playin' and see these two little white faces out there [laughter]." The Blue Notes were among the first local white kids to brave the trip out to see these R&B shows at the Evergreen Ballroom—and Engelhart took every opportunity to personally meet his idols. The first show that he ever saw at the hall was in 1956: James Brown and the Famous Flames. But on other Sunday nights he saw Lloyd Price, Fats Domino, Jackie Wilson—and another time, the Platters, with Seattle's Dave Lewis Combo opening the show. On one particularly memorable night, he made his way backstage to try and greet Ray Charles, and the resultant conversation was as short and sweet as it was inspirational. Charles asked the precocious kid: "So, are you a musician?" Engelhart replied, "Yes." "Oh? Well, what kind of music do you play?" "The blues." And, then after a significant pause, Charles inquired: "You're white, aren't you?" "Yes." "Well, it doesn't matter, if you *feel* it."

In time Engelhart would work up the courage to try and mount the Evergreen's stage himself—and on the night of February 2, 1958, he achieved that far-fetched goal. "I was so nervy when I was nineteen years old that I walked up to B.B. King and asked him if I could sing with his band. And he said, 'Sure. Whudya wanna do?' And I said, 'Well, mostly I just do some of the stuff you do.' He said, 'Well, go on up and *do* it!' I mean, *this* was a really an unbelievable thing. But it really happened, and Buck was in the audience. So I got up there and it was great. He had like this big fifteen-piece band then, and I was just in seventh heaven. So I sang a couple songs—and into the second one I heard a *guitar* behind me, and I turned around and it was B.B. King, and he had this big smile on his face!"

But of all the many shows the Blue Notes attended at the Evergreen, perhaps none left such a deep impression on them as the night of February 22, 1958, when they witnessed performances by Little Willie John and Bobby Darin and, most importantly, Little Richard's band, the Upsetters. In addition to the sound of their fabulously rich horn section, the Upsetters' choreographed dance steps just slayed the young band. At their very next rehearsal they got busy practicing their own steps. They added Buck Mann and his baritone sax to the tenor sax of Dutra's replacement, Tom Giving, in an attempt to emulate the rich "sax choir" sound of their R&B heroes. Then, when Ormsby finally dumped his old lap steel and acquired a Fender electric bass guitar, the Blue Notes really began attracting attention. "We were in the garage rehearsing after school one day," recalled Engelhart, "and Robin went out of the garage and came back in, and he says, 'Come here—you gotta *see* this!' I went out and I didn't know what was goin' on— there were about forty kids *dancing* in the alley behind my dad's garage. So Robin—being real shrewd—said, 'Let's rent a hall.' So that's how we got started. We just started renting halls and making our own posters."

The Northwest's original DIY band, the Blue Notes found that their efforts to polish their own version of an R&B stage show not only won them fans amongst their age group, but made them Tacoma's hottest musical property. The media soon took note of all this action. But their elders' total befuddlement about what it meant for some local white guys to have formed a rockin' R&B band was crystallized in a newspaper article that was published with this inflammatory headline: *Thrill Jive Addicts.* Furthermore, that notice also misidentified them as "Pierce County's candidates for the hall of fame in the field of modern jazz."

Meanwhile, the good news was that the two old cowboys who'd given the Blue Notes their first break at the Crescent wasted no time in inviting the combo to appear on their KTNT-TV variety program, *The Bill & Grover Show.* If it seemed odd to anyone that a white teenage R&B combo was appearing on a TV program that had a distinct C&W motif, the Blue Notes never caught wind of any such sentiment. Their hosts made them feel right at home. Now, whether the show's audience could appreciate the boys' choice of material or not, *no one* could deny that they were—at the very least—extremely novel.

"The Blue Notes were the only band around that area for at least a year that actually played that kind of music," Engelhart proudly reflects. "Well, there *were* other young bands—but they were all sitting down with their dinner jackets and reading sheet music from the '40s. We were kind of an

The Blue Notes on *The Bill and Grover Show*, KMO-TV, 1958.

oddity. Later we heard about this group out in Lakewood, a Tacoma suburb." And that new rock 'n' roll band—the Wailers—would prove to be one that music fans would definitely be hearing a lot more about. In fact, they would soon upstage the Blue Notes and then go on to challenge the top Seattle bands as well.

CHAPTER 5

Wailers House Party

I n the late 1950s rock 'n' roll was the most exciting thing in the world for many teenagers. Some of its earliest pioneers, however, were no longer exactly spring chickens: Bill Haley, Fats Domino, and Chuck Berry were all over thirty years old. So, it was really only a matter of time before those stars' musical progeny would rise up to carry the torch forward. Among the leaders of that "next generation" to emerge and gain degrees of national notoriety were South Carolina's Joe Bennett and the Sparkletones, Philadelphia's Freddie Bell and the Bellboys—and Tacoma's Wailers.

Of these, it was the Wailers who would have the biggest impact—and one way they achieved that was by *not* highlighting a bandleader's name and instead presenting themselves as equals, thereby crystallizing the very concept of a teenage rock 'n' roll *band*. And as a band, the Wailers would certainly have an interesting career arc—highlights would include early gigs at Harlem's famed Apollo Theater and on ABC-TV's *Dick Clark Show*—and (in what must have seemed to be a century later during the psychedelic '60s) other shows at San Francisco's Fillmore Auditorium and Los Angeles' Whisky A Go Go.

Still, the Wailers' origins were as humble as they come: The group evolved out of a Dixieland stage band formed at Tacoma's Clover Park High School. The band's co-founders were an acoustic bassist named Woody Mortenson and a trumpeter named John Greek, who began by casually hiring a varying cast of other players and booking themselves variously as the M-G Trio, the M-G Quartet, the M-G Quintet, or the M-G Octet, all depending on a particular gig's musical requirements—and payroll limits. The personnel lineup varied according to who was able and willing to do one-nighters on short notice, but a key discovery for Greek was the band's first guitarist, Rich Dangel. "One day he came up and asked if I'd be interested in coming and playing on Saturday nights at these sock hops that they did, so they could do a rock 'n' roll tune or two," Dangel recalled. "And I knew a few tunes like 'Honky Tonk.' So [Greek] said, 'I'll pay ya five bucks to come in and do two or three tunes this Saturday night.' And so I did that, and pretty soon people were asking for *more* of that sort of thing and *less* of the Dixieland music."

As the formative band shifted their musical focus, a few players dropped out and a few others joined in. Among the latter was a kid named Kent Morrill, who could not only pound out a mean rock 'n' roll piano but also sing in a mercurial high tenor. Then, with the addition of a couple guys from Stadium High School—Mark Marush on saxophone and Mike Burk on drums—the combo's lineup gelled. The band took on a new name, the Nitecaps, and played a few early shows at the local Frosty Freeze, where they were compensated with free ice cream.

The Nitecaps' first real gig was a Wednesday night show at McChord's enlisted men's nightclub, the Snakepit, and the following Friday they played a dance in the grange hall out at Clear Lake near Eatonville. It wasn't long before Tacoma's reigning teen band, the Blue Notes, caught wind of the Nitecaps' existence, and, not sensing any danger to their status, Engelhart magnanimously invited the new band to open a dance that his combo had scheduled for the very next weekend at the Lake City Community Center at American Lake just outside Tacoma. The Nitecaps accepted gratefully— and also coincidentally settled on a new permanent name that night: the Wailers. Soon thereafter, in October 1958, the newcomer band played a post-ballgame dance at Bellarmine High that won over the hearts of that large school's music fans. Word about the exciting new band spread like a prairie fire, and a couple of weeks later a crowd of 1,800 kids swarmed the All-City Halloween Dance at the Tacoma Armory—1,800 *white* kids, that is.

And that's about where the first indication of a division of audience share—and a point of future tensions between the two combos—would become apparent. "The difference between us and the Blue Notes at the time was we were definitely more rock," contended Greek. "The Blue Notes were into a harder blues/R&B [sound]. Which is why, I think, we always outdrew the Blue Notes—I mean *eight* hundred to *two* hundred. They wound up where they couldn't even play in town if we were playin'— which kinda frustrated them, I think."

"The Wailers caught on real fast," said Engelhart, "and they were a real pain in the butt for us for a long time. But see, we were playing a more 'black' music—we were more of an *R&B* group. We were playing what was

considered 'race' music.' I had three horn players and Robin out in front—
we patterned ourselves after Little Richard's band, the Upsetters. And
when the Wailers came along, they were playing Duane Eddy and more
teenage-type things—so they caught on with the younger kids faster than
we had. They were smart, because here *we* were playing *R&B*, but there
were no black kids at the dances—I don't remember *any* black kids ever
coming to any of our dances. So the Wailers come along, and they're playing exactly what those young white people wanted to hear, and they did
way better as far as local dances."

Another sign that the Wailers were experiencing a meteoric rise came
after they were invited to do a spotlight set during a couple Saturday night
dances at the old Midland Community Hall. This room had long been a
country joint where Pop Avera and the Wildwood Boys had their weekend
dances broadcast live over Tacoma's KMO radio. But as Avera watched his
crowds dwindle and the Wailers' snowball, he let the upstarts have the hall
all to themselves one night a week. And that move proved to be the first
step toward his own band's extinction. The numerical disparity between
the size of the country audience and the new rock 'n' roll audience was
undeniable, and before long the Wildwood Boys got edged out of both the
hall *and* their KMO radio slot. From there, the band played the odd gig at
places like the Crescent Theater, the Parkland Theater, and Puyallup's Liberty Theater. But soon the Wailers took to copying the Blue Notes' earlier
bootstrap DIY tactics—they rented venues like the Fellowship Hall or the
Tacoma Armory, brought in rented Coke machines, and printed and distributed their own posters to advertise a series of what they promoted as "Wailers House Parties."

With all that activity going on, even the *Tacoma News Tribune* couldn't
ignore their town's rock musicians any longer. In 1959 they tracked the
Wailers down for an interview, and Greek informed the reporters that "rock
'n' roll is just catching on in the Northwest and is becoming more and more
popular every day. Even older people are admitting they like some of it. A
year ago Tacoma had no rock 'n' roll combos—now there are half a dozen,
and Seattle has eight or ten." And it was those Seattle and Tacoma bands
who were helping forge an indigenous new blend of driving jazz- and R&B-
tinged rock 'n' roll that soon acquired the descriptive name of the "original
Northwest Sound."

CHAPTER 6

That Sound

It remains an interesting mystery exactly why the Pacific Northwest's vibrant jazz community never really established a definably unique regional sound. Although the jazz played along both Seattle's Jackson Street and Portland's Williams Avenue from the 1920s through the 1950s was vibrant and plenty entertaining, those fine players just never took their collective music that one extra step.

Instead, the task of creating a Northwest Sound would be left to the next generation—players whose musicality was admittedly informed by jazz traditions, but who would lean more toward the emerging trends of rhythm and blues, and then rock 'n' roll. In fact, this regional musical mutation—which was forged in the rowdy dancehalls of the area's biggest seaport towns of Seattle, Portland, and Tacoma—was initially referred to by a few hip West Coast players as the "Sea-Port Beat." In its earliest phase, the music was based on a shared repertoire of recent and current R&B hits and a lot of "rude jazz" saxophone-led tunes—in other words, just the sort of music that was imported here by the particular hit-making R&B stars who had willingly braved the wilds of the Northwest Territories back in the 1950s.

The "Sea-Port Beat," or "original Northwest Sound," as first defined by Seattle's Dave Lewis Combo was essentially a regional sub-strain of rock 'n' roll that was firmly anchored in the West Coast R&B previously honed by Ray Charles and Richard Berry—along with the horn-driven sounds of the bands of Big Jay McNeely, Bobby "Blue" Bland, and Hank Ballard. But the critical ingredient that the young Northwest players brought to this mix was a tendency to take all those artists' greatest songs and alter their overall vibe in a way that appealed instantly to their own audiences' needs. And what the kids of the Northwest reacted to best was a song that rocked hard and had no room for rhythmic subtlety.

The first generation of Northwest rock bands typically squared off any song's beat and shed some of the complexities that more seasoned musicians who originally composed and cut these songs had included in their arrangements. Sure, the simplifying process may have altered the compositions, but that change proved to be a definite plus in the minds of the Northwest groups' young fans. To these teens, whatever might have been lost in this morphing process was more than made up for in raucous energy and sheer danceability.

The best example of this de-evolutionary process is the case of Richard Berry's "Louie Louie," which was adopted as a centerpiece within a core list of songs that were considered Northwest teen-dance essentials. Probably not too long after Berry had introduced the song in person at his dances here in 1957, the Blue Notes' singer, Rockin' Robin, came across a copy of the Flip label record while working part-time as an errand boy for the Broadway Record Shop. He loved the tune and added the disc to his growing collection of R&B records—a stash that his band often delved into for new material for their set lists.

Once the Blue Notes got their hands on a song, they began to reinterpret it. In the case of "Louie Louie," they kept the original lyrics—which relate the saga of a sad-sack sailor who is pouring his lonely heart out to "Louie," his patient bartender—but dropped the exotic Caribbean aspects of Berry's rhythmic arrangement. This was the beginning of an inexorable process that subsequent bands would continue with until the tune became a simple, straightforward, and subtlety-free garage rock pounder that drove kids to the dance floor—and adults to fits of frustration . . . except, it would seem, in one notable instance, when "Louie Louie" played a role in saving the day at an adults-only event.

It was the winter of 1959 when members of the elite Seattle Yacht Club showed up with expectations of dancing the night away to the classy sounds of the Woody Herman big band. Herman and his band, however, got snowed in at some distant airport and were forced to cancel. Panicked, the club's managers cast about frantically for a short-notice replacement—*any* replacement. And the group they settled on was a rookie band called the Regents, who'd only just formed. Young and brave, the combo took on the task—even though they knew exactly three songs, which they proceeded to perform in rotation (and at varying tempos) all evening: Ray Charles's "What'd I Say," "Roll Out the Barrel," and "Louie Louie." Grateful to have any music at all, the older crowd got into the spirit of things and danced well into the wee hours.

"Louie Louie" seemed to have that magic ability to rile people up—both those who loved it and those who didn't. And in fact, it was "Louie Louie" that resulted in the Blue Notes getting banished from performing in their own hometown—a place that was probably never too thrilled about the idea of an R&B band from the "wrong side of the tracks" luring the fair city's white youth to the "dark side" of youth culture in the first place. "The city council finally kicked us out of Tacoma and wouldn't let us play any more dances there," laughed Engelhart. "They were so worried about us playing all these dances that they passed an ordinance that you had to be eighteen to go to a teenage dance. And, then some promoters wanted us to play at the New Yorker Café. And of course you had to get a permit for it and all of that—and so of course they promised the officials that no one under eighteen would come in. *Of course* they let in *anyone* who had a dollar. Well, then these plainclothes police came up to the stage, and they said to me, 'Okay, partner. That's it. You'll never play in Tacoma again.' And—'cause the place was packed, Robin said, 'Let us do one more song so that there's not gonna be a problem.' And he finally talked them into it. So we did 'Louie Louie' for about *forty-five minutes* [laughter]! And these guys [laughter] . . . Oh! They literally wouldn't let us play dances inside the city limits. They wouldn't let us play in town."

The Blue Notes' immediate recourse was to scout out other locations to play, and their first discovery was a winner. "We went right outside the city limits on Old Highway 99 and played at a place called the Little J.E.M."—a hamburger shack plopped halfway between Tacoma and Fife—where "you could see the city limit sign right from the place!" It was about July 1958 when the exiled band began their series of "Teen Age Hop" gigs at the Little J.E.M. and forever after that one song, "Louie Louie," would retain a special place in their repertoire and in the hearts of their fans.

The Blue Notes and the Regents were hardly the only Northwest groups to have adopted the song—up in Seattle, the Dave Lewis Combo had begun playing it at the Birdland in 1957, and in their wake, others, including the Playboys, the Frantics, the Thunderbirds, and the Gallahads, helped it become firmly ingrained as a primal, social teen-dance ritual across the region. But "Louie Louie" is merely the most prominent example of the type of song that laid a foundation for the advent of an eventual Northwest Sound. Taken as a whole, those hard-core R&B songs provided the teen players with a rich musical vocabulary that they utilized as building blocks to create their own musical language.

CHAPTER 7

Come Softly to Me

B y the late 1950s, the Northwest teen scene was really beginning to show some promise, but the local music industry was still lacking a few components necessary for viability. For example, while there were more than a few locally based record companies around by this point, none were truly rock 'n' roll- or R&B-oriented, and even fewer had anything like a professional publicist with enough natural chutzpah to promote a band in an effective manner. And so, those labels were perfectly incapable—as every Northwest rockabilly band with a record learned at the time—of overcoming the habitual reluctance of area radio stations (and record shops) to support the few youth-oriented records that *had* been produced locally. This stalemate spread directly to the print media, which had a tendency to downplay, or outright ignore, any musical activities other than those that pleased the mainstream's tastes.

All these factors worked together to create a self-defeating, stigmatic mind-set—one in which people naturally came to doubt that *any* locally produced recording could *ever* succeed. Adding to this poisonous situation was the fact that when the area newspapers did occasionally sit up and take notice, their coverage was dependably laced with strained tolerance or cruel disparagement. In particular, the *Seattle Times'* arts and entertainment editor (and resident curmudgeon), Louis R. Guzzo, with his negative attitude, was deeply responsible for helping induce a community-wide inferiority complex about what might even be *possible*. Guzzo insisted upon discounting anything that he didn't understand about the younger crowd's artistic efforts—which was nearly everything—and for years subjected local up-and-comers to naysaying in his columns.

Guzzo proudly relished his chosen role for decades, using his bully pulpit to insult everyone from the first generation of polite, clean-cut, suit-wearing local combos right up through the hissing, snarling, spiked-leather-clad punk rockers of the Reagan-era 1980s. Despite Guzzo's relentless efforts to steer his readers toward worthy art—meaning most anything that was *not* locally generated—his evil spell was broken in 1957 with the "discovery" of Seattle's fantabulous local lounge diva, Pat Suzuki. Hired by the Colony Club—a downtown dinner joint run by Seattle's top jazz impresario, Norm Bobrow—Suzuki had already been enchanting crowds there for over a year without any sort of media hoopla. Indeed, the room had been packing in the crowds who were thrilled by her singing, but by then the locals didn't even trust their own native instincts. They had been slowly brainwashed—thanks to Guzzo and his ilk—into disbelieving that they could possibly be witnessing a genuine talent who might break out into the big time.

That impasse was finally overcome only after the Northwest's biggest entertainment star, Bing Crosby, attended Suzuki's show one evening while back in town for a visit. Luckily for Suzuki, word leaked to the newspapers that Crosby was prowling around town, and when reporters caught up with him and asked what he thought, his quote—"Great bet for the big time. I really mean that"—finally rang the alarm and woke everybody up. Maybe, just maybe, another talent could emerge from this region. After all, Crosby had gone from his hometown of Tacoma to become one of the twentieth century's greatest stars of radio, records, movies, and television. Though a man of many talents, what Crosby was *not* was prescient: It was he, after all, who (later, in 1962) cheerfully opined that "rock 'n' roll seems to have run its course." Regardless, now that Crosby's endorsement had been secured,

44

the local media *finally* felt safe to jump on the bandwagon—and in the process they tried to make up for lost time by going thoroughly overboard in hyping Suzuki. Still, the general enthusiasm was *very* refreshing—and contagious: The next thing anyone knew, Suzuki had been whisked off to Hollywood and signed to a major-label deal by RCA Records. She made her national television debut on ABC-TV's *Lawrence Welk Show*, and was named America's Best New Female Singer in *Downbeat* magazine's annual DJ poll. Funny, isn't it, what a little hometown boost can do for an artist's career?

Word quickly spread throughout musicians' circles about how Suzuki had been signed to RCA on the basis of demo tapes that had been cut right here in Joe Boles' basement studio. Up until this point, local studios had always been considered a joke, and anyone with serious aspirations soon heard that you had to go to Hollywood, New York, or Nashville to cut a legitimate record. Well, at least that was what everyone from Bing Crosby on down—including the handful of other Northwest talents who achieved fame in the 1950s (Seattle country singer Bonnie "Dark Moon" Guitar; Camas, Washington, folk-pop star Jimmie "Honeycomb" Rodgers; and Dallas, Oregon, pop idol Johnny "Cry" Ray)—had been doing for decades in order to break out nationally.

So when people began to eventually connect the dots and realize that Pat Suzuki *and* Big Jay McNeely (and Bonnie Guitar) had each gotten huge career boosts directly *after* recording with Joe Boles, musicians of every stripe began beating a path straight to his West Seattle door. It was late 1958 when the next momentous session occurred in that modest wood-paneled rec room—and it came about only after a label with adequate capital and effective distribution channels was finally established in Seattle.

Dolton Records' origins trace back to the C&C Distributing Company at 708 Sixth Avenue, which had been founded back in 1946 by Lou Lavinthal (and his partners Stan Solman and Stan Jaffe), and which by the mid-'50s had grown to be the region's biggest independent record wholesaler. At the time, only a few major record companies—RCA, Capitol, Columbia/Epic, and Decca/Coral—had their own exclusive distribution networks for getting new discs to both radio stations and retailers. However, the vast majority of "independent" labels—like Imperial, Modern, and Dot Records—employed the services of firms like C&C to do their legwork around the nation's many varying marketplaces.

As it happened, C&C had recently hired a young new sales account representative named Bob Reisdorff, who quickly proved his worth and was promoted to the position of promotion manager. Always pushing ahead, Reisdorff soon began publishing a little mimeographed newspaper that he called the *Platter Pulse*, which was intended to get the region's radio biz focused on whatever particular indie-label records C&C was promoting that month. Along the way, Reisdorff began demonstrating an uncanny ability to spot promising tunes before they scored as legit hits, and by 1958 he decided that the next step was to form his own label. He simply believed that he could produce hit records just as well as any of these guys in New York and Hollywood—and that confidence convinced his bosses at C&C, who bought in, and committed to throwing their corporate weight behind the new venture.

With the label's business concept firmly set, all Reisdorff needed now was a likely talent to groom, record, and promote. Making his weekly rounds for C&C, Reisdorff met everyone in the biz, and in time he began hearing tips and receiving tapes from all sorts of "talents" wanting to make a hit record. But his interest wasn't fully piqued until early in the summer of '58— a season when Pat Suzuki made a triumphant return for an extended engagement at the Colony Club. The Colony had put out notices that they would be auditioning for several dancers needed for Suzuki's show. One successful applicant was a dancer/singer from Olympia High School named Gretchen Christopher—and fate intervened soon thereafter when Suzuki fell ill one day and Norm Bobrow asked Christopher (whose mother was with her as a chaperone) to fill in and headline the show that night.

Seattle Post-Intelligencer columnist Emmett Watson just happened to be attending. Impressed with the young fill-in act, he raved about Christopher in his next essay, giving her prominent coverage that would have been highly welcome under almost *any* other circumstance. But when the Washington State Liquor Control Board took note of Christopher's reported age of seventeen—and, thus, her legal status as a minor—her short-lived nightclub career was halted in its tracks. Luckily for her, other people beyond Watson and the WSLCB enforcers were discovering her, including Bob Reisdorff, whom Bobrow had tipped off about a demo tape that the teen had recorded at home with some friends—a trio called Two Girls and a Guy—and was now lugging around.

"She had this tape that she'd asked Norm to listen to," recalled Reisdorff. "The title was 'Come Softly'—and he was chuckling about it. He said, 'Can you *imagine* calling a record [laughter] "*Come* Softly"?!' So he said to her, 'You should have Bob Reisdorff listen to it 'cause he has connections.' So

Gretchen brought this thing to me. And it was just *beautiful*. I thought it was a natural hit."

"Come Softly" was an original doo-wop tune that had been written by two pretty cheerleaders, Christopher and her friend Barbara Ellis, and their school pal, a trumpeter from the Oly pep band, Gary Troxel. Formed to perform at a school assembly—with the backing of the Blue Comets, a combo that boasted guitarist Donny Ulrich (who had already played with Little Bill Engelhart)—the trio were an instant hit on campus. After they made a second appearance at a postgame school dance with the Blue Comets, their fellow students begged them to record the song. The trio cut it a cappella on Christopher's father's home tape recorder and then hurried on down to the broadcast studios of Olympia's tiny AM station, KGY, where the DJ indulged them with an airing.

Reisdorff also liked the song—but he was cautious enough to seek out a second opinion from the one person in town who had a lengthy track record in the production of hit songs—Bonnie Guitar. An excellent musician who had been playing country music locally since the late 1940s, Guitar had enjoyed her own bouts of national fame—her 1957 Top 10 national hit "Dark Moon" had led to television appearances on New York's *Ed Sullivan Show* and California's *Town Hall Party* program, tour dates with Gene Vincent and the Everly Brothers, and a staff position in a hit-making studio, where she soaked up many of the fine points and technical tricks behind successful recording techniques. Beyond all that, Bonnie had also worked with Dot Records—a big-time label that had not treated her in the most honorable way, either as a recording artist or, later, as an A&R executive scouting out and producing other talents for them.

Now back home in Seattle, she was raring to go with the next opportunity that came her way, and the little gem that Reisdorff brought her was just exactly that. After one listen she seconded his original opinion, declaring: "This is *absolutely* a hit sound." Furthermore, Bonnie stated that she knew *exactly* how the single ought to be produced: with warm production values that would bring out the doo-wop song's natural intimacy. Pleased with that assessment, Reisdorff made an offer: Dolton would bring her in as a partner, and she could supervise a recording session over at Boles' studio. In full agreement, Dolton proceeded to sign the trio—who were renamed the Fleetwoods.

During that session, Bonnie worked out an incredibly sparse pop instrumental arrangement that featured the innocent and wispy harmonies of the

Fleetwoods, Troxel rhythmically rattling his key ring, and her own simple gut-string guitar as instrumental backing. Reisdorff *loved it*, and in January 1959 he took the tape down to Hollywood, where he thought he might just be able to license "Come Softly to Me" directly to a big-time label and delay activating his own label. To his utter surprise, though, all he received from his cherished industry contacts there was an earful of discouragement: "*Don't* waste your time, Bob." "*Don't* blow your money." "*Don't* start a label." "There's *no* hit there." Ouch. "I was a little jarred by that reaction," said Reisdorff, "but I was back in Seattle in the next day or two, and I went straight from the airport to all the key radio guys I knew and I said, 'Will you play this for me?' And they all played it. And they said, 'Listen, the switchboard's all lit up.'" With the powerful KING station among those giving the single a heavy push, Dolton raced to get some 45s pressed, and from there the tune's popularity began to spread—first statewide, and then down the coast.

Billboard took note of the action in mid-February, and that publicity helped Dolton attract distribution channels nationally. The usual route for a small indie label with a promising hit on its hands is to find an established label that can license and rerelease the song with a bigger marketing push and make the record into a nationwide hit. With this single, finding a willing label was not the problem—it would be simply choosing from amongst *all* the labels that were clamoring for a piece of the action. And, in fact, it suddenly seemed that every shark in the music biz was circling the fledgling company. These guys could smell a potential windfall ten thousand leagues away, and among of the first to make contact were the Dot and Era labels—neither of which was a very palatable option. Dot was the cutthroat label that had maimed Bonnie Guitar's "Dark Moon" hit back in 1957 when they suddenly released a second version by another singer and those two discs had to share the glory. And Era was infamous for adding overdubbed orchestral string arrangements on top of recordings (which would have simply drowned the wispy Fleetwoods), or, if unable to secure a deal with the original label, simply issuing a rush-released copycat cover version in an often successful ploy to steal the original's thunder.

Unimpressed by Dot's or Era's overtures, Reisdorff handled the disc's promotion for its first six weeks and then entered discussions with his old pals Al Bennett and Snuffy Garrett, down at Liberty Records. At which point Era's owner, Lou Bedell, threatened Reisdorff, saying, "Bob, if you don't give it to me I'm going to *cover* you." "And so," said Reisdorff, "I stalled him. I must admit. You have to play their game. I stalled him as long as I could—

at least long enough to get pressings so that Liberty could get its DJ mailing ready. You know, they play such *awful* games in Hollywood. It's a very dog-eat-dog world. There's so much conniving in the record business, and it was pretty widespread and pretty disgusting."

And it was disgusting to watch as Era flooded the radio market with promo copies of a quickie remake of the song by none other than Ronnie Height—a former member of Seattle's Five Checks who'd relocated to Hollywood. Though the remake didn't possess half the charm that the Fleetwoods' disc did, Era had successfully confused the marketplace, and in the following days more than one station resisted Dolton's outreach, explaining that they had already committed to airing Height's version. Liberty responded with a redoubled effort to spread their promo copies far and wide, but in a few markets—like Chicago, where 63,000 copies of Height's 45 were reportedly sold—they were simply beaten to the punch.

This brazen display of music biz hardball shocked Seattle's newbie record execs—all the more so when Height's single began to show up in a number of West Coast radio markets. Now the very real possibility was raising its ugly head that Dolton might just have their hit stolen right out from under them—especially when Gone Records suddenly issued *another* version (by their top act, Richard Barrett and the Chantels), and it began charting on New York radio stations. This was getting to be ridiculous. However, it seems that the record biz always has one more surprise up its sleeve. And so, even though Dolton was already shaken by these unexpected events, the plot thickened again when a henchman from Dick Clark's office let it be known that they were "probably" going to go with the Chantels' version on ABC-TV's *American Bandstand* show.

Reisdorff knew that if that happened, their hopes for the Fleetwoods' record were shot. By that time, Clark had managed to carve himself a uniquely powerful niche as American youth culture's pop czar. Dolton was adamant that their hit—which was No. 1 in Miami, Cleveland, and Seattle, and had already shipped over 100,000 copies—would not be hijacked. Reisdorff sprang into action, hitting the road with the Fleetwoods on an emergency promotional concert tour around the country and simultaneously launching phase two of his game plan. And that meant: "I had to stop Dick Clark from putting the Chantels' version on," said the Dolton exec. But that goal was even complicated further when Clark's agent made contact again in order to mention that there was a chance that any problems still facing the Fleetwoods' 45 might be forestalled—*if*, that is, a certain business arrangement could be worked out. Maybe one in which the song's publishing rights were transferred from Reisdorff's publishing company—Cornerstone—over to a different firm.

Well, that was the final straw. Reisdorff had realized that he was operating in a new arena now—one that the big boys thought they ruled—and even that Dolton might eventually be forced to come to some sort of terms with his competitors. But not just yet—and certainly not without a fight. Reisdorff simply figured, Why produce a hit just to have the rewards grabbed by some song-publishing gangsters? And so Dolton came out with both barrels blazing and a commitment to make as big of a stink about it all as necessary. Furious—but realizing Dolton had had no *physical* evidence that Clark's people had ever tried to pull any funny business—Reisdorff needed to find a way to put pressure on Clark. And the path he chose was that of pitting the ABC network's natural corporate adversary—the NBC network—against them. And by leveraging the pride that management at KING Broadcasting Inc. (Seattle's NBC affiliate) was feeling for helping birth a hit, Reisdorff convinced them to enter the fray. In fact, Dolton won the support of all of the NBC affiliates in the Northwest—along with a number of station managers in Los Angeles—and even Washington's then-governor, Albert Rosellini, who immediately wired Clark to "remind" him that "Come Softly to Me" was *already* a Fleetwoods hit.

By March the dust had settled: ABC and Clark had apparently been given the necessary prodding to do the right thing, and the Fleetwoods' 45 entered both the *Billboard* and the *Cash Box* charts. The group was soon summoned to the *Ed Sullivan Show* in New York City. From there, "Come Softly to Me" soared to No. 1 on the *Billboard* pop charts, became a huge international hit, and sold a quick million copies. And—as an ironic capper to the tale—it was none other than Clark himself who later made a televised gold record award presentation to the group on the April 11 episode of the *Dick Clark Show*. Looking back on the entire escapade decades later, Reisdorff recalled with a twinkle in his eye that the *real* payoff was "when I met Dick Clark in Philadelphia—and the first thing that he said to me was, 'I never had *so much* pressure to play a particular version of a record as I got from you! [laughter] He said, 'I heard from all *kinds* of people.'"

The Fleetwoods went on to many more successes: performing everywhere from the Hollywood Bowl, to Madison Square Garden, to the Whisky A Go Go. They were named Most Promising Vocal Group of the Year 1959 by *Cash Box*, and the trio cut eight more Top 40 singles—including the No. 1 gem "Mr. Blue"—and thirteen albums. In time, historians would begin weighing in on the group's contributions: In 1994, Glenn Gass wrote that the Fleetwoods hits' "close-miked intimacy and tame but catchy rhythmic backing create an unpretentious charm that eluded the more contrived efforts of the 'teen idol' era." Michael Kelly's 1993 book, *Liberty Records*, went even further in praising Dolton's first hit: "This song was a groundbreaking rock 'n' roll event. Until this record, the vast majority of rock 'n' roll had been of the hard-driving, bluesy variety. . . . True, there were [other] rock 'n' roll ballads . . . [but] these songs were still forcefully delivered. 'Come Softly to Me' opened up new vistas of possibilities for the music."

This much is inarguably true: The success of the Fleetwoods' debut record did, among other accomplishments ascribed to it, force open the eyes of the Northwest music scene to "new vistas of possibilities." In fact, "Come Softly to Me" can serve as a metric for how far the local music industry had come: With Dolton Records' freshman effort, they brought home the very first gold record award ever earned by a local production. And that was a milestone that would proudly stand as an inspiring, if longshot, goal for countless other Northwest songwriters, bands, producers, engineers, and labels to try and equal.

CHAPTER 8

Young Blues

The out-of-the-blue left-field success of Seattle's Dolton Records instantly made all those old provincial doubts about the hopes of striking gold with homegrown musical talent perfectly obsolete. And that dramatic shift of perceptions affected not only locals, but the entertainment industry establishment in Hollywood and New York City—if something as golden as the Fleetwoods could be reeled in from the Great Northwest, goodness knew *what else* might be lurking around in the backwaters of that unexplored territory.

The bigwigs down at Liberty Records, in particular, were certainly open to damn near *anything* that Dolton presented them. If Bob Reisdorff's and Bonnie Guitar's prescient pop vision saw merit in some particular recording they'd produced, Liberty assured them that they'd be willing to finance the pressing and distribution of it to the national market. Luckily for everyone involved, this reputation that the Dolton brain trust was gaining for having the Midas touch would turn out to be quite well deserved—each of the first *seven* Dolton 45s issued would score on the *Billboard* and/or *Cash Box* charts and become national or even international hits, including those by some of the Northwest's finest young rock 'n' roll talents, like the Frantics.

As early as January 1958, the Frantics felt that they were ready to cut a record, and so they booked some time at Joe Boles' studio—but neither that session nor another at Chet Noland's Dimensional Sound studio led to a recording contract. But when Art Simpson, a KOL DJ, heard and liked the band, he told them to contact Bob Reisdorff—which they did. He signed them, and they were soon at Boles' house recording their first instrumental single, "Straight Flush" / "Young Blues."

Under Reisdorff's guidance, proper promotion of the band and their Dolton 45 began. Thanks to the success of the Fleetwoods, KING radio was given the opportunity to debut the label's latest disc, and then Reisdorff's friendly contacts at other area radio stations—like KOL, KMO, KXRO, and KJR—also began airing the Frantics' hot two-sided instrumental disc. It was March 1959 when the Frantics followed the path that their labelmates, the Fleetwoods, had taken by debuting their disc on KING-TV's new *Seattle Bandstand* show. Modeled after Dick Clark's national program, the local version was a weekly two-hour teen record-hop show—hosted by KING radio DJ Ray Briem—that aired on Saturday afternoons at 1 P.M. Like any DJ worth his salt, Briem was no slacker when it came to hype. He told one local newspaper that his show "has become a real star-maker. The Fleetwoods made their first appearance on the show. Now their 'Come Softly to Me' is pushing the million-seller mark. 'Straight Flush' by the Frantics is No. 2 on the local charts and skyrocketing. The song was first heard on *Seattle Bandstand*. . . . Seems like Seattle is loaded with talent and the rest of the country is beginning to find out about it."

Before long, Dolton's second release began getting airplay in scattered markets around the country: It soon made its entry into *Billboard*'s Top 100 pop charts. Reisdorff kept pushing, looking for any opportunity to promote his acts. So when Briem called in to ask if the Fleetwoods and Frantics were both available to perform at a very special show he was planning, the answer was an emphatic yes. And so, on the fabled night of February 23, 1959, both groups were booked to share the billing at a dance to be held up at Parker's Ballroom—a gig that was to be headlined by big-time singing star Bobby Darin. By this time, the Frantics had already solidified their reputation as superior musicians and they were often hired to support touring stars ranging from Frankie Avalon to Gene Vincent—but that night with Darin was special because Darin dug his support band so much that, after doing their set together, he rejoined the Frantics while they wrapped up the night with a final closing set. "After he does *his* show," Frantics bassist Jim Manolides recalled, "he came back out and joined the band! He sang Ray Charles' 'I've Got a Woman' with us, and then he started playin' the piano a little bit, and he was singin' and playin' the drums! He just loved it and had a really good time."

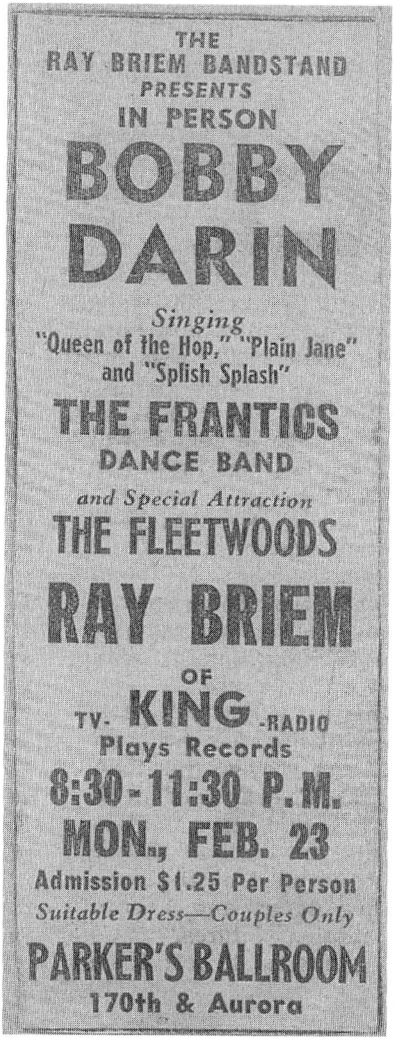

Seattle newspaper ad, 1959.

CHAPTER 9

I Love an Angel

Dolton Records' remarkable winning streak continued as the spring of 1959 unfolded. Following the chart success of both the Fleetwoods' and the Frantics' debut releases, the former group struck again in May with Dolton's third release, "Graduation's Here," a single that reached *Billboard*'s No. 39 position—and from there everything seemed to accelerate.

Down in Tacoma, the Blue Notes had watched all this action bubbling and were disappointed after they contacted Dolton Records only to be spurned by Reisdorff. The label head did, however, suggest that they first go over and cut a demo tape at Joe Boles' studio—or, at least that's how he remembered the encounter. Interestingly, Little Bill Engelhart recalled that the band had asked around *on their own* and discovered that Joe Boles' Custom Recorders was a good place to work. None of this would matter, of course, except that things proceeded from there to get quite complicated, and these conflicting recollections ended up becoming a sore point that would make future relationships between all the parties involved rather sticky.

The afternoon session itself, however, went *very* well: "The Blue Notes," explained Engelhart, "were basically an instrumental group—which most groups were back then. We had Rockin' Robin with us, and I sang a little—but it was mostly an instrumental group. And we just wanted to see what we sounded like, so we went up to Joe Boles' studio in West Seattle. We'd saved up our money and booked a couple hours of time. We went through all the instrumentals and then Joe came in and said, 'You've got a little extra time. Do you have anything else you'd like to do?'" One can easily imagine poor Rockin' Robin—who had, thus far, patiently waited with nothing to do—and his reaction to Boles' inquiry. He must have been simply chomping at the bit to get his crack at recording. But instead of letting him have a chance at the microphone, the band decided to cut a promising teen ballad that Engelhart had written, called "I Love an Angel." "So we did it," laughs Engelhart, "and Joe comes *flying* out of the control room. He was all excited—he said, 'Is that an *original?*' And we said, 'Well, yeah, it is.' And he said, 'Everybody sit down. I'm gonna make a call.' And so he called Bob Reisdorff and Bonnie Guitar from Dolton Records and they came down and just *flipped* over this song. [Reisdorff] had contracts with him and everything!"

In fairness to Reisdorff, his sudden flip-flop toward the Blue Notes can be partially credited to Boles' clean engineering work—a job that highlighted the sweet appeal of Little Bill's youthful voice singing those endearing lyrics—"I love an angel, but does she love me?"—coupled with Lasse Aanes' crisp drumming, and a "sax choir" chart by Tom Giving that is to die for. Conceivably patterned after the killer sax lines in James Brown's first hit, 1958's "Try Me," the song's horn arrangement—featuring Giving and Frank Dutra (who had just rejoined the band) on twin tenors, joined by Buck Mann's grunting bari sax—sounded *stunning*.

Dolton expressed an interest in working with the Blue Notes, and after suggesting they modify their name to Little Bill and the Bluenotes, Reisdorff pulled out a contract. "They sent me home that day with a recording contract for my dad to sign," said Engelhart. "I was the oldest—and I was nineteen—so you can *imagine* the excitement. In fact, I remember at one point asking, 'Well, are we going to have a record?' And they said, 'Of course yer gonna have a record.' So we flipped out! We went home that day in the car and hardly anyone said a word we were so excited. We were gonna have a *record!*" That was a tremendously exciting development, but of all the quiet band-members riding back to Tacoma in the car that day, one imagines that the quietest of all was Rockin' Robin. The band's nominal front man and main singer must have been wondering where exactly he fit in now that the freshly renamed group's debut disc would be featuring the vocals of their *guitarist*.

Meanwhile, other dark clouds were forming on the band's horizon. Unbeknownst to them, Boles had suddenly experienced serious second thoughts about having steered the Bluenotes to Dolton. Boles must have kicked himself plenty for ever having called the label. It was he, after all, who'd demonstrated the ability to spot this potential pop hit in the making. And so, according to Reisdorff, soon after everyone had cleared out of his studio, Boles got right back on the phone in an effort to reclaim his discovery. "Joe jumped in there and wanted to take the record himself!" exclaimed Reisdorff. "And I went to him and I said, 'Joe, what are you doing? I'm using your studio exclusively. I'm *sending* you people. I don't expect you to intercept me.' And Joe was upset about it, just terribly upset. He had stars in his eyes. So I said, 'I'll tell you what I will do'—and I shouldn't have done it, because there was no reason to do it—but, I said, 'I'll give you a penny a record.' Which I *did* do. But it should not have been done. Now, Joe was not a bad man, but he did a bad thing [laughter] because it was not like him. He was always a very nice man. But he liked that song a lot—he was going to put it out on his own label. And I think that would have been a mistake."

Having ironed out that wrinkle in their relationship, Dolton brought the Bluenotes back to Boles' studio on March 28, and this time Bonnie Guitar oversaw the session in which a final master track was cut from scratch. As producer, she was a taskmaster, making the boys play the song dozens of times to achieve pop perfection. Then, at day's end, Reisdorff assured the band that he'd call them the minute their 45s were pressed up and available. After receiving the word, the guys raced back to Seattle, picked up a box of their discs, and, while returning home, decided to drop by Tacoma's top radio station, KMO, to see if they could prompt some interest. "So we walked in there," recalled Engelhart, "and this disc jockey, Jack Morton, was sittin' in the booth, and he waved at us, and we held up our record and he motions us in. So we go into this small control room. He says, 'Well, whatcha got there?' 'We got our *new record*!' And he says, 'Well, let's put it on.' The guy didn't even *listen* to it first. He played it when we were all standing there and then when we were going home and we were listening to the radio, he played it *again*! So by the time we pulled up in front of Lasse's girlfriend's house, all of our girlfriends were there waiting—'Oh boy,' you know, 'we heard yer record!' I mean, the *thrill* of hearing it on the radio the first time was . . . well, I never have had anything quite like that since in the business."

Following KMO's lead, Seattle's KOL and KING also began airing the single, and then things really took off when the *Dick Clark Show* featured it on TV for a couple of weeks. "I Love an Angel" broke onto *Billboard*'s Hot 100 on June 22, 1959, and everything should have been peachy in the Bluenotes' camp. Rockin' Robin, however, wasn't so thrilled. Feeling shunted, he began to whine about how *he* wanted to record something, about how the Dolton know-it-alls had interceded to rename the band, about how Engelhart's name was in a larger type font than the band's on the

45 label, and about how they now had Little Bill wearing a *different* stage out-fit than the rest of the band members. Everyone knew that Rockin' Robin was disgruntled, but Reisdorff thought the guy was just plain *unpredictable*. He began to quietly advise Engelhart that he should dump the Bluenotes and start over with a fresh, and less scruffy, combo. But meanwhile, both the Frantics and Little Bill and the Bluenotes were invited to appear on an "Open House for Mental Health" fund-raising TV telethon that was being hosted by Bob Barker and broadcast live on KTVW.

Against his better judgment, Reisdorff went ahead and committed the two groups to perform. The Frantics' booking schedule was open for that date, but there was one complication for the Bluenotes: "We were playin' in Centralia the night before," recalls Engelhart, "and we'd been doin' about five one-nighters right before then, so we had to go on at like three in the morning. That's when we were scheduled to go on this telethon, so we all got packed up down there at one in the morning and we drove and drove and drove" back to Seattle. The Bluenotes' first set of songs—which were played at around 3 A.M.—drew a good number of phoned-in pledges, enough that the telethon's stage director asked if they'd hang around and play again. And so, the band reappeared at about 6 A.M., and then again at about 9 A.M., and once again at 10 A.M. By that point the game but exhausted band began wondering aloud, "Why don't we get Robin on?" Engelhart told them, "'Well, I'll talk to Bob.' So I went over and said, 'Bob: Can we get *Robin* on?' And he said, 'No. Robin's too crazy. You never know what he'll say.' And I said, 'Look, I'm really under a lot of pressure here with these guys, you know, and this would really alleviate a lot of it 'cause it's staring to look like I don't want to let Robin on cause he might show me up. And it's *not* like that. We're a *band*.' So, he says, 'You *promise* Robin won't say anything crazy?' And I said, 'I promise you' [laughter]. So we went on again and Bob was standin' right behind the camera and Robin got out there and we did 'Dizzy Miss Lizzy' and he was all over the place! He was real wiry and boy he got 'em goin.' So the MC from Hollywood comes over and he goes, 'My God, you guys are just unbelievable!' And he's talkin' to Robin and he says, 'Now, let me get this straight. You guys just did a few nights out on the road. Last night you were in a town called Centralia. Now where's that?' And Robin says 'Well, about a hundred and fifty miles south.' And the MC says 'You come up here today and you guys go on at three in the morning and here it is eleven thirty.' He says, '*How* do you do this?' And Robin says, real straight-faced, 'Oh, we take pep pills' [laughter]. And we didn't! But Robin had a real weird sense of humor. Reisdorff almost fell down behind this camera and he said, 'I *told* you he'd say something like that!'"

That live broadcast incident must have been the last straw for Dolton, because when a subsequent opportunity arose for them to bring all three of their hit bands out to make joint appearances on the *Spokane Bandstand*, *Portland Bandstand*, and *Yakima Bandstand* TV shows, the traumatized Reisdorff opted to load up a car caravan that included all the members of the Fleetwoods and Frantics—but only Engelhart would be there to lip-synch "I Love an Angel" while the rest of the Bluenotes were left behind.

Liberty Records' distribution efforts had guided "I Love an Angel" onto the national charts, and then, having bee licensed to various European record markets, the tune also began to take off as a radio hit in England and Germany. Liberty became so convinced of the record's potential that they invited Engelhart down to Hollywood for a face-to-face let's-get-acquainted meeting, and the young singer saw all this as indicators pointing toward his inevitable stardom. Such dreams, however, can easily be shattered, and upon his arrival in California, Engelhart quickly sensed that his hosts at Liberty's headquarters were now suddenly less enthusiastic than they had been in their earlier solicitous kissy-kiss phone calls. The idea that the label now looked at him and seemingly saw his physical profile to be a deal-breaking marketing challenge in a finicky teen-idol biz—one that mainly rewarded all-American pretty boys like Bobby Vee and Bobby Vinton—was just another of the numerous rude awakenings that the smallish, gaunt singer who walked with distracting steel crutches had had to bear in life.

But Engelhart was now facing other truths—in the wake of that meeting, Liberty's promotion machine apparently broke down and his hit song lost its chart momentum after peaking in August at the *Billboard* chart's No. 66 slot. Worse yet, he would now be returning home to Tacoma to face the fact that he'd totally burned his bridges with the Bluenotes, who had moved on without him by adding Bill Johnson as their guitarist. But that wasn't the only change that the Bluenotes had experienced in Engelhart's absence—Rockin' Robin had finally split and joined another band—one that Ray Briem was already touting to a local newspaper as the region's next big thing, saying, "Keep an eye on the Wailers. This is a group of Tacoma teenagers. . . . [W]e hope to have them on *Seattle Bandstand* in the near future."

CHAPTER 10

Tall Cool One

Nineteen fifty-nine was very good to Seattle's Dolton Records and their little roster of teen talents. But while the label had led this dramatic outbreak of music business successes emanating from the Northwest, they were in fact not alone: Down in Tacoma, the Wailers had been hustling to score their own recording contract.

In fact, back in the spring of 1958, the band had signed a management deal with Attlio "Art" Mineo, an old-school Tacoma big-band leader and the owner of the New Yorker restaurant. Mineo had moved here from the Big Apple, where he'd had some experience playing with big-time orchestras led by Paul Whiteman and Vincent Lopez. In the mid-1950s he'd even formed a short-lived song publishing partnership, Bolmin Music, with Joe Boles. So while Mineo *did* seem to have a showbiz connection or two, there was just something about the way that he was always name-dropping that made folks uneasy. Well, that and all the rumors that swirled around Tacoma about his and the New Yorker's minor-league mafia underpinnings.

Regardless, when the Wailers felt that they were ready to cut a record, Mineo—who had parted ways with Boles after some sort of falling-out—opted to take the band over to Lyle Thompson's Commercial Recorders in downtown Seattle. And it was there that on August 25, 1958, a master tape was made of a very cool original instrumental called "Scotch on the Rocks." Mineo was impressed, and he very confidently assured the boys that scoring a record deal would be a snap. But Mineo's supposed ins with various industry heavies somehow failed to convince the powers-that-be at numerous labels—including Atlantic and Dolton Records—each of whom declined to sign the Wailers. Finally, though, he was able to announce to the band that he'd negotiated a deal: They would be recording for the otherwise obscure New York–based Golden Crest Records.

Although the label's name was not exactly a household word—and the company had a nonexistent reputation in the rock 'n' roll world—the good news was that Golden Crest's eager head honcho, Clark Galehouse, soon arrived in Tacoma toting a portable tape deck. The gear was soon set up at the nearby Lakewood Knights of Columbus Hall, where the Wailers were booked to play a Saturday night dance—and after the gig ended, at about 2 A.M., the tapes rolled while the boys cranked out their set one more time. A total of five songs were captured that night: "Scotch on the Rocks," "Dirty Robber," "Roadrunner," "Mau Mau," and "Snakepit."

"Scotch on the Rocks" was the song that everyone thought was the potential hit—but its booze-oriented title was deemed inappropriate for the teenage market and it was renamed "Tall Cool One"—a title that could *at least* be conceivably interpreted as referring to an innocent mug of cold root beer. Musically, "Tall Cool One" featured a jazz-tinged instrumental riff that grooves along until it is utterly overrun by a wailing saxophone squall— just the sort of harsh sonic detail the afforded the band's stodgy hometown paper, the *Tacoma News Tribune*, an eagerly awaited chance to zing the young rockers a bit by complimenting old Mineo's acumen, carefully noting that while his "own inclinations lean to a more musical type of performance . . . he recognized a lively possibility when he heard the Wailers."

Local teens deemed the tune to be quite acceptably musical, however, and within weeks of its release by Golden Crest, "Tall Cool One" began to climb up the playlists at KMO and a few other Northwest radio stations. By the first week of May it was sitting at KJR's No. 1 slot—and the single's *flip side*, "Roadrunner," was at No. 5! Within in its first ten days in local record shops, "Tall Cool One" sold an astounding 20,000 copies. And from there the record took off nationally: Stations all across the country picked it up, and the single soon hit No. 45 on the *Cash Box* chart, receiving a positive review in that magazine: "The Wailers serve up a lidful of solidly rocking instrumental music. All the necessities of infectious rock 'n' roll are here: honking sax, twangy guitars, pounding drums." On May 18, "Tall Cool One" entered the *Billboard* charts, where it had a strong thirteen-week run, ultimately peaking just inside the nation's Top 40 at No. 36.

Golden Crest was ecstatic, and Clark Galehouse raced back to Tacoma for a second session, which yielded some more good instrumentals, including "Tough Bounce," "Long Gone," "Swing Shift," "Driftwood," and "Gunnin' for Peter." The label was all keyed up over their newfound success and they seemed determined to go all out in pushing the Wailers' career—*if*, that is, the combo would agree to immediately relocate to New York. But consid-

ering that the band-members' ages ranged from sixteen to eighteen—and most were still obligated to attend school through May—that would be a difficult demand to honor. One further complication was that Mineo was suddenly huffing and puffing and claiming rights to a full 50 percent of the band's earnings. Luckily, Mineo was effectively squeezed out without any Godfather-like repercussions, and when school finally let out, the Wailers crammed themselves (and all their gear) into a shiny new trailer-haulin' '59 Pontiac Fury station wagon (purchased with their cash advance of $1,200) and headed east to New York City.

Upon the boys' arrival, Golden Crest took them directly over to the offices of one of top talent agencies in America, General Artists Corporation, which also had big plans for the Wailers. First the band hit Philadelphia for a June 11 appearance on the *Dick Clark Show,* and from there the hit the *Milt Grant Show* in Washington D.C., the *Buddy Dean Show* in Baltimore, the *Roy Lamont Show* in Richmond, Virginia, and then record-hop shows in Ocean City, Maryland; Harrisburg, Virginia; Fort Wayne, Indiana; and Jackson, Michigan. Somewhat later they played a two-week engagement at the Cold Spring Resort in Hamilton, Indiana. The Wailers also went back to New York City for appearances at the Apollo Theater and on Allen Freed's popular *Big Beat Show* on WNEW-TV.

On June 26 Golden Crest released "Mau Mau" as a follow-up single, and by mid-August the song had gone Top 10 on Seattle radio, causing it break onto *Billboard*'s charts, where it peaked at No. 68. In the meantime, the Wailers were taken into Golden Crest's modest studio out in Hunting-ton Station, Long Island, to record more songs—and this time their record-ings would have considerably better fidelity than the field recordings made previously in Tacoma. Plus, the new batch of songs was showing the band's growth as rock 'n' roll composers: "Beat Guitar," "Wailin,'" and "Shanghied"

were all cool instrumental rockers of the first order, while the atmospheric mood piece "Devil's Island" featured the scary sounds of rattling prison chains—and a title that the timid Golden Crest exec replaced with the less provocative one, "High Wall."

When issued as a new single, "Wailin'"/ "Shanghied" also met with favor, and *American Music* magazine complimented the band in a terse platter-chatter review, in which it awarded the group a B+ : "[The] combo, which has shown its instrumental mettle with such noise-makers as 'Tall Cool One' and 'Mau Mau,' can click big with this driving statement. 'Shanghied': Stuff teen successes are made of." "Wailin'" also received a B+: "Here, too, there are sounds of big-beat note. Feature of the drive is a good 'click' sound behind the sizzling guitars. Voices shout. Two strong works." Encouraged, Golden Crest indicated that they were ready to move forward with the release of a full album—in fact, they offered to invest further in the band by hiring them private tutors to help with their schooling, and even to give them choreography lessons to sharpen up their stage act. But by the end of all that road travel, and following all the other excitements they'd experienced in recent weeks, the Wailers were tired and homesick, and back to Tacoma they went.

No doubt disappointed in a band that seemed to be caving just as they sat on the cusp of big-time fame, Golden Crest nevertheless moved forward with the March 1960 release of their debut album, *The Fabulous Wailers*. Although the LP was packed full of all the band's great tunes, it also featured a memorable black-and-white cover photo of the Wailers—one that has been since credited with helping establish the very concept of the "rock band." It features five hip guys posing with their instruments—lots of shiny guitars and other instruments—but more importantly, it just screams "band" at you. A group of equals joined together to play rock 'n' roll. No star like Buddy Holly out front—just the Crickets. No Gene Vincent getting all the glory—just the Blue Caps. Indeed, no Little Bill stealing the spotlight—just the Blue Notes. Or in this case, nobody hogging center stage—just an all-for-one, one-for-all rock 'n' roll band: the Fabulous Wailers.

Issued at a time when most teen-oriented artists—even those who'd already scored a string of hit singles—never got an album issued, *The Fabulous Wailers* was an oddity, a rare occurrence in the biz, and one that even Golden Crest didn't know how to capitalize on. Promotional efforts were invisible, and resultant sales were marginal. In fact, it has long been speculated that *The Fabulous Wailers* really never sold all that well—except to other young *musicians*, who recognized that the band's unique and brilliant

sound owed little debt to either the Duane Eddy school of Western buzz/ twang guitar rock or Johnny and the Hurricane's braying saxophone-led hits. The Wailers simply had a rock 'n' roll sound like nothing else around— and bands in the Northwest, across the country, and even in England loved them. Though their album never scored on the popularity charts, it did get recognized as a landmark—even the Beatles' guitarist, George Harrison, once enthused that he'd had the LP "since day one." Coincidentally, in 1964—right when the Beatles were storming the American shores—the Wailers' five-year-old single "Tall Cool One" broke out as a Top 40 radio hit once again in Detroit, leading it to another ten weeks on the *Billboard* chart, which prompted Golden Crest to reissue the LP.

And in one last respectful salute to the band's earliest recordings, *Hit Parader* magazine took a moment during the radicalized haze of August 1968 to note that "the Wailers' hit, 'Tall Cool One' . . . set a new standard of quality for the rock instrumental idiom, which had previously consisted almost entirely of such novelties as 'Tequila'. . . . 'Tall Cool One' itself was quite a ways ahead of it's time in the way it builds to a climax from a very, very soft opening. . . . *The Fabulous Wailers* LP was astounding when it was issued in 1959. And cut for cut, it remains the best LP by a white rock instrumental group made before the coming of the modern blues and San Francisco scenes."

CHAPTER *11*

How Long

Dolton Records had single-handedly kick-started the percolation of an optimistic new mood throughout the region—and then when Golden Crest Records jumped in and showed that the scoring of big-time hits by teenage talents from the Northwest was no fluke, lots of folks sat up and took note. One young musician—and leader of the Johnny Millward Combo—penned an essay for the "Younger Set" column of the June 1959 issue of the Musicians Union's newsletter, *Musicland*, which took stock of the progress made thus far—and also issued a challenge to the community: "In the last few months amazing things have been taking place in a city usually known for its natural beauty. Now Seattle has come up with another 'natural,' that of being the new influx of local talent on the national 'pop' scene. The growth of a new recording company has given new birth to the Northwest. In just a few months the growth of [Dolton Records] has been amazing and has listed among its recording stars the Fleetwoods and the Frantics, both having nationally distributed hits. As these groups worked their way to national prominence, other North-west groups became stimulated, and now we can hear them on almost any jukebox. What effect has this had on Seattle and what can be the result of this niche Seattle is carving in the 'pop' or 'rock and roll' field? For one thing, it is healthy and acts as a catalyst to the music business. Recently in the *International Musician* [magazine] Seattle was featured as one of the brightest spots for music in the United States. The rise of [local labels] makes the light even brighter. With national recognition of Seattle musicians, Seattle itself may take a second look at its own talent. . . . So far Seattle has taken only a condescending attitude toward its own musicians. . . . Why is it that the largest city in supposedly the fastest growing area in the nation cannot support and aid its own talent? . . . How come there are only very few nightclubs . . . and why is it that these clubs have such a hard time making ends meet? . . . I hope that you will take time to think about the condition that Seattle is in. Seattle can become one of the real hot spots in the nation, but it will take an organized effort by each and every one of us. Let's get on the ball and put Seattle on the map once and for all!"

Well, yes, thanks to Dolton and Golden Crest, Seattle *was* now on America's pop culture map, and the first three quarters of 1959 had—with the phenomenal concurrent national success of the Fleetwoods, the Frantics, Little Bill and the Bluenotes, and the Wailers—provided more excitement for Northwest rock 'n' roll fans than any time in memory. And as summer drifted toward fall, the rock 'n' roll action only intensified. In September alone, Dolton Records scored again twice: the Fleetwoods' "Mr. Blue" shot straight up to the nation's No. 1 slot, and the Frantics (with a new drummer, Don Fulton) returned to the *Billboard* Hot 100 chart with their second single, "Fogcutter." This was a fine instrumental tune named in honor of a famous cocktail that had first been concocted at Trader Vic's Restaurant—a historic nightspot that, way back in 1948, had been the very first to be granted a liquor license to serve cocktails in Seattle.

But even the route taken to produce those hits had a few bumps along the way, as trouble was still brewing within one of the professional relationships that had launched all this recent success. It seems that the previously productive working arrangement between Dolton and Joe Boles had been strained enough over their recent "I Love an Angel" clash that Bob Reisdorff pivoted and began taking all of the label's recording business to another of Seattle's studios, Northwest Recorders. This was a small studio that had opened for business back in 1948 in the rear section of Oliver Runchie's Electricraft Inc. hi-fi supply and electrical fix-it shop at 622 Union Street. Northwest Recorders' new employee, Kearney Barton, had cut his teeth as an engineer in the early '50s working at KTW—a 1,000-watt classical music radio station—but in 1958 he'd accepted an offer to move over and run the recording studio, which up until that point had mainly been recording old-fashioned pop vanity projects on their Listen Records label.

"At that time, there were only about three studios in town," recalled Barton. "When I started there I had never run a studio and I had to teach myself to do the actual recording and disc cutting and so forth. Well, I was just setting up—and Bonnie Guitar and Bob Reisdorff came in to do a demo. Bonnie liked the sound I got on her voice, and then they tried the Fleetwoods. And I started doin' all of their things after that. Bob Reisdorff and Bonnie Guitar kinda taught me recording—you know, what *they* were looking for." The Dolton execs found Barton easy to work with and, in fact, the studio's central downtown location was so darn convenient that before long the label moved out from their original C&C Distributors based headquarters and into a small office space in the same building as Northwest Recorders. The setup was ideal: Dolton would now literally be only a few short steps away from a perfectly decent studio. And the priority project for Dolton now was to cut enough tracks to fill out a debut LP for the Fleetwoods.

As things turned out, Dolton's sense that a couple of the group's new tunes—"Mr. Blue" and "You Mean Everything to Me"—were strong contenders was spot-on: Issued together as a single, the former began its twenty-week chart run in the first week of September, and a few weeks later the B-side, "You Mean Everything to Me," also hit the charts. Suddenly Dolton had a two-sided hit on their hands. Not bad for Barton's first effort! On a serious roll, Dolton proceeded to release its first of many albums, *Mr. Blue*, and just like clockwork, its soaring sales also earning the Fleetwoods yet another gold record. And not long after that, Dolton struck again with the Frantics' third hit single, "Werewolf," which *also* entered the *Billboard* charts.

It was at this point that Reisdorff realized that Dolton's string of successes was not an anomaly—that the label really did know what they were doing, and that he could make the leap to running it as a full-time venture. When giving his two weeks' notice to C&C, Reisdorff suggested that they hire Jerry Dennon, Portland's ace record promo man, as his own replacement. Dennon was a young man with great connections in that market, and he understood record sales. In 1958 he'd quit college to work for KOIN-TV, but had soon been hired by Portland wholesaler BG Record Service to push records to area shops and radio stations. Dennon began publishing his own little industry tip sheet, *On the Record Beat*, in an effort to tilt attention to records BG wanted to push. By getting to know every radio station's program director, he began to have considerable impact on what records sold in his market. "I was being quite effective doing record promotion," recalled Dennon, "and the secret to what we were doing, and the reason I had a uniqueness at the time, is very simple—I, as a promotion man, knew how to get a PD's attention. *And* I published a newsletter, and the only way to get their name in it was *they had to be nice to Jerry*. Okay? So if I was lucky enough, I could not only get the record on the air, but I could also make sure the record was in stores. Because *I* controlled the distribution. All those were important ingredients."

Jerry Dennon at KRKO Radio, 1962. (Photo by Herald Studios, Everett, WA.)

It was in the late summer of '59 that C&C hired Dennon and he relocated to Seattle to become their Northwest promotions manager. And it was in that role that he began to get to know Bonnie Guitar—whom he sensed was harboring some resentment over the way Dolton was being run. Sure, the label had been wildly successful—*Cash Box* even took note of Reisdorff and Bonnie's acumen and featured them on the *cover* of their March 5, 1960, issue—but the duo was already beginning to butt heads over the future direction of the label.

By this time Bonnie had surely proven her skills at picking tunes, and her chops in the studio were indisputably valuable—so it would seem inevitable that she would desire more input on A&R decisions. But Reisdorff—though no musician—was a great promoter who also possessed an ear for pop. So a major point of contention was that Bonnie was discovering more local talents than Dolton was able to deal with, and one day, when she mentioned her frustrations to Dennon, the two began scheming. They thought that perhaps by working together—she overseeing music and recording, and he handling promotion—they could launch a new label of their own and position themselves to compete with Dolton. With only a concept and a name derived from a contraction of Jerry Dennon's name— Jerden Records—they began to devise a way to launch their enterprise. But before they were ready to reveal their plans to leave Dolton, Reisdorff caught them examining rough graphic sketches for the Jerden label design and threw a fit. C&C immediately axed Dennon and quickly settled their accounts with Bonnie.

Still starry-eyed over the Fleetwoods' continuing success, Jerden Records' first move was—*surprise!*—to sign a teen trio that Bonnie had discovered down at Vancouver's Frontier Room club, and who were dead ringers for the Fleetwoods. Darwin and the Cupids were brought up to Northwest Recorders, and after a few hours' work with Barton, Bonnie and Dennon both were convinced that the trio's "How Long" was a surefire hit. Still, it took a few months for Jerden to raise the funds required to get the record pressed and promotional materials produced, but upon the single's release in June, radio stations including KJR and Vancouver, B.C.'s C-FUN pushed it up their charts and Seattle's newest label was off and running. The real question was: Could it actually be possible that another Seattle label could duplicate Dolton's magic—and accomplish that feat by pushing a Fleetwoods soundalike group?

Well, in fact, for the first couple weeks it looked like Jerden just might pull off the scam. With "How Long" gaining support daily on more and more stations all over the Northwest, Jerden was able to quickly cut a deal with Dolton's own distribution partner, good old Liberty Records—but, alas, perhaps *too* quickly. "Liberty was the label that Dolton was distributed by— and in hindsight I suspect that was a stupid move on my part," confessed Dennon. "At the time, we were thrilled to get a national distribution deal for our first record, but the reality was, we were competing with a substantial star [Liberty/Dolton's Fleetwoods]. Liberty distributed our record nationally and, well, nothin' ever happened. And looking back now, I'm not sure the whether the record would have happened or not, but my sense is, had we gone to somebody else, we probably would have had a better shot. Anyway, I think that ended our relationship with Liberty and the big time."

Even though Liberty had failed Jerden by not taking their regional hit and expanding it nationwide, Dennon was not prepared, just yet, to throw in the towel. He carried on by issuing a couple 45s without success, plodding ahead until Jerden's final financial reserves ran out. About that dispiriting period Dennon has ruefully admitted, "We had some wonderful grandiose thoughts that just didn't materialize." And so, just before the year's end, Jerden Records folded. And although Dennon and Bonnie each went their separate ways, both ended up in Hollywood—Bonnie as a recording artist with RCA Records, and Dennon as a promo man for such independent labels as Era and Fabor Records. And just as Bonnie would return to the nation's popularity charts with a long string of country hits, so too would Dennon eventually return to the Northwest, where he would become as successful, and hardball, a businessman as the Northwest's music industry would ever likely see.

CHAPTER 12

Rock and Roll Radio

The musical sounds that had ruled the Pacific Northwest's airwaves during the first four decades after the radio industry began broadcasting locally in 1921 were mainly classical standards, easy pop, church hymns, and country-and-western hits. But by the late 1940s—a period when many thousands of new arrivals had settled into Seattle—changes were evident on the radio, and opportunities for hearing authentic black-oriented music on the airwaves increased a degree.

Perhaps the earliest-known source of these new sounds was the pioneering black radio DJ Bass Harris—whose on-air moniker was reflective of his sonorous and remarkably low-pitched voice, and who, although employed by a mainstream station, KOL, nevertheless managed to spin some interesting tunes on his late-evening shift. Mind you, in comparison to certain stations in heavily black communities like Memphis, New York, or South Central Los Angeles, Harris's playlist was rather tame, but even songs by the likes of Louie Armstrong and Louie Jordan were welcomed by a populace starved for any music with a beat.

Following in Harris's footsteps were two other black DJs, Bob "Bop" Summerise and Fitzgerald "Eager" Beaver. Summerise had gotten his start back in the late 1940s at Bremerton's KBRO; then in 1952 he bought Seattle's hippest record store, the Groove Shop, at Twelfth and Jackson, and renamed it the World of Music. Promoted as Seattle's "Rock & Roll Headquarters," the shop became the local jazz and R&B community's living room—a friendly place where music fans could hang out and hear and buy all the latest hot tunes.

By 1954 Summerise's radio career had taken a big step up—with his new *Cool Breezes* show on Tacoma's KTAC at Seventh and Broadway, he began attracting a loyal following. And it didn't hurt matters at all when he also began courting the younger crowd by doing his show from a booth above Tacoma's cruising hangout, the Burger Bowl. As Summerise later told the *Seattle P-I*, "On Saturday nights the parking lot would be packed with kids. They'd sit in their cars and tune in to the show. I'd sit on top of the Burger Bowl and look out over the whole thing, making jokes about who's in that car or that car." To local teens the deal was basic and *irresistible*: You bought a burger and the DJ said your name on the air. Now *this* was a guy who understood the teenage psyche!

But Summerise wasn't the only one who "got" it: "Eager" Beaver had also been building his radio by playing all the jazz and R&B tunes that other stations had been ignoring. Beaver's debut in radio had been back at Puyallup's KAYE, and by 1952 he was spinning discs on his *Eager Beaver Show* at KFIR in North Bend, Oregon. In 1955, Beaver was back in the Tacoma area, where he and a few partners founded their own Broadway Broadcasting Company and—using a gambit similar to Summerise's—he began to win over the kids by doing remote broadcasts from another popular burger joint, the Last Round Café, as well as from the Broadway Record Shop.

By the fall of 1954, rock 'n' roll had picked up enough steam as a fad that even one white radio DJ, Robert "Red" Robinson, also began airing the music on his *Theme for Teens* show at Vancouver, B.C.'s little 5,000-watt station, CJOR. Then in 1956, Robinson moved up to the 50,000-watt giant CKWX, where he was positioned to help promote local concerts by the likes of Bill Haley and His Comets, Little Richard, Chuck Berry, Fats Domino, Elvis Presley, Buddy Holly, and Sam Cooke. Although Robinson's popularity grew to the extent that rock 'n' roll's detractors took to calling him silly names like "the Platter Prince of the Pimply Set" and the "the Pied Piper of Sin," it would be yet another white DJ—Pat O'Day—who would rise through the ranks and ultimately have the biggest impact of *any* of these disc jockeys on the rise in the Northwest's teen scene. Indeed, by the 1960s O'Day (who was born Paul Berg) would come to dominate the region as only a very few other top DJs would ever be able to do elsewhere in America.

Berg's first lucky break in the biz was provided by a veteran Seattle radioman named Wally Nelskog, who'd been the host of KRSC's popular 1940s dance music show, *Wally's Music Makers*—a program that he later moved over to Seattle's long-established AM giant, KJR. And from there, Nelskog had managed to cobble together the largest regional chain of radio stations in the Northwest—fourteen stations that came to be called the "Cutie" network (including Seattle's KQDE, Everett's KQTY, Renton's KUDY, and others like KUTI, KUTE, KQDY, et al . . .). But the historical significance to all this is that while most other local stations were studiously avoiding the airing of any records that bore even a whiff of rock 'n' roll, Nelskog committed his chain to adopting the brand-new Top 40 format—one that essentially committed a station to playing *whatever* songs happened to be any week's forty best-selling discs. No longer would the on-air staffers have a say in what records they spun: If the tune was popular, their station would be playing it.

Years after the fact, *Seattle Magazine* illuminated the situation with this look back at how the DJs at one major Seattle station reacted to all this change: "In the mid-fifties, KOL, like several other stations, got stuck playing rock 'n' roll records without ever intending to. Plugged into a format that called for playing the 'most popular songs', KOL discovered one day that 35 of the top 40 hits were [rock 'n' roll]. The DJs hated the music. Bob Waldron, who was on in the evening, spent most of his time bad-mouthing the records he played, and Ray Hutchison, the daytime guy, kept wondering aloud whatever happened to Kay Starr. And all the time, kids were calling up, requesting the original version of 'Louie Louie,' by Richard Berry. . . . It must have been *awful* for everybody over thirty."

Radio DJ, Paul Berg, at Yakima's KUTI, 1957. (Courtesy Pat O'Day.)

79

And while this arrangement obviously made for some very grumpy DJs, the "Cutie" network made the most of the situation and can be credited with bringing some of the first rock 'n' roll music to our local airwaves. Nelskog was continuously on the lookout for new talents who would enthusiastically embrace the sounds his station were airing. With that as a goal, it would seem to be merely a matter of time before he would cross paths with young Berg—who had literally grown up in a broadcasting booth, as his father had been a preacher with a weekly radio show, and whose favorite local air personalities, as a teenager, had been KJR's Nelskog and Bob Salter.

After graduating from radio school in Tacoma, Berg had been hired in September 1956 by Astoria, Oregon's KVAS, where, in between reading lost-dog reports and funeral home ads, he spun a few records. Eventually, the management at KVAS agreed to his *Paul's Platter Party* concept of a live remote broadcast of a Tuesday night sock hop. After a season in Astoria, he was hired away by KLOG in the sawmill town of Kelso—a podunk place where he soon made a discovery that would impact both his own career and the nascent Northwest teen scene.

To supplement the meager income he pulled in spinning country discs at KLOG, Berg hit upon the idea of throwing a teen dance featuring a local rockabilly combo, Vinny Duman and the Rhythmaires. And that first event turned such a good profit that Berg instantly deduced that promoting dances was a *far* more lucrative vocation than that of being a disc jockey. The real key to such an operation was, of course, controlling both aspects: locking down the dance hall so other would-be promoters couldn't compete, and simultaneously serving as the information conduit by promoting his *own* dances over the radio. All was going well for this new enterprise when, in August 1957, a car suddenly pulled up at KLOG's broadcast studio one day, where he was working alone. Inside that car was none other than Wally Nelskog—who had been scanning various stations as he drove up the highway only to discover a natural-born, and fabulously glib, motormouth named Berg. The radio exec walked in, introduced himself to his longtime fan, and proceeded to hire Berg on the spot to come and work at KUTI up in Yakima.

For Berg, this big chance to move up in the biz and take on his first air shift spinning Top 40 sounds was utterly irresistible, and he moved to Yakima. But then disaster struck: Just as Berg was settling into the new town and job, Nelskog—with zero warning whatsoever—suddenly sold KUTI, and Berg found himself without a job. After a harsh Christmas season, during which the desperate DJ was grateful to land even a seasonal job at a local department store, Berg lucked out in mid-1958 and was hired at Yakima's KLOQ. And it was while at KLOQ that he met up with concert and dance promoter Pat Mason and got his first real up-close look at that facet of the music biz. Mason hired Berg—initially to do radio ad voice-overs to promote his Yakima Armory dances, and then eventually to serve as MC at shows featuring the bands of Bill Haley, Gene Vincent, Jerry Lee Lewis, Fats Domino, Eddie Cochran, Lloyd Price, and the Everly Brothers.

During the time Berg spent around the far-more-experienced Mason, he learned a lot about how the public dance biz worked. In fact, at one point he wondered aloud as to why the promoter brought all these rock 'n' roll stars to seemingly every small town in the region but never seemed to tour them through the state's biggest population center, Seattle. Mason's response—"*That* town will eat you alive"—was probably based on past experiences with the big city's event-planning codes, security requirements, liquor rules, teen-dance ordinances, et cetera. But the central point was, that adamancy about not working the Seattle turf caused Berg to begin pondering if perhaps there was an opportunity over there. . . .

Meanwhile, like many other stations across America, both Seattle's AM giants, KOL and KJR, had followed the "Cutie" chain's lead and adopted a Top 40 format. And so by the fall of 1958, various other local radio station managers had realized they needed some young blood on their staffs, and thus Seattle's underdog station, KAYO, soon recruited Berg from Yakima. But the whole radio-biz playing field was still quite unsettled: With a growing national backlash against rock 'n' roll by politicians and other moralists, pressure mounted to the extent that a remarkable number of stations across the country suddenly began abandoning their winning Top 40 formats and switching to easy pop.

The whole anti-rock trend was partially fueled by the sort of sentiments expressed by the likes of Jim French, a prominent radioman at Seattle's KIRO, who editorialized his hatred for the music in an essay in *Advent* magazine, writing that rock 'n' roll was "sick. . . . This music is often extreme, generally objectionable, and frequently vulgar. It is performed by 'artists' who seldom have any qualification other than a typically nasal, childish delivery, and a perfunctory acquaintance with a guitar or piano. . . . The youngsters whose musical tastes are reflected in the 'charts' . . . WILL GROW UP. As their appetites broaden, they will desert the tastes of their childhood and actually look upon them with some embarrassment. . . . It's obvious that someone involved must take a stand."

81

In Seattle, KING radio took a stand by claiming to have conducted a quick "scientific" poll that, believe it or not, supposedly discovered that their audience *really* preferred the music of Tommy Dorsey and Vaughn Monroe as compared to rock 'n' roll. Station management announced that henceforth "raucous rock 'n' roll will be completely excluded." That KING would drop Top 40 was really no great surprise, but that even Seattle's premier AM powerhouse, KJR, also dropped rock 'n' roll from their playlists was shocking. To Berg—who arrived in Seattle only to discover that his new employer, KAYO, was also suddenly experiencing cold feet—the situation was a nightmare. Reporting for duty, Berg faced KAYO's general manager's pronouncement that "the listening public is turning off rock 'n' roll music" and therefore KAYO would also be switching to the "sweet side" of a new Top 50 format.

And, as if that wasn't stupid enough, as Saint Patrick's Day 1959 approached, the station began hyping their call letters with a promo campaign based on the concept that KAYO was *Irish*. Even worse, management informed all DJs to select new Celtic-sounding on-air names—monikers that had to begin with the letter O. *Oh, lordy*. The passage of time has obscured what the other poor jocks came up, with but Berg instantly showed his keen sense of humor by lifting the name of a Seattle school—O'Dea High— and he was soon hosting the KAYO *Housewives Hit Parade* show as "Pat O'Day." Meanwhile—with KING, KJR, and KAYO having willingly abandoned their formerly sizable shares of the local youth radio market by fleeing for the shelter of easy pop and country music formats—the area's lone Top 40 holdout, KOL, had by early '59 shot straight to No. 1 in the ratings. It somehow took several months for KJR to realize that KOL was now plundering the teen audience alone, and they soon came crawling back to rock 'n' roll.

But KJR was now stuck in catch-up mode, and the well-funded station's tyrant of a program director (and morning-man DJ), "Jockey John" Stone, was getting testy about having to compete head-to-head against KAYO's popular *Housewives* show. He soon convinced KJR to steal O'Day away from their competition. None too pleased with O'Day's sudden defection, KAYO threatened a lawsuit to prohibit him from using the air name that he'd been gaining notoriety with, but O'Day bravely told 'em to shove it, and he worked under that name for the remaining decades of his career. And those would be decades that saw O'Day become one of America's most influential DJs—a gatekeeper who could make the right record into a serious hit—and the founder of a Seattle-based teen-dance promotion empire that would be unequaled anywhere else in America.

Once he was comfortably ensconced over at KJR, O'Day got down to business—that is, the teen-dance business. After poking around a bit, he discovered that there were perfectly logical reasons why no private businessmen—including, of course, the region's most active dance promoter, Pat Mason—were really milking Seattle's potentially lucrative market. Instead, it seemed that the majority of teen sock hops and the occasional dance were sponsored by organizations like the Parent Teacher Association (PTA) or the Catholic Youth Organization (CYO). And that, O'Day was to learn, was the lingering result of civic issues with deep roots in the town's history. In fact, ever since its first dancehall was established, the city of Seattle had had civic discord over the issue of public dancing, and in the 1800s various draconian laws were enforced to restrict dancing by minors within the city limits. Then there was the law—still on the books in the 1950s—which required a youth dance producer to guarantee that 50 percent (or, optionally, even more) of the proceeds be earmarked for a local charity—a nonprofit organization which would then, in effect, become the dance's *sponsor*.

This was the system under which some of the area's first rock 'n' roll sock hops were consequently thrown at Seattle Parks Department field houses under the aegis of area Catholic schools and the public schools' PTAs. In addition, occasionally some venturesome social club or other such organization would surface and throw a few dances at community rooms like the Carpenters Hall, the Morrison Hall, or the Palladium Ballroom—but they presumably soon realized that the economic odds were stacked against them and gave up. Eventually, though, as rock 'n' roll became more and more popular, attendance records started being set at PTA dances, and radio stations began dabbling with the music, a few enterprising local DJs—led by KAYO's "Big Daddy" Dave Clark, KOL's Dex Allen, and KJR's Lee Perkins—took the plunge and, playing by all the rules, began hosting their own sock hops.

That was pretty much the lay of the land when O'Day rolled into town. Having hosted plenty of sock hops and dances already in Astoria and Vancouver—and then emceed Pat Mason's concert/dances in Yakima—the new KJR DJ already knew that under the right circumstances throwing a dance could be a very lucrative sideline. But he'd never before faced anything like Seattle's onerous 50-percent-to-charity stipulation. The obvious quickly dawned on him: Why reinvent the wheel? Instead, why not use the same nifty solution that had been pioneered by an earlier generation of Prohibition-era entertainment industry entrepreneurs?

And that solution was simply to escape the various laws, ordinances, and other capricious city red tape by doing business in rooms located just *outside* of the city limits. In fact, that is the very reason why Seattle's best old roadhouses—Parker's Ballroom and the Spanish Castle Ballroom—are not actually *in* Seattle, but rather were built out in the woods on the old highways, and beyond official city limit lines.

With that realization, O'Day had a dance spot—now all he needed was a band . . . and a natural choice was the band he'd recently met while still working over at KAYO, when the Wailers had stopped by to giddily show off their new "Tall Cool One" 45—a disc that had become a big hit in the intervening months.

And so it was that O'Day ended up eyeing the fabled Spanish Castle as a potential site. Problem was, the room was *still* featuring old-fashioned swing dances with Gordon Greene and his twelve-piece Spanish Castle Orchestra on Saturdays. However, that left open the possibility of a Friday night event—and thus, in the fall of 1959, O'Day rented the hall, booked the Wailers, and aired countless plugs during his radio shifts. The turnout was great, and both the band and O'Day pocketed a tidy profit. Thus began the golden era of Northwest teen dances. . . .

CHAPTER 13

Love You So

On February 3, 1959, a trio of rock 'n' roll's brightest hopes—Buddy Holly, Ritchie Valens, and J.P. "The Big Bopper" Richardson— perished together in an icy Midwestern plane crash. "The Day the Music Died" caused more than a few folks to think that rock 'n' roll might be on its last legs.

What was certain was that by that turn of the decade nearly all of the original rockin' rebels had been neutralized, muted, or enabled to self-destruct. At the time, the U.S. Army was actively exorcising Elvis's rock 'n' roll spirit; Chuck Berry was jailed for messing around with girls who were "Almost Grown;" Little Richard had gone Jesus—and Jerry Lee Lewis and Gene Vincent were both trouble-magnet jailbirds whose records were periodically banned and tours canceled. Finally, Vincent was maimed in a car wreck that also killed Eddie Cochran, while old Bill Haley and His Comets had simply faded out of stylistic favor.

On a business level, both Holly and Richardson were artists whose hit records were producing revenue for, respectively, Decca and Mercury Records—both major labels well enough established to withstand the loss of any *one* top artist from their roster. Valens, on the other hand, was *the* moneymaker for the small-time Hollywood-based Del-Fi Records. And so, his tragic loss was felt not only by his family and fans but by Del-Fi's owner, Bob Keane, who necessarily kicked off an immediate search for new talent. Over the following few months, Keane turned up four different teenage acts from the Northwest: Chan Romero, the Swags, Ron Holden and the Thunderbirds, and the Gallahads.

The first of these bands dropped right into Del-Fi's lap when a package arrived one day from Billings, Montana, with a letter from a radio DJ named Don "Weird Beard" Redfield, who stated that he was the manager of a local seventeen-year-old rocker named Robert "Chan" Romero and his band, the Bell Tones. One can easily imagine the howls of glee that rang out at the Del-Fi offices after Keane listened to the enclosed demo tape and heard a *miracle*—the Chicano kid from Montana was a dead ringer for Valens. Within days Keane was on the phone, and by April 1959 Romero was recording at Hollywood's Gold Star Studios. Hoping to replicate the exciting sounds—and the success—of Valens' records, Keane hired the same studio pros who had played on those hits. But Romero's debut Del-Fi 45, "Hippy Hippy Shake," rocked *far* harder than anything the deceased star had ever done, and American radio found Romero's minute-and-three-quarters blast of pure red-hot Chicano rockabilly music to be too intense. Few stations outside of Southern California gave it much play. But if the song was too wild for most radio markets, it did become a fave rave in England, and in fact, music historian Rob Finnis noted in 1982 that "'Hippy Hippy Shake' has been acknowledged by several luminaries of the Mersey-beat era as being the record which indirectly sparked off the entire movement. It became something of a standard in beat circles, and in 1963 the Beatles recorded an un-released version for Parlaphone while the Swinging Blue Jeans revival . . . made the UK top three." As for Romero? He toured with Jerry Lee Lewis and, ironically, eventually ended up joining Buddy Holly's band, the Crickets.

By that point Keane had signed the Swags—a Bellingham band who'd opened for Valens back when he'd come through the Northwest in November 1958. The Swags had a sound not unlike that of the Wailers—based more on the guitar-heavy music of Link Wray and Duane Eddy that the other Northwest teen R&B bands were exploring—and Pat Mason hired them to open big gigs for Gene Vincent, Johnny Burnette, and other stars at the Beacon Ballroom or down at the Seven Cedars Ballroom in Mt. Vernon—shows that attracted up to 1,500 teenagers. It was through their manager—Jim Bailey, a radio DJ down at KAGT in Anacortas—that the Swags really began to get ahead. Bailey booked live TV appearances for them on the Seattle, Yakima, and Portland *Bandstand* shows, and he also formed West-wind Records. After a recording session in Seattle with Kearney Barton at Northwest Recorders, Westwind issued one single, "Rockin' Matilda"—which was a rock instrumental version of the hoary old folk chestnut "Waltzing Matilda"—and by mid-1960 it was doing well in the Anacortas-Bellingham area. But then Bailey *somehow* persuaded KJR's John Stone—who was already gaining a reputation for denying airtime to local records—to give the thing a little play, which got Keane's attention. A deal was struck, and the 45 was rereleased by Del-Fi, who managed to get "Rockin' Matilda" aired on Dick Clark's *American Bandstand* for two consecutive weeks.

Keane's next discovery from the Northwest came about because of the untiring efforts of two enterprising young local fellows named Larry Nelson and Chuck Markulis. This duo already had a keen understanding of how the record biz worked—and, in fact, had already experienced the whole roller-coaster ride inherent in trying to launch a band and score a hit record. Back in 1958, Nelson and Markulis, along with a few other Everett Community College students, had formed their own multiracial doo-wop group, the Shades. From the get-go, hopes were high: Less than a month after forming, and after only one live performance at an Everett High School assembly, a local newspaper excitedly speculated that "in the near future, perhaps, Everett will have a claim to fame in the Rhythm and Blues world with these kids."

Energized, the Shades began working on a demo tape and, while on a deal-hunting trip to Hollywood, actually signed up with seminal Los Angeles–based R&B firm Aladdin Records. Upon its release in April 1959, the Shades'

The Shades, 1958. (Photo by Robinson Studios, Everett, WA; courtesy Larry Nelson Estate.)

"Dear Lori" / "One Touch of Heaven" 45 met with a surprisingly positive response from various radio stations. But the problem was that there was no consensus on which side was the best. Everett's KRKO highlighted "Dear Lori" as their "Pick of the Week"; KAYO's Pat O'Day opted for the flip side and began airing "One Touch of Heaven": It immediately entered the station's Top 10. Then Everett's KQTY—which had been airing both tunes—settled on the B-side and it climbed to No. 14.

It looked as if a genuine hit—or two!—was in the making as the Shades' songs began to pop up on additional playlists down the West Coast and in a few other markets. But before long, the discs' momentum waned and the Shades faded away. But Nelson and Markulis had joined the Dolton gang as one of the Northwest's first, and very few, management teams that had any real clue about the rock 'n' roll record biz. Wisely realizing that singing might not be their strongest suit, in that spring season of 1959 Nelson and Markulis decided that they could form their own label—just look at Dolton's crazy streak of wins!—and they opened up a small storefront office in downtown Seattle with a sign on the door that read NITE-OWL RECORDS. And that's when Nelson—who'd also taken on a part-time job with the sheriff's office at the King County Jail—and Markulis began scouting out local sock hops for promising R&B talents.

This was a search that didn't take long at all, but the surprise was that they didn't discover their first talent at a dance or anything like it: Nelson found Ron Holden—the teenage black singer with the Playboys combo— in the hands of the King County sheriff. "Somewhere around May, I was singing with my band at the Encore Ballroom at Eleventh and Pike," recalled Holden, "and during the intermission we went out to the parking lot to drink some whiskey and maybe smoke some of those funny little cigarettes. So the boys in the band and a couple girls were in the car. All the windows were steamed up, and so one of the security policemen at the place came around the corner, pulled us all out. He checked everyone's ID. He immediately recognized me as the singer in the band. It turned out that I was eighteen and a half and *everybody else* was eighteen or under. I was arrested for contributing to the delinquency of minors. They hauled me off to jail and I got ninety days, which I served at the King County Jail."

Luckily, Holden was befriended by Larry Nelson, the deputy who'd fingerprinted him and who began making a point of getting the kid out each day for a cigarette break. At the same time, Holden continued to pen flowery love notes to his girlfriend, and one day he offered one up to the jailbird doo-wop group that had formed on his cell block: "My darling . . . I love you so. . . ."

"So one day, I come out to have my cigarette with Larry," chuckled Holden, "and he starts telling me that he's going to retire in the next month or so and that he's going to start a record company. And I said, 'Gosh, you should hear this song we got back here.' So he heard it and the next day he said, 'I like your song. When you get out, I want you to come see me.' Then he retired, and in a week or two I went to see him. He said, 'I want you to record the song, and I have a band over here I want to introduce you to.' And he introduced me to a band called the Thunderbirds." That was a white north-end group who featured a wild black pianist named Little Willie Bell—and because the Playboys had necessarily replaced their singer (with a Jackie Wilson–style raver named Aaron Stewart) while he'd been "indisposed" all summer, Holden was grateful to have a new band to work with.

Nite-Owl didn't waste a second after Nelson heard Holden and the jailbirds singing "Love You So." A session was booked with Fred Rasmussen at his North Seattle home studio, Acme Sound and Recording. The goal was to cut Holden's "Love You So" and *anything* else the Thunderbirds could whip up for a flip side. By all accounts, this was to be a tortuously chaotic and grueling experience for everyone present that day. "We did it in Fred Rasmussen's living room," laughed Holden. "For nineteen hours there were fourteen people in this room—which was about ten by twelve [feet wide]! It was the engineer, his wife, his daughter, and his dog sitting there on the couch, and a couple of the guys' girlfriends. Larry Nelson was playing the claves and Chuck Markulis was playing the tambourine. The Thunderbirds' pianist was Little Willie—he *looked* like Little Richard and he *played* like that! He and I were in the alcove, and the other guys were all in the other room. And every time the dog would bark, we'd have to start over! On 'Love You So' it was up into the *nineties* on takes! It was ridiculous!"

Finally, with takes of "Love You So" and "Louie Louie" both in the can, the guys were asked to cut one more tune, and because they and Holden hadn't rehearsed anything else, Holden improvised a rockin' little ditty they whipped together called "My Babe." The session mercifully completed, Nite-Owl arranged for 5,000 copies of the label's debut single to be pressed and so, with all that effort invested, it came as a keen disappointment when KJR's John Stone specifically refused to air "Love You So," and then Seattle's other top stations, KAYO, KOL, and KING, all unanimously agreed. The song was not a hit, they said—its intro section was too long, and it had an odd beat that wasn't even rock 'n' roll. Nite-Owl asked them to flip it over and try "My Babe"—word came back that the B-side rocked too hard. The only local DJ who gave the record a fair shot was Bob Summerise, who finally debuted the disc on his late-night show. But without much radio support, Nite-Owl found that record retailers weren't interested in stocking the thing. Still, the young label never gave up trying to promote their first record—and the fact of course is, they were not the only local label to have trouble trying to promote a record by a teenage rockin' R&B group.

Undaunted by the setbacks Holden's 45 was experiencing, Nite-Owl persevered, and while checking out a sock hop sponsored by Renton's KUDY, Nelson and Markulis stumbled across the Gallahads. This was a black teenage doo-wop group comprised of Garfield High School pals Bobby Dixon (lead), Jimmy Pipkin (tenor), Ernie Rouse (bass), and Anthony "Tiny Tony" Smith (baritone). They had sung at a few school assemblies, community Fun-Fests, the Central District YMCA, and some after-school dances that were called "mixers." Then KUDY DJ "Hey Hey" Steve Wray took an interest and began booking the Gallahads at various station-sponsored sock hops. Soon after, Nite-Owl booked the group (supported by the Thunderbirds) with Barton down at Northwest Recorders, and the label had their second release, "Gone," another excellent local R&B 45 that sank without any local radio support. But after a demo tape of the Gallahads' new song, "Lonely Guy," was cut in Nelson's living room and mailed down to Del-Fi Records in September '59, Keane asked them to come to Hollywood and record. The excited teens jumped into an old '49 Ford, drove down, cut a couple tunes at Gold Star, got a chance to do a spotlight set during a break by James Brown and the Famous Flames at the 5/4 Club, and then returned home to await their Del-Fi record's release. "Lonely Guy" began receiving some airplay at scattered stations in late '59.

In the Northwest, KQDY came through with some air support for the Gallahads—and then, to everyone's puzzlement, its sister in the "Cutie" network, KQDE, suddenly added Holden's "Love You So" to their playlist. At that point, Seattle's big record retailer, the Ware House of Music, agreed to stock the Nite-Owl disc. "We convinced Barry Ware to put twenty-five copies in his record store," said Holden. "At this time, KAYO disc jockey Pat O'Day broadcast his program from the fishbowl window at that store—and he played his records directly off the sales chart. The Top 40 of *that store*. They put our record on their *Battle of the Records* feature: Top of the hour, every hour, they played a new record against an established record, and the winner of that hour would go on to the next hour."

And the determining factor in this contest—phoned-in votes from listeners—was one that was easily manipulated: "The telephone calls come in and 'Love You So' wins, wins, wins!" laughed Holden. "My little friends did call, but it wasn't a *totally* stacked deck: It *was* a concerted effort!" And those calls (and sales) pushed the tune up to KAYO's No. 33 slot the first week, to No. 22 the following week—then the B-side "My Babe" and "Love You So" *both* shot up to tie at No. 11—and finally "Love You So" hit No. 1, while "My Babe" rested at No. 2. KJR, however, was a little slow out of the gate, not touching the disc until January '60—but it was KJR's chart that the record industry big boys kept an eye on: "All the major [labels] came in," recalled Holden. "They wanted to buy this local hit *because* I was holding *their* hits out of the No. 1 spot! Decca, Capitol, Chess/Checker, Argo—they all came to town, and what they each wanted to do was sign me and like, build me over a five-year period. Which is the [proper] way to do it. Well, we were so dumb we kept putting everybody off, and so along comes Bob Keane." "I was up in Seattle," recalled Keane, "and my distributor there said, 'How'd you like to pick up the No. 1 record? And the other side is No. 2.' I says, 'You've gotta be *kidding*.'" So we went around to the big local retail house where they sell records there. And we met a young man who had the Nite-Owl label, and they'd cut these two songs, and they were No. 1 and No. 2 at the time." Pretty impressive chart action, that's for sure, but upon hearing the A-side, the Hollywood pro had his doubts: "I remember the big hit was "Love You So," and when I first heard it, almost a minute went by with just this [intro] vamp. And I couldn't believe it, because my theory was, the disc jockeys are going to—well, if you don't sell it in the first fifteen grooves, you're not going to listen to it any further. And I said, 'Well, look, I don't know about that song'—because I didn't hear it. I mean, in my mind it wasn't a hit. I figured something must be going on because he was a local boy or something . . . but I said, 'I can't ignore it,' so I picked it up."

"And so," recalled Holden, "Keane says, 'I've got ten thousand dollars and I'll take it and run with it. Let's make a *hit*!' And we said, 'Hey, is this what we wanted or what?' We took the ten thousand, signed a lease deal, and he took it to Hollywood and made it a national hit." Rereleased on Keane's new Donna label in late March '60, "Love You So" suddenly broke into the Top 5 all down the West Coast, and Holden's tune soon entered *Billboard*'s charts and began chugging into the nation's Top 10. All this action led to appearances on both the *Dick Clark Show* and *American Bandstand* for Holden, who then embarked on what became a long, long, series of R&B

road tours with the James Brown and Jackie Wilson bands that began in Detroit and then moved on to Florida, Mississippi, and Texas.

"In May of 1960 I had the No. 7 record in the country—and Ray Charles had "What'd I Say" out (which was No. 30)—and I was *headlining* a show that he and his band were on!" exclaimed Holden. "Then in June, I worked the Apollo Theater for two weeks with Jackie Wilson. And we were doing seven shows a day!" In September, Holden was the focus of a three-page feature in *Hit Parader* magazine in which the writer stated: "Show business is truly one of the oddities of nature. One minute, an obscure talent sits dreaming of success in a remote little city and knowing well that the top of

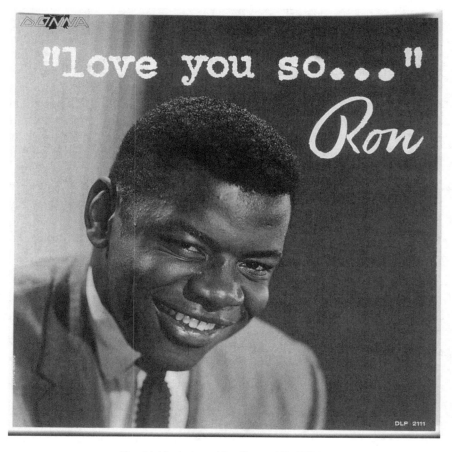

Ron Holden's *Love You So . . .* LP, 1960.

the ladder is beyond reach. Then along comes a promoter with just the right combination to unlock the doors. . . . In one fast swish, you're riding on a cloud and you've struck it rich."

Well, Holden certainly enjoyed all his successes—"My Babe" had become a good-selling favorite in England, and one of his many follow-up 45s, "Gee But I'm Lonesome," also charted in America—but in his subsequent four decades in the biz, he never did exactly strike it "rich." But, then again, few if any, musicians who worked with Keane ever did rake in the dough they probably should have. "Love You So," however, did become a classic that was reissued many times over the years on various golden oldies compilation LPs.

It was on August 15, 1960, that the Gallahads' "Lonely Guy" finally entered the *Billboard* charts at the No. 111 slot—and in order to push the song up into the Hot 100, Del-Fi asked the group to come back down to California. The plan was to promote the 45 by booking the group at a few teen dances and TV sock hops there, but the wait for action to occur had taken its toll: Smith had married and taken a job with the US Postal Service. Dixon dropped out, Ray Robinson was added to fill the tenor spot, and Pipkin was now singing lead. When these new Gallahads arrived, Hunter Hancock began giving the group radio time and even took them around to a number of lip-synch parties at high schools around town. And between Hancock, and then Wolfman Jack's support, "Lonely Guy" became the No. 1 song in Los Angeles for about eight weeks, leading to the group's appearance on the *Wink Martindale Show*, and another *Bandstand*-type TV program, which the Gallahads appeared on every Saturday for months.

"Then in 1961 our second single, 'I'm Without a Girlfriend,' came out," recalled Pipkin. "I was back home again then, and Ernie [Dixon] got on the phone and called me one day and said, *'Jimmy, turn on the TV! Dick Clark's playing 'I'm Without a Girlfriend!'"* Excitement understandably reigned in the Gallahads camp over that brush with the big time—Smith even rejoined them—and the group continued making live appearances at the Birdland and elsewhere around the Northwest. But after cutting a couple more singles—including a take on Richard Berry's "Louie Louie" rewrite, "Have Love Will Travel"—it became clear that the doo-wop days had finally drawn to a close. Still, the good news for the individual members of the Gallahads was that as experienced singers, they each found themselves in considerable demand as the dance combo scene was shifting too, and many of the formerly instrumental-oriented bands began to see the advantages of having singers out front.

CHAPTER 14

Walk—Don't Run

Even considered as a whole, the quantity and great range of rhythm and blues, jazz, and doo-wop that emanated out of the inner-city nightclubs, taverns, and dancehalls along Tacoma's Lower Broadway and Seattle's Jackson Street and East Madison neighborhood scenes back in the 1950s was still, at most, only *half* of the musical equation in the Pacific Northwest. This other, larger, and concurrent realm was country-and-western music—and it too would play a role (albeit a much less significant one than R&B) in influencing the rise of the upcoming rock 'n' roll generations.

As one measure of how robust and healthy the region's country scene was, just consider that *three* of America's premier Southern-based singers—Willie Nelson, Loretta Lynn, and Buck Owens—each moved north to Washington state in the 1950s and found the place to be so supportive and nurturing that they managed to either cut their first recordings here and/or build upon their local successes and launch their subsequent national careers after gaining experience in our dancehalls. Of the three, Buck Owens had the greatest impact locally—frustrated by a stalled-out career in Bakersfield, California, he started from scratch by moving to Puyallup in January 1958. Investing in a tiny local radio station, KAYE, he worked as a DJ while he formed a band and then took on a house band gig at Tacoma's Britannia Tavern. Before long he was also hosting the *Bar K Jamboree* show on Tacoma's KTNT-TV. His band, the Bar K Gang, now included Tumwater's Don Rich (neé Ulrich), whose superb fiddling and chicken-pickin' guitar work ultimately made him Owens' longtime musical partner. Also of note were the fine drummer, Skip Moore, and a Native American guitar genius, Nokie Edwards. Soon, Owens and band—with a few brand-new compositions like "Under Your Spell Again" in hand—were booked at Joe Boles

Joe Boles in his home studio, 1950s. (Courtesy Virginia Boles.)

Custom Recorders in Seattle. In July of 1959, Hollywood's Capitol records bit and called Owens back to California, where he rerecorded the tune. By June 1960, he was wrapping up his Puyallup business affairs and heading back home to the streets of Bakersfield, where he became one of the decade's biggest stars.

It was during that same summer season that Moore and Edwards also felt the tug of stardom. But in their case, it was while playing in their next ensemble—a rock 'n' roll band that would soon gain worldwide fame as the Ventures. Formed, as they were, on the fringes of the Sea-Tac country music scene, the Ventures reflected little of the predominant musical influences that most of their generation's bands did: i.e., a rude-jazz- or R&B-tinged sound—they did, however, eventually record "Louie Louie"—not to mention their versions of the Wailers' "Tall Cool One" and "Wailin'"! Their classic sound instead emphasized very intricate and clean guitar work and snappy drumming. But if they were an anomaly on the local teen scene, the

Ventures made up for it by eventually becoming recognized globally as the biggest-selling instrumental rock group of all time, credited with sparking the entire surf rock movement of the early 1960s. The Ventures recorded 250 albums over a five-decade-long career in which some thirty million units were sold.

The Ventures' musical odyssey stemmed from very, very humble beginnings. Just consider the fact that this was a quartet led by two Tacoma musicians—Don Wilson and Bob Bogle—who had only played guitar for about a year and a half before hitting the big time. But at least they chose the right role models: Wilson dug Duane Eddy's trademark deep buzz/twang, while Bogle admired Chet Atkins' versatile style and also studied under the Frantics' ace guitarist, Ron Peterson.

It was in 1958 that the two budding guitarists met, discovered a mutual interest in music, bought their first cheap electric guitars and amps, and started dreaming about being rock stars. Months later, while working day

Promotional photo for the Ventures, circa 1960.

jobs over in the tiny college town of Pullman, Washington, they began practicing together in the banquet room of the Washington Hotel—and their unique sound instantly began attracting crowds of students, as well as job offers. Billed initially as the Impacts, and later as the Versatones, the duo soon found a temporary drummer named Buddy Dumas and began playing the Pullman Elks Club.

Back in Tacoma, the pair found their first bassist, Earl Herbert; a new drummer, George Babbitt; and a weekly radio gig performing each week on KAYE. One of that station's talent contests promised the winner a one-off fifteen-minute on-air showcase, complete with the backing of the Versatones. The winner turned out to be a fourteen-year-old Kent-based singer named Nancy Claire, who specialized in Brenda Lee's country/pop repertoire. The spotlight set by Claire led to a *weekly* fifteen-minute show and then to an hour-long show—and before long, Claire and the Versatones were performing live at the Belfair Barn and at country dances at various grange halls and rodeos. Then, after each Saturday's KAYE radio broadcast, the act began to make regular appearances on the *Bill & Grover Show* from Tacoma's KMO-TV studios.

All this action for the young band encouraged them to take the next step of trying to score a record deal. The obvious place to go was the red-hot Dolton Record company up in Seattle. Unfortunately, when Wilson and Bogle trudged their guitars and an amp over to Dolton's offices and played a few tunes for Bob Reisdorff—including a jazzy instrumental called "Walk—Don't Run" they'd found on a Chet Atkins album—he basically rebuffed them. "We brought 'Walk—Don't Run' to Reisdorff," laughed Wilson, "and he turned it down! He said, 'Well, I already got an instrumental group called the Frantics. I can't really use another instrumental group.' But, he says, 'You guys are *good*. You oughta keep it up.' So we did." Nonplussed, the adventurous band—now called the Ventures—simply moved forward by forming their own company, Blue Horizon Records. They cut a couple tunes on September 20, 1959, at Joe Boles' studio, and self-issued their first 45. KJR's program director, John Stone, rejected the young musicians' disc, as did nearly every other area radio station—no surprise given that the two forgettable tunes ("Cookies and Coke" / "The Real McCoy") barely even *hinted* at the instantly recognizable and winning sound the boys would soon patent. The record sank without a trace, leaving the Ventures stuck with nearly five hundred unsold copies of the 45, but still, they weren't discouraged.

For the moment, they were busy trying to replace Babbitt, who had been squeezed out when the band got a gig in Tacoma at Mike's Blue Moon Tavern: As a minor, the sixteen-year-old couldn't legally be on the premises. Struggling to find a drummer of age, the Ventures ended up using a succession of pickup drummers for a spell. They used a fill-in drummer for a November 28 television appearance in Tacoma on KTVW's *Dance Party* show, and a month later, on New Year's Eve '59, when they played their first big teen dance, held at Fort Lewis. It was at the point in time that Buck Owens' Bar K Gang were headlining the Britannia six nights a week. But when Owens opted to instead take on a regular Saturday gig playing the huge dances at Bresemann's Pavilion out on Lake Spanaway, the Ventures—still without a regular drummer—were hired to fill in at the Britannia performing a grueling noon-till-midnight bandstand shift. And it was due to that connection that the group happened to struck up a friendship with Owens' band mates Skip Moore and Nokie Edwards.

Despite the fact that their debut 45 had failed to set any fires ablazin', the Ventures decided that it was time to head back to Boles' studio—this time with the intent of cutting "Walk—Don't Run." Once session time was booked, Wilson and Bogle bravely asked Owens' rhythm section if they'd like to help out: "We went to Skip Moore," recalled Wilson. "He was working in a self-serve gas station—and I remember going to him and saying, 'We need a drummer to do this session. We want to record "Walk—Don't Run."' And he said, 'Well, I don't know. I'm kinda busy.' And I said, 'Well, I'll tell you what: We'll either give you twenty-five dollar or a *fourth* of what the record makes.' And do you know what he took? He said, 'Oh, no, just give me the twenty-five bucks.' So I said, 'Okay.'"

And so it was that in March 1960 Boles cut the quartet doing brilliant renditions of "Walk—Don't Run" and another instrumental, "Home"—each featuring stellar guitar work by Bogle (lead) and Wilson (rhythm), tight bass playing (Edwards), and stunning drumming (Moore). Still, having learned from their previous experience of trying to market a record, the Ventures knew that, at the very least, they probably needed to work with a distributor who had *some* promotional experience. Maybe Seattle's Jerden Records could help. "Reisdorff had already turned us down," laughed Wilson, "so what we did was we took 'Walk—Don't Run' to Jerry Dennon. And that was after it was recorded! We were trying to get somebody to handle it, you know? He said, 'No. I don't think so. It doesn't sound like a hit to me.'" Kicking himself to this day, Dennon fully admits this error, confessing that at

that point in time "my head was so into Darwin and the Cupids that I could-
n't even *hear* this 'Walk—Don't Run' thing. They were saying, 'Help!' And
I *coulda* said, 'Okay, I will. I'll put it out. You don't worry about it.' Instead
[laughter] I was putzing around with Darwin, and 'Walk—Don't Run' went
right by me!"

Still stung by the failure of their debut 45 to sell, the Ventures saved
their money again, and this time decided to press a mere three hundred
copies of their second Blue Horizon single. This time, however, they were
determined to bypass KJR's pigheaded program director, John Stone; the
Ventures managed instead to meet with the station's new afternoon man,
Pat O'Day. "Donny Wilson and Bob Bogle brought the tape by the station,"
recalled O'Day, "and I said, 'The thing's a *hit*! Here it goes!' We put it on the
air *instantly*. We always played an instrumental going up to the newscast at
the top of the hour, so we put it on every hour as that filler there, and of
course, you know what happened after that. What was happening in Seattle was so startling—there was *no* question: It was a stone smash."

"So we got to Pat at KJR," agreed Wilson, "and he said that they'd play
it just before the news and wouldn't announce who or what it was—they'd
try to get a reaction through the phones. People would call up and say,
'What is that? I like it.' And as it happened, a *lotta* people called." Among
the first callers to dial KJR's broadcast booth's phone number was Reisdorff
from over at Dolton's headquarters. He'd been listening to KJR and now—
a mere week and a half after Blue Horizon had issued the 45—he finally
heard the magic. "When Reisdorff called the station," Wilson recalled, "he
said, 'Jeez! What is *that*?' And Pat O'Day told him, 'Well, it's a local group.'
And he was *amazed*. Reisdorff called my mom—she was doing our legwork
for us then, because we were too busy—and he didn't even remember us
having been in his office. He said, 'No, I couldn't have heard that. That's a
natural hit.' And we said, 'Well, yeah, you did.' So he says, 'Jeez, I want to
make a deal with ya.' So we got together with him and we signed to Dolton
Records."

As a next step, Reisdorff wanted to double-check and make sure that if
he rereleased the song, Liberty Records, as potential national distributors,
would be 100 percent fully and completely behind the record. "And so,"
recalled Wilson, "Reisdorff sent it down to Al Bennett, who was the president of Liberty, and he played it and he said, 'No. It's *not* a hit. I don't want
it.' And Reisdorff said, 'You put it out and I'll *guarantee* it. If it loses money—
I'll pay!'" "Walk—Don't Run" became an instant smash, selling millions,
spending eighteen weeks on the *Billboard* charts (finally peaking at No. 2)

and simultaneously breaking out as a hit everywhere from England to Germany to Mexico to Japan.

And so, even though Dolton and Boles weren't technically working together any longer, with the Ventures acting as a sort of bridge between the two former collaborators, the two had combined their skills once again to launch an important Northwest band into the wide world of pop music. But because the Ventures now needed to embark on the first of countless national concert tours—and because Skip Moore was apparently satisfied with his twenty-five-dollar fee and filling station job—the boys set out to recruit another Tacoma country drummer, Howie Johnson, whom they'd seen playing at the Circle Tavern.

Still feuding with Boles, evidently, Reisdorff rushed the Ventures into Seattle's Northwest Recorders to cut additional tracks with Kearney Barton for a debut LP. Meanwhile, the band was called to appear on the *Dick Clark Show* in New York City. Following that, the Ventures moved to Hollywood, where, on June 25, they performed (along with the Fleetwoods) for Alan Freed's *KDAY Spectacular* at the famous Hollywood Bowl. By that point, Reisdorff had gotten the band signed to the same major talent agency that the Wailers had signed to—GAC—and their monthlong tour began with skating rink and armory dates in Arizona, New Mexico, and Colorado. While these weren't exactly the hottest rock 'n' roll markets in the world, it was a fine start for the guys: "It started getting exciting right away," recalled Bogle. "I remember the fans were screaming so loud we could hardly hear our amplifiers most of the time. And they'd try and tear yer clothes off. We had to have constant security. We *loved* it! We had a lotta fun. We were kinda overwhelmed by all of it, but we adjusted pretty rapidly."

Well, they all adjusted except for Johnson, who was still recovering from a broken neck he'd suffered in a car wreck prior to joining up. Tired of the pain all the travel caused, he resigned. Another change occurred when Edwards—who had proven his superior skills with a wide-ranging grasp of jazz, classical, flamenco, country, and rock 'n' roll guitar chops—and Bogle switched roles. With Edwards on lead, Bogle on bass, and the addition of Mel Taylor (a drummer they recruited in California), the Ventures' classic lineup was now set. It was in October 1960 that Dolton Records continued with their winning streak with the release of the Ventures' single "Perfidia," a disc that enjoyed a thirteen-week run on the *Billboard* charts, which resulted in a No. 15 hit. That same autumn, Dolton began discussions with Liberty Records about a topic that would ultimately have a jarring impact on the Northwest music scene.

When the talks concluded, Liberty had bought Seattle's most success-ful pop record company. The specific deal included stipulations that would soon see Dolton abandon Seattle, and Reisdorff run Liberty's Dolton divi-sion from a brand-new office complex in Los Angeles. Although this was probably a good business move for Dolton's founder/owners (*and* for the Fleetwoods and Ventures, who moved south as well), the day Reisdorff closed up shop in Seattle also was a sad one for town's fledgling music industry—not to mention all of the other young Dolton acts who were unceremoniously dumped. A thrilling era for area music fans had come to a close, and no one could even begin to guess whether or not another local label would ever be able to rise to the challenge—Jerden, after all, had *already* tried and failed, and Nite-Owl had experienced mixed results before shutting its doors. Perhaps it had been both a blessing and a curse that Dolton Records had made it all look so easy.

CHAPTER 15

The Turnaround

In the brief but productive two years that Dolton Records had been active in Seattle, the label's success had served as a wonderful example—one that got people to thinking that maybe, just maybe, the town *could* really support a vibrant music industry. And so, even though Dolton's bugout in late 1960 put a damper on things, its departure would also prove to have a silver lining—the simple fact that the label had raked in a fortune quickly brought others out of the woodwork to try giving the pop music crapshoot a go.

In fact, with Dolton suddenly out of the picture, it seems everybody and his brother began activating labels and scouring the area searching for the next rising star. Among the new local labels to try to get in on the action were Alki, Camelot, Cascade, Hemlock, Julian, Maverick, Mecca, Shadow, and Star-Hi—and a couple (Seafair-Bolo and Penguin) even ended up scoring a run of sizable regional hits.

The Penguin label was founded back in 1959 by Jim Hammer, a young employee of KOL radio who had watched Dolton's success and made his move to sign up a few "second-generation" bands, including the Continentals, the Royals, and the Dynamics. The Continentals were a north-end band formed by some Blanchet and Lincoln High School kids—including Eldon Butler (sax) and Don Stevenson (drums)—who got their first gigs playing on the CYO "circuit"—at a point well before they were fully qualified for the job. "The first dance we played," laughed Butler, "we knew a *couple* tunes! You know, 'Blue Moon' and 'Louie Louie'—but we just kept adding to our repertoire." To find R&B songs with which to update their set lists in those early days, the band ended up doing what many a band after them would: They went to check out Seattle's top bands: the Frantics, Ron Holden and the Playboys, and the Dave Lewis Combo.

And of all Seattle's leading bands, it was Lewis's that set the bar the highest: "Back in those days," recalled Butler, "Dave Lewis was just playing so far over everybody's heads, you know? His chord structure. His rhythm. The musicians he had with him were just . . . I mean, here *we* were studying "Louie Louie," and these guys were playing *music*. Yeah! He was tops! Now, the Frantics had this thing called 'Fogcutter,' and since we were kinda their protégés—I mean, those guys were working all the sock hops and we were coming up through the parochial school circuit—we kinda just did some of the songs they did. And some of our own things. And we did some of the songs the Playboys did—you know: You *had* to do 'Louie Louie,' okay? *Even* in '59 and '60." Soon the Continentals had a couple of what might generously be call "original" teen R&B tunes: "Cool Penguin" (which was essentially "Fogcutter" turned inside out) and "Soap Sudz" (whose inspiration Butler says came from the Playboys: "When they did 'Louie Louie'—after they'd done about eighteen repetitions—they all traded off fours or eights [bars], and after trading it around, they'd wind the whole thing up. So that's what we did").

"Jim Hammer was an assistant engineer at KOL, and I think that he somehow decided that since a competitive station [KING] was pushing the Frantics, *his* station needed something to push. He said, 'We're gonna make this record.'" After a session with Joe Boles, in May '59 Hammer rushed to get "Cool Penguin" / "Soap Sudz" pressed as Penguin Records' debut: "And then it got on the station," said Butler. "*Instant* play. There was no problem. I think 'Cool Penguin' finally went up to No. 7—Blanchet girls called the station *over and over*. I think we only made about fifteen dollars from it [laughter] but we were *rock 'n' roll stars* and that was *fine!*" Typical of radio station politics, KJR, KING, and KAYO (and most of the area's other stations) showed no interest in Hammer's band's 45—and so by June, "Cool Penguin" was a solid Top 10 hit *only* at KOL. But that fact enabled Hammer to strike a national distribution deal down at Era Records, and once the single was reissued and given another push—one that got "Cool Penguin" aired on ABC-TV's *Dick Clark Show*—the Continentals were on a roll and were hired for a number of big out-of-town gigs, including performances in Vancouver, B.C., with the Fleetwoods, and a Paul Anka concert at the Spokane Coliseum.

Hammer's next discovery was the Dynamics, a group originally formed as the Keynotes by a few Sealth High School chums, including Terry Afdem (piano), and by mid-'59 they'd added a few more, among them Afdem's thirteen-year-old brother, Jeff, on saxophone. Now called the Dynamics, the band cut a couple original instrumentals, "Aces Up" and "Baby," which were issued in July by Penguin. And in a repeat of his previous success, Hammer was able to strike a national distribution deal for the Dynamics with the New York–based Guaranteed Record Co. Penguin issued another single—"Thunder Wagon" / "Teen Beat"—cut by a Tri-Cities-based combo, the Royals—that September. But any sense of excitement and impending fame felt by either the Royals or Dynamics came to a sudden halt when Hammer was mysteriously murdered in his hotel room while working in New York City.

Also inspired by Dolton, Tom and Ellen Ogilvy's Seafair Records—and the sister labels they owned in partnership with Joe Boles (Nolta, Virgelle, and Bolo Records)—were gearing up to issue what would end up being *the* most consistent stream of high-quality Northwest teen R&B ever offered up by any firm in the Northwest. And just about the first move they made was to scoop up a couple of Dolton's castoffs—the Frantics and Little Bill Engelhart—along with two of the now-defunct Penguin label's acts: the Continentals (who had added Keith Shoemaker on sax, and Marius "Butch" Nordal on keyboards), and the Dynamics (who had begun rehearsing with a few singers, including Randi Green, and the Gallahads' Tiny Tony Smith). Bolo Records quickly issued what would be the Continentals' second and final single: "The Turnaround" was a dance-oriented instrumental that became a minor radio hit on KQTY—the only Seattle radio station to jump on it. A pair of Dynamics instrumentals, "Onion Salad" and "Lonesome Llama," that Seafair released in June 1960 met a similar fate. But the labels didn't lose heart, and instead intensified their scouting for new talent.

It was in January 1961 that they released an instrumental single by the Dave Lewis Combo (with new additions: bassist Chuck Whittaker and guitarist Jerry Allen). One side, "R.C. (Untwistin')," was a twist-era tune titled in tribute to Lewis's hometown musical hero, Ray Charles. Everybody who had ever heard the song on record (or at dances) thought that it was perfect. Everyone, that is, *except* the big radio stations KOL and KJR—the latter even went so far as to inform the label that it was just "too R&B" for their listenership. The record, however, did end up being a moderate hit at the Central District's new FM station, KZAM, which was managed by veteran R&B DJ Fitzgerald "Eager" Beaver—and also made history as the very first one aimed at the area's black community. Now, *finally,* there was a station that could—*if* you happened to own an FM receiver—fill the gaping void caused by mainstream radio in its shunning of black-oriented music in Seattle.

Meanwhile, the Dynamics had experienced a few rounds of personnel changes that would dramatically raise the band's stature on the scene. New additions included Pete Borg (bass) and a couple of blacks—Ron Woods (drums) and Tiny Tony Smith (vocals). Eventually, when Smith drifted away around June 1961, the band added the Ogilvys' teenage son, Jimmy (who would later adopt his grandmother's maiden name, Hanna, as his own stage name). And because of his parents' involvement with the scene, working with the likes of Bumps Blackwell (whose Junior Band they'd recorded back in 1947), Big Jay McNeely, and Dave Lewis, Hanna had been exposed to sounds that would profoundly affect his musical tastes.

As a white kid growing up in the C.D., Hanna became deeply immersed in the subculture of Seattle's black music scene and developed a keen appreciation of black music forms—but he *really* got fired up one night after going out with friends to Seattle Armory dance featuring the Wailers. "That was the first band that I heard *outside* of the black district. The Central District experience was mainly where I was coming from, you know? I mean, that's *all* I listened to—outside of the [white] people that recorded with Dad. And so my real experiences with *other* kinds of music didn't really happen until ninth grade, when I heard the Wailers play. That was probably the first time outside of the Central District, where I saw a lot of *white* players playing things that I didn't think they *did*." You know, stuff that Rockin' Robin and the Wailers *and* Little Bill and the Bluenotes had *both* been playing. Stuff like, well, "Louie Louie."

CHAPTER 16

Louie Louie

As the rocky new decade of the 1960s got rolling, several of the top Northwest rock 'n' roll bands were facing turmoil. Everybody seemed to be scrambling for new record deals, and there was a fair amount of "musical chairs" being played, with a remarkable degree of personnel-swapping under way.

Remember that soon after Dolton Records convinced Little Bill Engelhart to leave the Bluenotes and go solo, his former band mate, Rockin' Robin Roberts, joined the Wailers. Then when his dreams of meteoric teen idol stardom were dashed, Engelhart joined up with Seattle's top band, the Frantics, and began doing dance dates with them. Before long, they hooked up with a brand new label, Topaz Records, which had been formed by Gretchen Christopher's boyfriend, John Hill, and was based in Dolton's old downtown digs. It was August 1960 when their recording of Engelhart's bluesy original tune "Sweet Cucumber" was issued—but that summer saw the Frantics getting a number of attractive gig offers from California, and their new singer wasn't so thrilled about road work just then. And so Engelhart began looking around for other local opportunities. "I talked to Pat O'Day and he asked me to come out to the Spanish Castle," recalled Engelhart. "He wanted me to meet someone, and I said, 'Okay.' So, I walked in and he says, 'This is John Stone, and he has a band.' And he says to John Stone, 'Bill's gonna be the singer with yer band' [laughter]. It was like, 'And *that's* that!'"

"Jockey John" Stone—O'Day's supervisor at KJR radio, and the guy there who had won few friends among local musicians and labels for his imperious manner and lack of interest in local recordings—had now somehow come to the conclusion that *he* was a singer who should lead a band and make records. Somehow, he actually finagled a recording deal with the venerated New Orleans label Ace Records. Having such little faith in Seattle's recording studios, he went to the expense of traveling alone to Gold Star Studios in Los Angeles, where he cut a couple tunes with some session pros. And even though the Ace 45 sounded about as soulful as Pat Boone, upon its release he even had the gall to program the damn thing on KJR.

"See, 'Jockey John' Stone was my program director for the first nine months at KJR," sighed O'Day. "And being my boss, he *forced* me to hire him and his band. That was an edict. And—*if you can believe this*—he took his record and actually listed it on his own chart at the station as a Top 10 record, when in fact it hadn't sold *any*! 'Together' was the side that *he* thought was the big hit. Boy, was it junk! 'Jockey John' Stone had quite an ego. He thought he was a really great singer. 'Jockey John' Stone was one of the worst singers in creation. But I used to have to *hire* him and *pay* him to come to a dance and sing his horrid songs [laughter]. So I figured, 'As long as I've got to hire these turkeys, we could have something here that makes sense.' So we got Little Bill in there."

The upside to all this was that O'Day had suddenly discovered a lever to use against Stone's power over him. Now, in order to keep getting dance gigs, Stone had to obey his underling. "So I started working with him and the Adventurers the next night as featured singer," said Engelhart. "What I did was my own show with them backing me. Usually John and I'd come out like the second and third set. 'Jockey John' Stone was much older than all the rest of us, and he was really a character. He'd talk about the band on the air—you know: Radio was *so* much looser then! So he'd just ramble on and on about where we'd played the night before and how it was a great band. We got to play with everybody 'cause it was like KJR had its own band." Stone's band, the Adventurers, were in fact getting to play some great gigs—including some backing Roy Orbison, Gene Vincent, and other stars. And all the while, Stone was abusing his powerful position at KJR— a habit that would soon bring about his downfall. "KJR had *a lot* of power then," said Engelhart, "and 'Jockey John' would literally just call up dance-halls and say: 'We'll be there a week from Saturday' [laughter]. And that would be it, you know—we'd be there!

"I was out at KJR this one time, and he was putting on this big show, and he had Bobby Vee, Brenda Lee, Johnny and Dorsey Burnette—I was the only *local* act at that show. He had *everybody*. And what he'd do was like call up Bobby Vee's manager—and I could only hear one end of the call, right?—'This is John Stone of KJR, we're having this big show here, and we'd like Bobby to come up.' And the other guy would probably be saying something like, 'Well, Bobby will need so much money.' And he'd say, 'Oh, no. We'll just pay the travel expenses up.' And then on the other end of the phone the guy was obviously saying, 'Forget it!' And John would say, 'Well, that's too bad. Because Bobby's record is No. 3 up here and it would be a real shame to take it off.' So, Bobby Vee and . . . well, they *all* showed up! But KJR had told John: 'If you're gonna do this—*don't* involve us.' So that night we walked into the place and John had put up all these big banners reading 'KJR Presents.' I think he got fired right after that. . . ."

Relieved of his duties at KJR after, as O'Day diplomatically put it, "he *forgot* to pay some of the acts," Stone moved away. O'Day moved up to the program director position, and the Adventurers moved on. This was a band that had formed in 1959 and was now becoming known for the great sax playing of Jim Michaelson and the exceptional guitar work of Joe Johansen, whose hard-core adoration of the blues would make him a key influence on the Sea-Tac scene. As it had for plenty of his fellow in-the-know peers, the Evergreen Ballroom had forever changed this former Mossyrock High School football star's life: "Let me tell you how much the Evergreen Ballroom meant to me," Johansen said years later. "Every Sunday night they had a rhythm and blues show come through—and the first one I went to was Bobby 'Blue' Bland and Little Junior Parker and Bo Diddley. Bo Diddley opens the show and has only got a maracas player and a drummer, and I'm goin', 'What the *hell* is this gonna to be about?' You know? And they get out there and they *cook*, you know. *Wow*!

"And then Bobby Bland came on, and he had this *great* guitar player named Wayne Bennett. So I got to study a lot of great blues guitar players down there. And then I went down there and saw James Brown and his Famous Flames. I'm just lookin' at this stuff, sayin', 'This is great!' For a young white kid to see that stuff for the first time—I'm just agaw. I also saw Ike and Tina Turner there. And Hank Ballard and the Midnighters. Fats Domino. Etta James. You know, *anybody* who was worth a damn. And then I saw B.B. King there. I was nineteen and I thought *I* was a pretty hot-stuff blues player. I'd been listening to B.B. King. I'd been listening to the blues. I thought I knew what I was doin'. Uh, it wasn't *quite* true." After the show, Johansen and Engelhart went backstage and met up with their idol— just as they would with other R&B stars on other nights at the Evergreen: "Little Bill introduced me to B.B. after the show, and he was a *real* gracious nice guy. He offered me a cigarette and . . . I didn't know whether to smoke it or save it [laughter]. I swear to God I had no idea. I was just so damn impressed with the whole deal. I just always thought it was great how nice these guys were. Bobby Bland: I spent hours talking with him. And his guitarist, Wayne Bennett, was real cool. And the guitar player with the Upsetters spent forty-five minutes after the show showing me how to play the song 'Hold It.' Freddy King showed me how to play 'Hideaway' at the Evergreen. Those kinds of lessons that you learn—man, *that's* important stuff."

The lessons that Johansen was learning began to have a direct effect on the Adventurers' sound, and though their first couple 45s—like "2:00 Express" and "Excelsior"—were basic rock instrumentals in the Frantics mode, a heavier R&B element began dominating sound. In fact, their fondness for hard-core black music had an immediate impact. One night the Adventurers met Nancy Claire, that young singer they had seen on TV doing all those icky Brenda Lee tunes with the Ventures. "I met them at a dance in Auburn and they had me sing," recalled Claire, "and Little Bill asked me to join up with the Adventurers, but then Joe Johansen said, 'Quit singin' those *cowboy* songs'—[laughter] that was his exact words—and he and Little Bill handed me Aretha Franklin's first record. It was called 'It Won't Be Long' and *that* was the beginning of my rhythm and blues. I hung up my Brenda Lee records [laughter], and from that point on it was Aretha, and Ruth Brown, Maxine Brown, Lavern Baker, and the other R&B singers of those days." Having finally discovered R&B music, Claire would go on to become one of the region's most in-demand singers, performing with various top combos including the Dynamics and Frantics.

Meanwhile, Rockin' Robin had now been with the Wailers for several months, and he was still harping about wanting to sing on a record. He simply desired nothing more than to have a record out with his name on it—and the song he was still nuts over was "Louie Louie." "Robin really discovered that song," recalled the Wailers' pianist, Kent Morrill. "He was workin' in a record store. When we wanted to rehearse and learn songs, we would bring records that we liked individually and the band would decide if they thought that was cool. We usually went along with whoever wanted to sing something. And I remember that Robin brought that record to us. He had a lotta the old Ray Charles, and blues singers that probably most people didn't know existed—things by Hank Ballard and the Midnighters and stuff like that—and that's where we got a lot of stuff."

The immediate issue that the Wailers were facing was that they were in a state of limbo—a sort of directional paralysis that was heightened by uncertainty over their legal relationship with Golden Crest Records. It had been a year now since the band had declined to relocate back to New York, and

Robin Roberts and the Wailers at Tacoma's Fellowship Hall, 1961.
(Courtesy Gary Tideman.)

although the disappointed label had ceased communicating with them—and the band figured that Golden Crest had broken their end of the five-year contract by failing to issue additional records by them (as was specified in the deal)—it was still uncertain terrain, and nobody seemed to really know if the Wailers were free and clear to record for some other company. Maybe even their *own* company.

Meanwhile, a bitter spat erupted within the band's ranks—and it all revolved around Rockin' Robin and his insistence on recording "Louie Louie." "Now, the main controversy I had with him," exclaimed bandleader John Greek, "was that he wanted to bill *himself* on a record!" "We were going to record 'Louie Louie' and he wanted to bill himself as 'Rockin' Robin and the Wailers.'" And Greek wasn't going along with the idea of downgrading the band's name in order to highlight their newest member. But that stalemate was merely one facet of the Wailers' mounting problems. Soon some of their parents began eyeing Greek's creative bookkeeping practices and began raising some questions like just how much in "beer expenses" should he have written off during a solo "promotional" trip to Los Angeles? Everything finally came to a head when those parents called upon Tacoma's Musicians Union, AFM 117, to sort things out. And that was not a forum that Greek welcomed. "There was a *hard-core* thing against us there too! There was a faction that was, you know, positive union. But there were some other guys, boy, they'd just as soon see us—and anybody else playin' rock 'n' roll"—gone." Maybe so, but after reviewing the case and making their decision, the Wailers weren't going anywhere: It was Greek who was expelled from Local 117. Exiled from his band, Greek moved to Hollywood in June, where he started a long career as a studio player.

But within days of Greek's departure, the Wailers contacted Buck Ormsby, who had been struggling to keep the Bluenotes going, and invited him to come sit in with them at their next dance. Ormsby's rumbling electric bass added a lot to the band's sound, and they hired him. His bulldog nature encouraged the band to finally renounce their contract with Golden Crest and make the move to launch their own label. As it happened, the band members who expressed an interest in this new business enterprise— a three-way partnership called Etiquette Records—were Rockin' Robin, Morrill, and Ormsby. It was in August that the first of two recording sessions with Joe Boles produced a version of "Louie Louie" along with a raving rendition of Ray Charles' "Mary Ann." The original intent was for Etiquette to issue those tunes as the label's debut; however, that master tape would in fact sit in the can unused for another six months while the band carried on bickering about how they would list the label credits: Would they read "Rockin' Robin'," or "The Wailers," or "Rockin' Robin and the Wailers"—or just *what* exactly?

What the young Etiquette executives didn't realize was that this gridlock had placed their project at great risk. And that's because in about March

1961, Engelhart and the Adventurers—being totally oblivious to the fact that the Wailers had cut a version of "Louie Louie" the previous summer—booked a session with Kearney Barton at Northwest Recorders to record the very same song, "Louie Louie," for Topaz Records. The band had run through the tune a couple times and gotten a satisfactory take on tape, and the recording was nearly done. All that remained to do was a little "sweetening"—the overdubbing of backing vocals by a local girl group, the Shalimars. "Well, we got it done," recalled Engelhart. "Boy, we worked on that. But we still had the girls' background voices being put on when my old friend Buck Ormsby comes by the studio and he says, 'What are you doin' down here?' And I said, 'We're puttin' the girls' voices on my record.' He said, 'Mind if I go up and listen?' and I says, 'No, I don't care.'"

Of course, when Ormsby saw and heard what was happening, he *freaked*. Not willing to take the chance that Topaz would ace out the Wailers' own dreams for Etiquette, he made an immediate preemptory strike by racing a pressed, but unlabeled 45 of the group's "Louie Louie" right over to Pat O'Day at KJR. "Well, so, the next day on KJR I heard a record of Rockin' Robin and the Wailers doin' 'Louie Louie!" an exasperated Engelhart said. "I don't know how they did it that quick—whether it was an acetate copy or a tape or what it was—but it *buried* me. I'll tell ya! The fuckin' guy! [laughter] I could have *killed* them!" Pat O'Day dug the tune and hyped it like crazy—and Etiquette rush-ordered an emergency pressing of their debut 45—singles that would, in fact, bear the imprint "Rockin' Robin Roberts." And though the Adventurers' Topaz single was pressed and issued within a few weeks, it never had a chance. Not only was it too late, but there was just no competing with the "lightning in a bottle" that the Wailers had captured for their recording.

And that's because the Wailers had radically transformed Richard Berry's low-key R&B groover into a haunting garage rock masterpiece. Instead of the original's offbeat island guitar figures, Rich Dangel applied blunt power chords to a stripped-down adaptation of the tune's main riff. But beyond that innovation, there was also Mark Marush's sax blatting those famous three intro notes, Mike Burk's perfect demonstration of the "Sea-Port Beat," and Morrill and Ormsby's background chanting of the timeless refrain: "Duh-duh-duh-duh . . . duh-duh." Ad infinitum. Topping all this off, of course, was Rockin' Robin's electrifying vocal. In addition to his frenetic overall tone, and the six ad-libbed "yeah"s he interjected every few couplets, there was also another hook that was nigh impossible to ignore: that invitational call to arms—"*Let's give it to 'em, RIGHT NOW!*"—just prior to Dangel's stinging lead solo. In essence, this first-ever garage version of "Louie Louie" was a *perfect* rock 'n' roll record.

CHAPTER 17

Go, Rockin' Robin!

With his new "Louie Louie" 45 suddenly sitting at No. 1 on KJR (and inside the Top 5 at KOL), Rockin' Robin must have felt vindicated for having wanted to cut the song—on a record emblazoned with his name, no less—for the past two years. Now look what was happening! Etiquette Records was off to an enviable start: In just a matter of weeks they'd sold nearly 15,000 copies of the single in the Puget Sound area alone. Hopes were high that the tune would soon break out in other markets, and the stars seemed to align in the label's favor when *Cash Box* gave the release an overall grade of "B+" and noted it as a "Fine Blues vocal by the songster on a catchy ditty that was an awhile back success by Richard Berry. Roberts receives striking combo support."

But damn! Despite phenomenal retail figures locally, the hit still wasn't spreading out beyond the Northwest. "'Louie Louie' was a song Robin believed in," sighed Pat O'Day. "He used to call me on the phone and say, '*How* can we make that thing break through?' He said, 'Isn't the evidence there, Pat, that it's a hit?' And I'd say, 'Robin, the evidence is there in *spades*. What we need is a record company that will believe in it.'" The time had come to seek a distribution deal and try to catapult the record to national hit status. And because Pat O'Day also believed in the tune, he offered to help by talking it up with his peers at other big radio stations around the country—and by pitching it to a few record execs in Los Angeles. "I took the record to Liberty, and I said, 'This record will sell you *five million* copies!' I said, 'Just get it out there and keep working it and working it; 'cause the thing is gonna hit. It's gonna sell and sell and sell!'

"I flew down there twice and just *begged* them. I said, 'Release it not just for the guys in the band, but for yourselves. Believe it. You know, Seattle's not *that* goofy—look at the sales numbers!' I think the sales on the single in the Northwest had passed the 20,000 mark, and if you realize that the Northwest was a 2 percent share of the U.S. record market at that time [and extrapolated from there], that added up to a million-seller! There's just *no* question as to how big it might have been. But I don't know what it was—maybe it was because Seattle was so vanilla white or something—but the rest of the country was following Seattle's lead on song after song after song, and KJR was one of the big breakout stations in the United States, but I would talk to the other program directors and they'd say:, 'Oh, Pat, that's just yer local group up there. You know, we listened to it, but God, that *ain't* much of a record!'"

The fact was, for all its apparent success with Northwest teens, not everybody could hear the record's charms. This wasn't anyone's fault—in fact, "Louie Louie" was such a hard-to-pigeonhole tune that doubts about its merits probably were reasonable. After all, the thing really was different, as O'Day well knows: "It didn't sound like any rock 'n' roll of that time. It didn't sound like anything we'd heard. You know, 'Is it black or is it white?' Or 'Is it . . . .*good*?' And I'd say, 'Gang—it's *magic*.'" O'Day's persuasiveness eventually prevailed—"There was one guy at Liberty that believed me, and he had it released"—and Etiquette finally got their national distribution deal. But it was a "deal" that had all sorts of tongues wagging in the biz. "In 1961, I was with Era Records in Los Angeles, and the record was No. 1 in Seattle and selling thousands and thousands of copies," recalls Jerry Dennon. "And I recall sitting at a meeting with the music director of the number one station in L.A., and the national sales manager and national promotions manager of Liberty Records. And basically the dialogue was, they were 'doing a favor' for Pat O'Day by taking it. They admitted that 'we really don't *understand* it.' So I'm sure they were just stroking O'Day by taking it. They didn't probably realize that the record had any potential outside the Northwest. They probably thought, 'Hey, you know, the band is obviously big up there, so let's not worry about it. Pat's gonna be happy.' Little did they realize what *they* were overlooking."

"So the Wailers' record came out, but Liberty was at that time going through a whole bunch of ownership changes and they totally dropped the ball," winces O'Day. "They never, *never* put *any* emphasis behind it. And it's too bad. As a result, they missed a record that was as big as anything they would *ever* have. And I guess if there's one thing that's a shame, it's all those circumstances that never allowed Robin's 'Louie Louie' to ever achieve its rightful No. 1 position in the country."

But even though industry doubts and missteps played a part in keeping Robin's "Louie Louie" from breaking out nationally, in a very real sense the song had already achieved plenty. By striking a responsive chord (or rather three) with local teens, the Wailers had managed to supersede the two biggest previous local guitar-driven rock hits—"Tall Cool One" and "Walk—Don't Run"—and establish "Louie Louie" as *the* signature riff of Northwest rock 'n' roll. Henceforth, "Louie Louie" would be a song that *hundreds* of Northwest bands adopted, a song that would be heard at *thousands* of dances over the following years, and one whose legacy would reverberate down through the ages.

CHAPTER 18

Paul Revere's Ride

One instructive measure of the "health" of the Pacific Northwest's evolving rock 'n' roll scene was the rate of growth of the teen-dance market—both the frequency of dances and the physical expansion of what was developing into a genuine circuit.

What had begun as a tour route for all the imported country-and-western (and then, later, rockabilly and R&B) bands that Pat Mason was bringing to the region throughout the 1950s was soon serving homegrown bands as well. With rentable community halls, old roadhouses, National Guard armories, and even some high school gymnasiums identified as available in just about every Northwest town that was big enough to boast a stoplight, a band working this circuit could now play dances all around the states of Washington and Oregon, and even over to the college towns of Idaho and Montana.

And *that* is exactly how and why early Puget Sound–area bands like the Dave Lewis Combo, Clayton Watson and the Silhouettes, the Wailers, the Frantics, and the Ventures began to have a direct influence on young musicians in those latter two states. In fact, Idaho's most famous rocker, Paul Revere, was inspired to begin his own rock 'n' roll career after attending a Jerry Lee Lewis dance in Idaho—one that featured the Silhouettes as the opening act. By his own admission, young Revere loved the music of his fellow wild-man pianist, Lewis—but on that night he was even *more* impressed by the local opening band. "There's a lot of things that I can remember happening way back then," recalled Watson. "Things like Paul Revere coming up to me at a dance—he was young too, younger than me by a couple years—and he said he 'wanted to start a band.' And, I'll *never* forget, he asked me, 'How do you go about it?' I *remember* that." Revere does too.

Revere was already jamming with some Caldwell, Idaho, guys who called themselves the Downbeats—but up until seeing the Silhouettes, he hadn't really taken that band seriously. And in fact the Downbeats were not even the most *active* Idaho rock 'n' roll band in the late '50s, and other combos of the day, including Daryl Britt and the Blue Jeans, and Dick Cates and the Chessmen, had their own teenage fans. But it would be the Downbeats (under a new name: Paul Revere and the Raiders) who would go on to achieve the greatest popular success of *any* Northwest combo—and, in fact, would eventually be ranked (along with the Beach Boys and the Byrds) as among the most successful American rock bands of the 1960s.

The Downbeats' origins trace back to 1957, when a local tough named Red Hughes managed to corral a few fellow jocks to back his efforts at singing. After jamming in the music room at Caldwell High after school, the guys invited the cat with the funny name—Paul Revere Dick—to join in. And that's when they discovered that he played quite a mean boogie-woogie piano. Meanwhile, the leaders of the Caldwell Elks Club decided to raise some cash by sponsoring sock hops for the town's younger set, and the Downbeats were asked to perform their first public gig. That event went well, as did subsequent high school dances and another show at the Oddfellows Hall.

Revere—who always had a real knack for business (he owned *three* barber shops by age eighteen!)—began sizing up the financial aspects of the teen-dance racket. And his conclusion was, Hell, there just wasn't *that* much to it. All he'd need to do in order to kick out the middlemen dance promoters was to rent a hall himself. And sure enough, the plan worked. The Downbeats were getting to perform more often, and the new revenue stream became so dependable that Revere decided to devote even more time to the band. He sold his barber shops and invested in the Reed n' Bell drive-in burger shack in the nearby town of Nampa.

And it was while running that new business that he struck up a friendship with the delivery boy from McClure's Bakery—a kid named Mark Lindsay, who would go on to become a teen idol of the first magnitude singing with Revere. But for the moment, Lindsay was just a Eugene, Oregon, trouble-boy who'd left home at age fifteen to stay with his grandmother in Nampa and was now singing occasionally with a country band called the Idaho Playboys. All it took, though, for Lindsay to realize that what he *really* needed was to be in a rock 'n' roll band was one sighting of the Downbeats performing at a dance, but Nampa only had *one* band, and Red Hughes—despite his obvious deficiency as a vocalist—was not the kind of guy whose toes you wanted to step on. Still, Lindsay was determined to get a shot with the band, and when Revere eventually invited him to grab his sax and come along to a rehearsal, he jumped at the chance. Lindsay's honking that day didn't exactly bowl over the Downbeats. But the band thanked him for trying out and invited him to attend their next dance anyway.

It was at that particular gig in 1958 when Hughes was very late to arrive, and the band asked the slightly beered-up Lindsay to help out by singing until their band mate arrived. And it wasn't more than a few songs into that set that the Downbeats saw their future right before their very eyes: Lindsay was a natural onstage, and his vocal skills were beyond compare. Hughes was booted out and the new kid was in.

By 1960 the band had developed a repertoire that included a number of the Wailers' tunes (like "Tall Cool One" and "Roadrunner") along with some original piano-driven instrumentals. Revere decided to book a couple hours of recording time at Boise's radio station, KGEM. "About that time we had a lot of original material that we were messin' around with," recalled Revere, "so we went into a recording studio. It wasn't *actually* a recording studio—there was no recording studio in Idaho then. This was a radio station that had a little room that they used to cut radio spots in. And so we all crammed into this 'studio' and set up the drums and the guitar amps and the whole thing, and we recorded this stuff in a couple of hours. We must have recorded ten or twelve songs. I mean, in those days if you didn't make a mistake that was *noticeable*, you would just say, 'Okay, that's good enough!'

"So I had a tape full of songs that I didn't really what to do with, but I thought, '*Maybe* we could make a record deal? I don't know!' So I jumped in my car and drove down to Los Angeles, and I just started knocking on doors. I didn't know what the hell I was doin'—I thought I had me a rock 'n' roll band and I thought somebody ought to hear about it. It was kind of a crazy trip, and a lot of experiences I had knockin' on record label doors were interesting. But someone had suggested this guy in Gardena, California, who had a pressing plant. A lot of the smaller labels got this guy to press their records up. But every once in a while this guy would put out a record on his own label, Gardena Records. So I went down there, and he instantly *loved* the stuff, and he wanted to put it out. The first record he put out was 'Beatnik Sticks,' which was kind of a rock 'n' roll version of 'Chopsticks.' He liked that."

Gardena's owner, John Guss, undoubtedly liked the fact that instrumental rock singles were popular at the time—but what he didn't like was the Downbeats' name. He agreed to issue their record but insisted on changing their name to something less, well, *jazzy*. Revere balked at his first suggestion—the "Nightriders" just seemed too, well, *country*. But then Guss tossed out another idea—one that had a certain positive ring to it, maybe even the magic ring of a cash register: "Well, how about *Paul Revere and the Raiders?*"

Back home in Caldwell, Revere and band were thrilled when in September 1960 their "Beatnik Sticks" 45 began charting on West Coast stations from Boise to Los Angeles to Vancouver, B.C.—and as a result, they were now able to score gigs in a broader area, first across the border in Ontario, Oregon; then in Baker, La Grande, Pendleton, The Dalles; and finally into Walla Walla and Yakima, Washington.

Meanwhile, Guss asked Revere to return to California with the Raiders to do a few promotional gigs—including the band's television debut on the *Wink Martindale Show*—and to enter a better studio and cut a follow-up 45. When the band arrived all loaded into Revere's T-Bird and Lindsay's Plymouth Valiant, Guss got them into a studio, and one of the tunes they cut was among Revere's earliest compositions, "Like Long Hair." This song was a clever knock-off of a beloved, if ridiculously pompous, classical piece by Russian composer Sergei Rachmaninoff, titled "C# Minor Prelude."

Upon the song's release by Gardena, it too was met with instant favor by the radio industry; Dick Clark even aired it on *American Bandstand*. In late March 1961, "Like Long Hair" made its entry onto the *Billboard* charts. Everything seemed to be snowballing, and the ABC network sent word that Dick Clark wanted the band to perform on his show. All signs were pointing toward an imminent breakthrough for the band.

Guss and the group were thoroughly ecstatic—well, for a few short hours anyway. Because when that day's afternoon mail arrived, Revere was suddenly staring at a notice from Uncle Sam instructing him to report immediately for military duty. This was a bombshell—first, the television opportunity with Clark was necessarily declined, becoming a major lost opportunity. And the Raiders still had two weeks of live bookings on their calendar—gigs that were fulfilled under duress with a substitute pianist—a then-unknown studio pro named Leon Russell picked up the slack for Revere.

In the end, though, Revere was exempted from military service due to his Mennonite religion (and Conscientious Objector status). Not fully off the hook, he was instead required to serve in an alternate capacity for two years by working in the psychiatric facility at Dammasch Hospital—which was located outside of Portland, Oregon.

That the Raiders—who'd just been named by a national poll of radio DJs as "one of the top up-and-coming instrumental bands in the nation"— were suddenly defunct (in fact, most members had headed back to their *logging* jobs in Idaho) surely exasperated Guss. "Like Long Hair" was now charting at the nation's No. 38 slot—a genuine hit that ultimately moved about 500,000 units—but there was no band to promote! Still, rather than throw in the towel, Guss gamely played the hand he'd been dealt and issued

The Raider's debut, Gardena Records, 1961.

additional Raiders 45s, and finally pulled all the band's tracks together (along with another called "Paul Revere's Ride," which mythologized the band-leader's original solo trip to California) on the *Like Long Hair* LP. And that was that. As far as anyone knew at the time, the brief, blazing career of Paul Revere and the Raiders was a closed chapter in the history of Northwest rock.

CHAPTER 19

World's Fair Rock

It was in anticipation of the vast legions of visitors expected for the Century 21 Exposition—or the 1962 World's Fair—to be held from April through October in Seattle that the Washington State Liquor Control Board *finally* loosened up their rules, which had long impacted the state's nightlife industry in a negative way. However, in a sort of one-step-forward, one-step-back routine, the nervous Seattle City Council simultaneously passed a law—the 1961 Noise Ordinance—that was presumably written with the best of intentions, but which would come in handy as a means to repress live music clubs for decades after.

Now venues could apply for licenses to pour individual cocktails—a practice that had been outlawed since 1948—and thus a whole new wave of nightclubs and bars arrived to join the old beer and wine taverns and outdated BYOB "bottle clubs." Being on the cusp of a hoped-for boom time now, the Northwest's nightclubs even began taking their first steps in hiring local rock-oriented bands. It was in March of '61 that the Frantics, whose youngest members had finally come of age, became Seattle's first white rock 'n' roll band to score a regular gig in a downtown liquor bar. The popular combo was hired at Dave's Fifth Avenue, and due to popular demand, their nightly engagement was extended for months.

Meanwhile, those rockin' R&B pioneers the Dave Lewis Combo were still pulling in largely black audiences over at the Birdland. Crowds of dancers *and* local musicians made pilgrimages there to see if they could work up the courage to climb on the bandstand, sit in with the combo, and see if their own skills passed muster with a very musically sophisticated and demanding audience. "You know," said Tiny Tony Smith, "the whole thing was, if they could get a chance to play like at Birdland with Dave Lewis, *that* was the whole thrill."

Among the many young local players who discovered the Birdland and began frequenting the joint were the members of bands like the Velvetones, the Pulsations, the Continentals, and the Dynamics. Lewis sometimes felt overwhelmed by the sheer quantity of players lining up to get up with his band—and even when he did call them up, he sometimes wished that he hadn't. Like when the Velvetones' guitarist, Jimmy Hendrix showed up. The Velvetones were a young, inexperienced combo who were largely self-taught—not knowing any better, they actually tuned their guitars to the key of C rather than the standard E. In addition, they struggled to get gigs and keep their instruments in shape—baritone sax player Luther Rabb once recalled some quite humble beginnings: "Jimmy used to carry his guitar in a plastic bag. It rains a lot in Seattle, you know." But for all the scuffling and lack of training, Hendrix apparently began exploring his signature sounds early on.

"Jimmy used to come to Birdland regularly when we were there," Lewis recalled. "The *thing* about Jimmy was, see, the music back in the '50s wasn't as technically involved as it is today, but it was formatted—in that there were certain patterns you played for, like, the blues—and when we'd have jam sessions on Sundays, Jimmy Hendrix would come up with his guitar, and he was playing it as a kind of style that he played even when he got popular. And we couldn't *relate* to it. So a lot of times he was asked to leave the stage. And, you know, the people, when they come into Birdland, they wanted to dance, and they couldn't relate to the loudness and the feedback responses. And that's what he was playing at the time. And we weren't really receptive to him, and I don't know, he may have resented us or thought that we weren't giving him a fair chance, but if you were in the time, you would know how it was."

Truth. Another contemporary player, Ron Holden—who had left town in 1960 to push his big hit, "Love You So"—remembered those early days very well too. "Hendrix used to come into the Carpenters Hall when the Playboys would be playing there. He'd come in there with just his guitar and cord and say, 'Hey, man, let me play.' And I'd say, 'Okay, man, but we're playing, like, "Blueberry Hill" so, you know, just be cool!' And so I'd count it off—a slow 'Blueberry Hill' tempo—and we'd get about three bars into it and he'd go right for the throat. He'd play a solo all the way through 'Blueberry Hill.' He'd play a solo all the way through 'Louie Louie.' So finally, I just had to tell him, 'Hey, man, I'm sorry but you play too loud! And you're soloing all the way through!'"

After such incidents—and others in which his pleas to jam with his other favorite local bands (including the Wailers, Adventurers, and Dynamics) were rebuffed—Hendrix must have felt as through his opportunities in Seattle were being stifled. After all, none of the string of three teen R&B combos that he became a member of—the Velvetones, the Rocking Teens (aka the Rocking Kings), and Thomas and His Tomcats—ever had any realistic chance at breaking onto the region's increasingly lucrative teen-dance circuit. By the summer of 1961, when he split to join the US Army, Hendrix did, however, leave his hometown with something other than bruised feelings and a battered cheap guitar, and *that* was a musical sensibility steeped the Northwest's "Louie Louie"–driven rock 'n' roll aesthetic.

By 1962 there were probably a couple hundred active teenage bands in the Northwest, but the one that scored the biggest hit record during that World's Fair summer was the Statics. Formed in Burien back in 1960, the Statics had already recruited the Gallahads' singer, Tiny Tony Smith, who agreed to front them part-time, but in '62 they added sax-man Neil Rush and his soon-to-be wife, Shoreline High School student and singer/keyboardist Merrilee Gunst—who had already played with a Kent-based band called the Aztecs and then Merrilee and Her Men. Now billed as "Tiny Tony, Merrilee, and the Statics," this band was red-hot. "Merrilee played the organ," Smith recalled, "and she would do a first show. Then I would do a second show. Then Merrilee and I did the last set together. And we would get *wild* at the end. See, we had all the steps down. See, *that's* what made the Statics a real dynamic group. I'd basically been the choreographer for the Gallahads, and I took all those steps and taught 'em to the Statics, and we had a basic *hard-core* front line of R&B steps. And that coupled with our sound made our show fantastic."

That fantastic show would earn them a region-wide reputation as a smokin' teen R&B combo—but it was *also* funky enough to actually get Smith in hot water with the law: "Tony got thrown in jail once down in Olympia out at the Evergreen Ballroom," said Neil Rush. "We used to do some pretty graphic steps—we'd do the 'bump-and-grind' kind of a thing. One of the things Tony used to do . . . well see, one of his girlfriends was about a six-foot-tall and very beautiful Amazon-looking woman, and she was dancing out in the crowd right in front of Tony. And Tony would take his belt, and he'd pull his belt out and stick it out like a dick. He used to wear three-piece suits, and he would have his belt sticking out about seven

Twist Adds Modern Touch

BY MOONLIGHT: Dancing Under the Stars is a popular new feature at the World's Fair. These youngsters were twisting to music from the International Bandstand in the fairgrounds' northwest corner. The outdoor dancing is free to fairgoers from 9 to midnight each Saturday night.

The Statics at the 1962 Seattle World's Fair. (Courtesy Merrilee Rush.)

or eight inches, and the cops came and hauled him away. They hauled his ass *away* for that one. We had to go down and get him out of jail."

But that incident was merely a one-off problem. A more persistent issue was that even though Merrilee was becoming a major attraction at dances, and even though their fan base was quickly expanding, the Statics' first few 45s were rejected for airplay on KJR by Pat O'Day, who told them that their recordings weren't airworthy. For their part, the band believed that the tunes were just too R&B-oriented for *his* personal tastes. True or not, that theory might at least help explain why the Statics' July 1962 single, "Hey Mrs. Jones"—a mildly risqué R&B song featuring an openly flirty (". . . Hey Mrs. Jones, can I come in . . .") vocal duet between a big black man (Smith) and a petite white girl (Merrilee)—struggled without mainstream radio support. Indeed KJR, KOL, and all the other big Seattle stations steered clear of the thing in droves. Fortunately, the town's new little R&B outpost, KZAM, jumped on the hot disc, and suddenly Bolo Records had the biggest local hit of the year on their hands.

Meanwhile, what had begun only a few short years prior as a simple series of teen dances promoted by O'Day had by now escalated into a rather substantial industry. The year of 1962 would, in fact, be a banner one for him. By promoting dances through his new company—Pat O'Day & Associates— he would manage to bolster his $12,000 salary as KJR's program director with an additional $50,000 of income. And one of the aces up his sleeve was an ongoing relationship with the Wailers. Thinking ahead to the upcoming World's Fair, O'Day had arranged to help cut what would become the Etiquette label's first album release, *The Wailers at the Castle*—which would prove to be an excellent record and a *perfect* piece of advertising for his dances down at the Spanish Castle.

Issued just in time for the fair's opening, the *Castle* album featured liner notes penned by O'Day, which hyped all the fun people could expect at a

The Spanish Castle, circa 1963. (Photo by Harry W. Wilson; courtesy of the Wilson Family.)

Wailers dance: "If you visit Seattle for the Fair, I hope you will find it possible to stop by the Spanish Castle . . . the Friday Night entertainment mecca of the Seattle-Tacoma area." Given that many tens of thousands of copies the LP were sold, it can fairly be assumed that the disc probably *did* attract some outsiders to the hall, but the record also had lasting appeal. As a historical aural document, the album (which was captured live "at the Castle" late one night with O'Day producing and Joe Boles engineering) perfectly showcases the musical changes that the Wailers had experienced in the two years since their instrumental rock days with Golden Crest Records.

In addition to featuring Rockin' Robin—and their gutsy new girl singer, Gail Harris—the band was displaying a much tougher edge on such instrumental songs as "San-Ho-Zay," by the Texas bluesman Freddy King. Guitarist Rich Dangel became so influential regionally that his adoption of that and other King classics like "Stumble" and "Hideaway" became mandatory local teen-dance standards—and one of Dangel's biggest fans, Jimmy Hendrix, even chose to cut "San-Ho-Zay" at one of his very first recording sessions after arriving in New York City in 1965.

But throughout the entire '62 World's Fair, Pat O'Day & Associates worked furiously to ratchet up their expanding teen-dance empire—and that meant promoting certain bands that O'Day favored—which in turn meant keeping their recordings on KJR's charts. And so, while the *At the Castle* LP didn't produce any new radio hits, there was still a business imperative to steer attention to his top-drawing band. And thus, in the spring of 1962, KJR's Fab 50 suddenly saw the miraculous (wink, wink) reappearance of a now-year-old tune, Rockin' Robin and the Wailers' "Louie Louie."

But that reprise of his hit was not enough was not enough to keep Robin from making plans for his future, and it was around this time that he took a break from the band to serve in the Marine Reserves down in Pendleton, Oregon. After returning to Tacoma and gigging a bit more, Robin announced that he would be moving away to study chemistry at the University of Oregon. Then, upon graduation, he began teaching at Oregon State, but Robin's rock 'n' roll dreams eventually led him to California, where he reunited with the Wailers once again to cut a couple new tunes. Then, sadly, while the singer seriously pondering leaving academia to rejoin the world of music, his quandary was unexpectedly resolved: On December 22, 1967, Rockin' Robin Roberts, age twenty-seven, lost his life as a passenger in a tragic car wreck on I-5 in California.

CHAPTER 20

Louie Louie
(A Slight Return)

Rock 'n' roll arrived in Oregon when KPOJ—a local radio station owned by the *Portland Oregon Journal* newspaper—began broadcasting *Dick Novak's Rhythm Room* show live from Amato's Supper Club in the 1950s. In1957, Novak started spinning discs nightly from Scotty's Drive-In, throwing his first teen dances; later in the year he switched over to Pioneer Broadcasting's KGW—where in 1959 he also became a cohost on KGW-TV's *Portland Bandstand* show.

That same year saw the launch of a powerful new Top 40 radio station, KISN, which featured the exciting DJ "Tiger" Tom Murphy, who wasted no time in promoting himself via a series of teen dances that showcased a young Portland combo called the Kingsmen. Formed by guitarist Jack Ely, drummer Lynn Easton, lead guitarist Mike Mitchell, and bassist Bob Nordby, the teenage quartet's struggle to come up with a suitable name was resolved after somebody spotted a newspaper ad mentioning that a nightclub group known as "the Kingsmen" were performing their final week before disbanding.

Prompted by the opportunity, Easton's mother dutifully went downtown to meet that older black group and explain the situation. The musicians assured her that the boys were welcome to adopt their name. Soon the new Kingsmen had built up a decent repertoire, and "Tiger" Tom Murphy began booking the boys at various dances. "KISN was *the* station in town," Mitchell noted. "KISN had no competition—until KGON came on the scene." It was September 1962 when that much older station, KGON, suddenly announced a switch to the Top 40 format—*and* the start of their *Saturday Night Dancing*

Portland's original Kingsmen, circa 1963.

Party show broadcast live from that old country hall out on Division Street, the D Street Corral.

Nineteen sixty-two also saw the Kingsmen score their highest-profile booking yet: a big fashion show at Portland's Paramount Theater, where they were co-billed along with the Ventures, whose other performance in town that week on the *Saturday Night Dancing Party* show would be released on compact disc decades later. Like young bands everywhere, the Kingsmen were big fans of the headliners and had even already incorporated a few of the Ventures' hits into their own set list.

One of the Kingsmen's early strongholds was the Pypo Club over in the coastal beach town of Seaside, where Rockin' Robin's "Louie Louie" 45 played *incessantly* on the room's jukebox. "We'd played the Pypo Club on a Saturday night and then went back there on Sunday afternoon to pack up our gear," recalled Ely. "While we were in there, fifteen or twenty teenagers were hanging out, and somebody put this song 'Louie Louie' on the jukebox. And when it came on the jukebox, everybody in the room got up and started dancing. I mean *everybody*. They didn't even care whether they even had a partner—they just got up and stood around their tables and started dancing. And I didn't think too much about it. Then the song ended and there was a few moments' pause—like there is on a jukebox while it puts away the record, recoils itself, finds the next record, and puts it on—and it was the same song again. And *again*. Somebody had plugged that jukebox

134

so it would play the same song over and over, and every time, everybody'd dance! And I looked at Lynn and said, 'We've *got* to learn this song.'"

First, though, the Kingsmen would have to get their hands on a copy of the year-and-a-half-old Etiquette 45—a record that, while a major radio hit around Seattle, had failed to become one in Portland. When none of the usual downtown record shops had the disc, Ely went across town to Bop City Records on N. Williams Avenue in the black community's Albina District to buy a copy. "We started playing the song and it had the *same* effect for us at dances as it had on those kids around the jukebox at the Pypo Club."

But the Pypo was not Oregon's only teen club at that point—in fact, Portland kids had been enjoying their dances at room called the Town Mart when a new "nonprofit" teen club called the Headless Horseman opened for business in 1962. And business was good. As of its opening night, the venue became the *largest* private-membership club in the whole state. The club's happy owners were three enterprising young men named Ross Allemang, Al Dardis, and Mike "Smitty" Smith—and both Smitty and Allemang were members of the house band. That's where Paul Revere—who had been set free by Uncle Sam that fall—and Mark Lindsay found some new recruits in their efforts to reconstitute the Raiders from scratch. Allemang came aboard as bassist, another pal named Steve West added guitar, and Smitty joined as drummer. He recalled that "the first time we got together it sounded good, and I knew that it was gonna go places, and so did everybody else. I was excited that first moment we sat down and played."

This Raiders band played regularly at the Headless Horseman, but soon they were in such demand that they ended up sharing house band status with a group led by vocalist Jim Dunlop—Gentleman Jim and the Horsemen, a band that had formed back in '61 out of the ashes of the Royal Notes (which had also included a keyboardist, Don Gallucci, who would soon join the Kingsmen, and who would later go on to produce Iggy & the Stooges' garage-punk masterpiece, *Funhouse*). Meanwhile, KISN radio had made moves to help consolidate its dominance in Portland's Top 40 market—including importing a Seattle DJ named Ben Tracy, who brought along *his* copy of Rockin' Robin and the Wailers' "Louie Louie" 45. And that is how the tune finally got some belated airplay in the Portland market.

"The first time I heard 'Louie Louie,'" said Revere, was when "a record was brought to me by a kid in Portland. We were playing at the Headless Horseman, and this one kid was always bringin' me records. You know, off-the-wall stuff that he had in his record collection. Usually he'd come up

135

with stuff that I liked and we'd learn it. He said, 'Have you ever heard of "Louie Louie"?' And I said, 'No. I don't think so.' And so he played me this record—it was the Wailers' version—I just went, 'Wow, that's *hot.*'"

Revere certainly did love the Wailers—back when his band was still with Gardena Records, they went so far as to issue a 45 featuring versions of "Tall Cool One" backed with "Roadrunner"—an exceedingly rare instance of a band covering *both* sides of another act's previously released single. Talk about paying tribute! But now the Raiders took on "Louie Louie" for the first time. "It took about two minutes to learn 'Louie Louie'—it was *three* chords [laughter]. Any idiot could learn it. Well, we played it at a dance that night and the crowd loved it. And so we played it a couple times. Then after intermission we decided to play a longer version. I think we played for about five minutes straight. It had the magic of the perfect beat to dance to at the time. I mean, it's the epitome of a great rock 'n' roll song. It's just a standard that will last for eternity. Those three chords will never die—as long as I'm around anyway. You can't possibly not like the beat or feel of 'Louie Louie'—if dancing is in your bones at all. It got to be a song that we played regularly—at least twice a night—at every dance that we played."

And so, 1962 rolled into 1963—the year that would see Portland's simmering teen R&B scene explode as the biggest battleground in Northwest rock 'n' roll history. The first skirmish occurred after the Raiders hooked up with a new manager, Roger Hart. Formerly a popular DJ at KISN, Hart had first gotten involved in throwing teen dances when he brought the Tokens to a rural grange hall just outside of Portland—a gig that drew a huge crowd who loved the national hit "The Lion Sleeps Tonight." But in the early spring of 1963, Hart took a leave of absence from KISN to accept a new temp job at Salem's KGAY—while KISN promoted Ken Chase (their DJ host of the *Lunchin' Munchin'* afternoon show) to the powerful program director position.

As it happened, both of these DJs were keeping a close eye on the developing scene. Inspired by the raging success at the Headless Horseman, Chase plunged into the dance biz by opening his own teen-club—which he dubbed the Chase—in a former Prohibition-era speakeasy that was located just outside of Portland in Milwaukee, Oregon. Meanwhile, the Wailers' "Louie Louie" had become so hot in the area that Hart hired them for a dance. "The first *local* group I ever hired was the Wailers. Brought them down and they were such a success it was like, 'Wow, I hafta find another group!' And then I stumbled onto the Raiders, and we hit it off, and I became their manager." As manager, Hart booked the new

136

Raiders into their first big dance over at Vancouver, Washington's Trapadero Teen Club, on March 30, 1963. With Hart pushing the dance on his radio show, the event was a great success and a fine start to a new partnership.

In the meantime, Chase had snapped up the Kingsmen: "By this time," said Ely, "we were the house band at the Chase, and Ken Chase was signed on as our manager—I mean, who was better for a manager than the program director for the local rock station?! And one who owned a teen club and could give you steady work?! So anyway—after I had been hounding Ken Chase to let us record 'Louie Louie' for I don't know how long, one Friday night he said, 'It's now time. It's time to record "Louie Louie." Let's do it tomorrow.' He had obviously called the studio and come up with the time of ten o'clock in the morning. We were gonna get our butts up outta bed and go down and record this song. And we were saying like, '*Tomorrow*? How can we get this all together by *tomorrow*?'"

"Get *what* together?" Chase must have wondered: This is, after all, "Louie Louie" we're talking about. And so it was that on the probable date of April 6, 1963, the Kingsmen entered an old three-track radio jingle–production studio, Northwestern Inc., and began working with the studio's owner/engineer, Bob Lindahl: "So we get down there and he sets our gear up in a circle around the room," said Ely. "He had an old ribbon mic on the bass drum and one other mic on the snare. He had a mic in front of each amplifier. Gallucci had a Hohner electric piano running through a Sears Alamo amp, and I was playing a Fender Jazzmaster through a Fender *Super* amp. Anyway, Ken Chase had in his mind that he wanted us to sound the same as we sounded in his club. Because he thought that the sound there had something to do with how the song affected people. Which was not true. So when he brought me in to sing, he took a Telefunken microphone and hung it from a soundstage boom right up near the ceiling. He stood me in the center of the circle under the microphone and had me lean back and sing up toward that microphone. It was more like yelling than singing, 'cause I was trying to be heard over all the instruments."

"And so Chase sat in the control booth with the engineer and said, 'Okay, start playing the song.' We started into 'Louie Louie,' and we'd gotten probably sixty bars into the song and he said, 'Stop, stop!' And we could see there was this huge argument going on in the control room, and suddenly Ken pushed the engineer out of the booth and shut the door. And he must have locked it, 'cause the guy couldn't get back in. Then Ken's voice came back on the monitors and said, 'Okay, from the top.' And so we thought that we were just kinda runnin' through the song again, you know? We had no idea that second time was going to be the take. We ran the song all the way through and he said, 'That's it. Pack it up. We've got it . . . sounds *great.*'" The band wasn't quite so sure. And for at least two good reasons: One was that Easton had (at 54.5 seconds into the song) allegedly dropped a drumstick during the second chorus and out of frustration yelled out something that—although very faint—sounds for all the world to be "FUCK!," and Ely had flubbed his part by losing his bearings (at 1:58) and fluffing the third verse by coming in a few bars too early. After bleating the lyrical line "Me see" prematurely, Ely dropped back, sat tight for two bars until the band came around again, and then got it right, yelping, "Me see Jamaica moon above."

Considered in hindsight, this whole mess is probably the sloppiest two minutes and forty-two seconds of rock 'n' roll ever captured on magnetic tape—and thus a stone classic. But at the time, "We were all pretty skeptical," said Ely. "But we did like we were told and then went into a listening room, an office where they had a speaker, and listened to it played back and we were all moaning, 'Oh God, that's *horrible.* That's the worst thing I've ever heard in my life. That sounds like crap.' But *Ken* was all elated—he thought it sounded wonderful." What is *not* debatable is that the Kingsmen's chaotic version—with its clubfooted drumbeat, insane cymbal crashes, ultra-cheesy keyboard figures, lead guitar spazz-out/solo, as well as Ely's remarkably slurred vocals—made for some sublime garage-band rock 'n' roll.

But the whole strange experience wasn't over quite yet for the Kingsmen: "So then we were walking out of the studio," recalled Ely, "and Ken came out and said, 'Well, it's gonna be fifty bucks. Who's got the money?' And we all looked at each other—I'm sure our mouths dropped down to our knees, you know? We'd figured that since *he'd* been pushin' us, *he'd* pay for it. Well, he didn't. So it was decided right then and there that each person would cough up ten bucks and we'd all own a fifth of the pie. The problem was, nobody had the ten bucks on 'em, so Lynn's mom—who had been the chauffeur that day—paid the fifty bucks, and we were to all pay her back. I'm sure the next week's pay *all* went to her."

Meanwhile, the Raiders and their manager were also becoming convinced that "Louie Louie" had a certain magical effect on their dance crowds. "One night Roger noticed how the kids reacted whenever we did 'Louie Louie,'" said Revere. "It was just the *perfect* dance song! And he says, 'You know, I think you ought to rerecord that.' And I said, 'Hey, no problem—you got the money, I got the time.' I think Northwestern charged thirty dollars an hour to record, so I says 'Roger, you got thirty bucks, we'll cut a couple of songs.' So we went in one night and did 'Louie Louie' and 'Night Train.'" It was on the probable date of April 13, 1963, when the Raiders set up their gear. "It took us about fifteen minutes to cut each one," laughed Revere. "There was just *nothin'* to it—we had been playin' them every night on stage. So we just tried to get a sound where the mix was halfway decent, and we played 'em. We did the music track first. Then we did the vocal on the second track."

In the end—that is, two hours and fifty-seven dollars later—the Raiders had the songs in the can—one of which Lindsay recalled Lindahl commenting on, by saying how odd it was that the Raiders were cutting same tune that another group, the Kingsmen, had just cut there just a week or so prior. No matter, though: Each band had their own following at their respective teen club gigs, and their arrangements of "Louie Louie" were actually rather dissimilar. While the Kingsmen's version bordered on gloriously undisciplined anarchy, the Raiders' rendition was positively tight and electrifying: From Smitty's rock-solid tub-thumping and opening command to "Grab your woman: It's 'Louie Louie' time!" to Lindsay's in-your-face sax blasts, all the way to that midpoint exhortation for dancers to "Stomp, shout, and work it on out!"—the recording revealed a band aiming for the big time.

But now the fate of these two Portland bands' "Louie Louie" recordings was in the hands of their managers. And so the ensuing Battle of the Louies commenced, with Chase airing the Kingsmen's tape on KISN while Hart aired an acetate disc of the Raiders on his KGAY shows. And beyond all that, efforts began to get the two songs issued in record form. Hart quickly formed his own label, Sandé Records, and arranged with Revere's old pal at Gardena Records, John Guss, to have a thousand 45s quickly pressed and shipped up from California, while Chase simultaneously called on his old record-distributor buddy Jerry Dennon—who had recently returned from Los Angeles to Seattle and reactivated Jerden Records—to see if he might step up.

Luckily, Chase's timing was perfect. Dennon had just released "David's Mood Pt. 2"—the new Dave Lewis Trio's radio hit debut 45, a great instrumental whose musical DNA reveals a family tree shared with "Louie Louie"—and following that success he was quite receptive to the pleas for help. After all, one hand washes the other: "Obviously, I wanted Ken to be happy with me," explained Dennon. "If I can do Ken a favor, he'll be a little more receptive to playing some of my records. So when he said, 'I've got a club and this house band called the Kingsmen—and if you could help do a record on them, you know, we could *guarantee* airplay on it,' et cetera, et cetera—well, we cut a deal." By May, fresh new pressings of "Louie Louie" by the Kingsmen on the Jerden label arrived in Portland—and the band enlisted their schoolmates to help create a "demand" for the thing. "About two weeks went by, and suddenly there was a box of records and we were givin' 'em to all our relatives and friends and everybody," recalled Ely. "And we were also calling all our classmates at school—everybody we knew— 'cause Ken needed some credibility in order to play our song on the radio. Even though he was program director, he had to answer to the general manager. So after school, from three o'clock on, all our friends were callin' the radio station saying, 'Play "Louie Louie" by the Kingsmen.'"

Having a Jerden 45 in the racks of local record shops was definitely cool for the Kingsmen, but Hart and the Raiders had even bigger opportunities unfolding. While settling in at his new DJ gig at Vancouver's KKEY, Hart shipped out the first promo copies of the Raiders' Sandē 45 to various radio stations and distributors. And, as simple as that, his phone rang with a call from the Los Angeles-based Arvee Records stating their interest in licensing the record. Pleased because Arvee had been doing well with a string of national hits like "Big Boy Pete" by the Olympics, Hart was busily discussing their offer, when moments later, his KKEY receptionist interrupted him to mention that someone in New York with Columbia Records was holding on the other line. Hart instantly dropped Arvee to speak with Columbia's A&R bigwig, who instantly offered a deal.

But the big question was this: Was Columbia—at the time under the leadership of famously square bandleader Mitch Miller—*really* the best label to get involved with? While the company had an illustrious and long-established history—it was after all one of the world's very first and pioneering sound recording firms—they'd long been focused on developing their sizable classical, country, and pop catalogues, and they'd *totally* missed the boat when it came to rock 'n' roll. In fact, their hottest properties going into 1963 were pop chumps Steve Lawrence and Andy Williams. *Ugh* . . . But still, Columbia did know how to sell records. And they did know how to develop *careers* for their artists. So it must have been tempting to try and believe that the label's new desire to sign the Raiders was the result of a studied and sincere recalculation of the teen market. Certainly, if the Raiders accepted the offer—one that included a commitment to cut whole *albums* of songs—they would make history as Columbia's first contractually bound rock 'n' roll band. Hart should have been ecstatic.

But he suddenly realized that his band was gone. After that months-long war between the two bands' two versions of "Louie Louie" fighting it out over various area radio stations, everyone involved was just *exhausted*. Although it seems that the Raiders' Sandē 45 had probably sold the most copies locally—and Columbia was circling the waters—Revere had apparently become concerned about his real estate holdings back in Idaho and had bullied the band into relocating back to Boise with him for the summer. While there, Revere—ever the businessman—decided to start a teen-dance club called the Crazy Horse so the Raiders would have someplace to rehearse. By the time Hart showed up carrying the good news about Columbia's interest in them, the Raiders' lineup had shifted: West and Allemang had been replaced by two members of Boise's Hitchhikers—Charlie Coe (guitar)

141

and Dick Walker (bass). The final step required before the group could return to Portland was that of finding a replacement house band for the Crazy Horse. When Revere hired the Sir Winston Trio, he was also crossing paths with three musicians who would each join the Raiders one day: Phil Volk, Drake Levin, and Michael "Doc" Holiday.

It was on May 23 that Hart concluded his deal with Columbia Records: The label advanced the band about $4,000 and a promise to give their record a strong national push. On June 11, the Raiders' "Louie Louie" moved from the Sandé imprint to Columbia Records. Meanwhile, Hart moved over to KGON, while Chase kept pushing the Kingsmen on KISN, and thus Portland's big radio stations continued favoring the "Louie Louie" 45s that were tied to their respective DJs' business interests. The field shifted when the town's underdog station, KGON, fully absorbed with trying to knock off KISN, hired Chase away from KISN to be their program director. In this all-powerful role, he could have simply elected to kill the Raiders' 45, but instead, he eased the Kingsmen's 45 into rotation by introducing the song in on-air battles that pitted all the versions—those of Richard Berry, the Wailers, the Kingsmen, and the Raiders—against each other, and exhorted listeners to phone in votes for their favorite. Thus the Kingsmen were suddenly getting plays on *both* stations, while the Raiders were still ignored by KISN.

That situation would change once again come the fall of '63 when Hart slid across the chessboard, once more signing on long-term with KISN— but even before that, additional plot twists were needed to further complicate things. The first blow came when Portland's AFM Local 99 belatedly discovered that the Kingsmen weren't even registered as dues-paying union members and forced them to join up. The direct consequence of this was that the band was obliged to charge a higher union pay scale—and suddenly Chase could no longer afford to book them regularly at his club. The Kingsmen lost their bread-and-butter gig at the Chase and another combo, the Jazzmasters, took over their spot.

But that was only the beginning of the Kingsmen's troubles. The military was also beginning to breathe down Ely's neck—but even worse, on August 16, Easton dropped a bombshell on his band mates: "I don't think it's a day either Lynn or I will ever forget," sighed Ely. "For a few months I had known that he was teaching himself how to play saxophone. Anyway, later at the Chase—they were closed on Monday nights—we were all set to rehearse, and we started to play and then he said, 'Wait a minute. I wanna talk to you guys.' So he said to us that he wanted to stop sitting back there playing drums

The wildest sound
for miles around

COLUMBIA
Recording Artists

PAUL   REVERE
&
RAIDERS

An early Raiders promotional photo, circa 1964. (Courtesy Jeff Miller.)

and he wanted to be out front playing sax. And sing. And be out front. And my first question was, to him, 'Well, who's gonna play drums then?' And he looked at me and said, 'Well, you are.' And I said, 'Come on! I fool around on the drums a little bit but you know, you've had classical and jazz training and yer ten times the drummer I am. I don't really wanna play drums.'"

"He said, 'Hell, you do good enough *for rock 'n' roll*,'" a disgusted Ely continued. "By this time Mike and Bob and Don were starting to go, '*This is nuts.*' They were getting this disgusted kinda attitude. And I said, 'Well, I don't mind doin' it on one or two songs, Lynn, but I'm a singer and that's what I want to do, and that's what we built this band on, and that's what we're gonna do.' And he said, 'Oh, no, we're not.' And I said, 'You can't talk like this. We've always discussed things, and we've always taken a vote, and that's just the way it is in this band.' He goes, 'Well, I am the band now.' And we all looked at him like, '*What* are you *talking* about?' He goes, 'Remember the time when we decided to take on the name the Kingsmen? Well, my mom and I went down to the county courthouse to register the name. And what we found out was, because everybody was a minor we all had to have a parent sign on the form. And at that time mom and I decided that it would be too much hassle tryin' to get *everybody* who has working parents to get them all together to sign in front of a notary public and then take that back to the courthouse. So the name "the Kingsmen" is registered to *me* with my mom as cosigner and you'll damn well do what I want. It's *my* band.' And everybody just looked at each other in shock. After the shock wore off, my hair got up, and I said, 'Well, I'll tell you what you can do with your band: You can shove it up your butt.' And I tore my equipment down. Nordby tore his equipment down. And we both left. And that's the last either of us were with the Kingsmen. At that time, our record was dead, it was going nowhere. Nothing was happening with it. The record was a dead issue."

By summer's end Jerden had probably sold six hundred copies of the Kingsmen 45 in Portland, and with the band now kaput, it seemed that this would be the end of their saga. Sandē Records had sold all of their original one thousand copies of the Raiders 45—and then when Columbia finally got their single on the radio in a number of West Coast cities—including the huge market of San Francisco, where "Louie Louie" went to No. 1—it looked like it might break out wider in California. But the Raiders were not in a much better position than the defunct Kingsmen to follow up on such progress—they were back in Boise experiencing personnel issues again, and on Labor Day weekend both Walker and Coe were ousted and replaced by Drake Levin (guitar) and "Doc" Holiday (bass) before the band hightailed it back to Portland.

Meanwhile, Jerden Records had never given up on the Kingsmen's single. Dennon instinctively knew that the only chance the Kingsmen's "Louie Louie" 45 had against Columbia's superior might and progress in Northern California was to head it off in the Southern California/Los Angeles market. But even that was easier said than done: As he pressed his contacts there for support, Dennon kept slamming into brick walls everywhere he turned. His industry connections simply thought he was off his rocker for even messing with the damn record. Who the hell were these *Kingsmen*? And why did these bumpkins up in the Northwest continue flogging that dead horse, "Louie Louie"? "I had friends in the record business like Russ Regen," said

144

Dennon, "who was with a big wholesale distribution company in L.A. I sent him one hundred records, saying, 'Gee, can you help me get this on the air?' I remember Russ telling me, 'You gotta be kidding! This is a Richard Berry town. Don't waste yer time.' And in other places—I'd sent 'em to a few friends in Pittsburgh and elsewhere too—it just wasn't worth their time to do anything [laughter]. I kept telling these people, 'I guarantee you, if you can get it on the radio, it will sell. Trust me.' But I did a lot of phone work trying to get people interested, with no success. Everybody laughed at me with this record."

As the Raiders' Columbia 45 continued to pick up steam, Dennon's last hope was that his Kingsmen 45 would break out over on the East Coast: "The Raiders' record was starting to get legs by this time, so I knew I was going to be history if we couldn't get the Kingsmen out nationally somehow. So it was very important that we make a deal and get on with it. How we broke the record is, a distributor friend of mine in Boston—basically he laughed at me too, but he said, 'To me it's a bunch of junk. But if you think you got a hit, you send me two hundred records for free and we can get them on the black station here. The DJ owns a record store and I just have to spiff him two hundred records that he can put in his store. Believe me, we'll *get* airplay, okay?' *And* that was the *only* time I participated in payola in my life, even though I had other opportunities later, with people coming to me, but we would never touch it with a hundred-foot pole."

It was October when that Boston R&B station did in fact come through with the airtime for the Kingsmen. Then, when the market's major station, WMEX—and their big-shot DJ, Arnie "Woo Woo" Ginsburg—latched onto the record, there was no turning back. Ginsburg highlighted the tune by showcasing it in his nightly feature segment, *The Worst Record of the Week*. And for emphasis he gave "Louie Louie" two consecutive spins on his influential hit-making show. Well, that was enough for Boston's teens, and their excitement over the Kingsmen's 45 was instantly manifested in radio phone requests as well as record shop sales. The song instantly turned from a potential "worst" record into one that was locked into heavy rotation. At that point a distributor named Bob Silverman tipped off one of his client labels—the New York–based Scepter-Wand Records—to the action this Jerden 45 was now seeing. Scepter-Wand (two sister labels, hereafter referred to as Wand) and Dennon struck a quick deal. Wand acted fast enough that before the week was out a reported 21,000 copies of the 45 would sell to Boston-area kids. By October 19, the Kingsmen's 45 was noted in *Billboard* as a "regional breakout" to watch—and certainly there must have been plenty

of eyes at Columbia watching what happened next as *their* potential hit began to slip out away from their grasp.

When the November 2 *Billboard* hit the stands, the Raiders' 45 appeared merely as a "regional breakout" from the Los Angeles radio market, while the Kingsmen's Wand 45 was noted as "bubbling under" the Hot 100, at No. 127. By the next week, the Kingsmen were up to No. 83, the Raiders trailing at No. 108. Then Wand scrambled to pull together a campaign to take the fight to the enemy by launching an offensive into the Los Angeles market—an effort that eventually succeeded: The giant Columbia machine was firmly vanquished. The finality of the situation was documented in the November 16 issue of *Billboard*, when the pop chart showed that the Kingsmen had vaulted up to No. 58, and the Raiders had fallen by the wayside. "Columbia beat us in some of the Western markets because they'd had months ahead of us," admits Dennon. "But I just don't think Columbia knew what they had. The other thing is that Wand was a hot little mostly black-oriented label and they knew how to merchandize, market, and run. They just beat the socks off Columbia. Columbia was used to doing it their way—very . . . deliberately . . . Johnny Mathis . . . Andy Williams . . . et cetera. And Wand just *killed* 'em. They took it and ran with it."

"Columbia *blew* it," roared Revere. "Columbia was *not* pushing this record. They did *not* believe in it. And that gave Wand Records a little time to get a foothold, and so the Kingsmen's version started getting airplay in the eastern part of the United States. So it was kind of a battle there for a while to see who was going to make it. But Wand was an R&B label, and they were very hip to what rock stations and what R&B stations to get to play this song. And they immediately got airplay. Whereas *Columbia* . . . I don't think they even had a *list* of rock 'n' roll stations to take the record to! So we ended up kinda getting lost in the shuffle." And that shuffling continued, with the Kingsmen climbing to No. 23, and then rocketing to No. 4. There was absolutely no doubt now: This recording of "Louie Louie" was going to finally achieve the major hit status that had previously eluded Richard Berry, Rockin' Robin and the Wailers, Little Bill and the Adventurers—and, most recently, Paul Revere and the Raiders.

But there was at least one other person—besides a few Columbia execs—who was quite surprised by this sudden turn of events: Jack Ely. Still bummed out about having been bumped out of his own band a few months back, he was nothing less than shocked when Ken Chase mentioned to him that his "Louie Louie" record had moved over to the Wand label and was climbing the charts in *Billboard*. Ely raced to a downtown newsstand, bought a copy of the magazine, and just about died when he saw the evidence with his own eyes. And his first reaction was a noble one: to try and make peace with his former band mates. Easton, however, had other ideas and was now busily attempting to regroup the band, this time with himself fronting the act and a couple of new players—Norm Sundholm (bass) and Gary Abbott (drums)—on board. Unbelievably, Easton was truly intent on going on without the singer of the band's hit being included. And then Ely heard secondhand that this new Kingsmen band had reserved the Chase on the nights of November 15 and 16 in order to cut an entire *album* for Wand. The gigs were well publicized, and a sold-out crowd showed up—among them, a beered-up Ely, who emitted just enough belligerence that the doorman barred his entry. The show, however, did result in the successful recording

of what became *The Kingsmen in Person Featuring Louie Louie*—an LP that Wand rush-released to get in on the remaining Christmas shopping season.

At about this point, the nation's top booking firm, the William Morris Agency, jumped in with a tour offer, which—after Chase was squeezed out—was accepted. The revamped Kingsmen headed out on a two-week tour to push their hit in the promising markets of Illinois, Minnesota, and North Dakota. This success was apparently too stressful for the boys, and upon their return from the tour, they broke up again. But then—after the December 14 *Billboard* showed the band with the nation's No. 2 hit—a *flood* of concert and television offers poured in, and the troubled band re-formed once *again* with a new drummer, Dick Peterson—who they discovered playing with the Majestics at the 1963 KISN Battle of the Bands event.

But the band's personnel upheavals were not quite over yet: With the Kingsmen looking at the immediate future touring to push "Louie Louie," the parents of their young keyboardist, Don Gallucci—who was still a sophomore at Franklin High—forbade any more travel, and the band was forced to scramble to find a replacement. Searching high and low, they finally found Barry Curtis, who had played in a few Yakima-based combos, including the Redcoats and the Klassics, and he was totally stoked for the big time. Easton called him with the offer, and Curtis recalls saying, "'You bet I'll do it!' I mean, *yeah*! That was the ticket *out*. I just *jumped* at that chance. I went to Portland, had no audition; we rehearsed about three days and hit the road."

The Kingsmen, circa 1965. (Courtesy Mulholland Studios.)

CHAPTER 21

Love That Louie

In the terribly tangled tale of "Louie Louie"—from obscure West Coast rock 'n' roll fetish, to national hit, and then global phenomenon—only one single fact is absolutely certain, and that is that in January 1964, the Kingsmen had the No. 1 record in America.

Or perhaps it was really only No. 2. Somehow it seems perfectly fitting that even *that* simple point is debatable. However, *Billboard*—which ostensibly calculated its charts by factoring in a record's sales figures as well as its airplay—listed the song at the No. 2 position for six weeks of its long four-month chart run. However, this was a record that was getting far more home spins than actual radio play and *Cash Box*—which based its charts solely on a record's *sales* figures—had the Kingsmen's "Louie Louie" sitting solidly at No. 1.

Regardless, the Kingsmen were on a roll: Their 45 had sold 600,000 units for Wand, they were busy doing big gigs from coast to coast, and in February they began some new sessions in Seattle for their next single release. After finishing up at Kearney Barton's new studio, Audio Recording Inc. (at 170 Denny Way), the band was just loading their gear back into their van when they were approached by a reporter from the *Seattle P-I*, who began asking a few questions about the fact that the UPI wire service had just posted a news flash that the band's "Louie Louie" had just been banned as *obscene*. For a moment or two the guys stood there stunned—but in time they would recollect an amusing incident a few months earlier, when Easton had received an odd phone call from some college kid in the deep South. Assuming that Easton was the hit record's vocalist—which, of course, he wasn't—the caller wanted to know just exactly what the "dirty lyrics" to the band's hit song were. The Kingsmen had initially laughed the call off, but now the matter was serious. As that *Seattle P-I* article noted, "A

Portland musical quintet making a recording in Seattle last night found themselves the center of a controversy in which the governor of Indiana charged their top selling record, 'Louie Louie,' was 'in questionable taste.' The core of the charge was that one set of words are heard when the record is played at normal speed while another version emerges when the record is played slower."

The paper went on to quote Easton's rebuttal, which "emphatically denied the group had made two versions of the number," by saying that, "'We took the original lyrics as written and recorded by Richard Berry several years ago and reproduced them faithfully for our record.'" But, it was already too late for those facts to get in the way of a media storm that initially centered around Governor Matthew Welsh, who was responding to a complaint that had allegedly been lodged by some deeply offended Frankfort, Indiana, kid who had apparently gotten curious about his copy of "Louie Louie" and begun playing the Wand 45 at the slower speed of 33 rpm, and then faster at 78 rpm, in an effort to pinpoint the muffled vocal lines.

But the central charge was that Jack Ely's vocals contained nasty words. Welsh, along with "an aide and officials of the broadcasting industry listened to the record at a slow speed" and they all "agreed with the boy's complaints." In fact, upon hearing the vile 45 Welsh's "ears tingled." The *Indianapolis Star* confirmed that the single "has been fingered by Indiana's first citizen" as being "pornographic"—and that Welsh called for a statewide ban on further radio airplay. The governor and broadcasting officials took immediate steps to have the record banned from Indiana radio stations. An investigation also was promised by the National Association of Broadcasters, and the US Department of Justice and the Federal Communications Commission were informed. James J. McManus, press secretary to the governor, weighed in by stating that the song's lyrics were—*get this!*—"indistinct but *plain* if you listen carefully."

In fact, those lyrics were so "plain" that nobody could seem to agree on what they actually said. And now with newspapers far and wide publicizing the scandal, every schoolkid in America was learning that *something* about "Louie Louie" was filthy—soon many were writing down what they *thought* they heard in order to compare notes with their pals. And what wild imaginations those juveniles have! Some deduced that the lyrical line "I smelled a rose in her hair" was really "I felt my boner in her there." And, too, the line "Me think of girl constantly" was deciphered as "Me fuck that girl all kinds of ways." Other ears heard Ely singing crudities like "She's got a rag on" and "I'm never gonna lay her again." And so on . . .

Well, given the governor's grandstanding and the subsequent publicity storm it sparked, three things happened. First, various self-appointed guardians of public morality launched additional bans of the record from Massachusetts to Florida. Second, as more and more kids passed around their vile notes, some were ultimately confiscated by parents and teachers who dutifully passed them up the chain all the way to the offices of US Attorney General Robert F. Kennedy and fearsome FBI head J. Edgar Hoover. Lastly, record sales *soared*. The whole brouhaha was a marketing man's dream come true, and at one point Dennon skillfully played the game, telling the *P-I* that "you can take any record, play it at a slower speed and imagine anything you want." Wand also did their best to sustain the controversy by coming forth with a public reward offering of a thousand dollars to anyone who could prove that the song's lyrics were "dirty." The whole mess really was a godsend of negative publicity, but the matter was still far from settled—at least as far as the government was concerned.

As it happened, 1964 was an election year, and so various politicos couldn't resist getting into the fray: the US Post Office (USPS), the FCC, the Federal Trade Commission (FTC), and Hoover's FBI each began conducting their own investigations. The owner of Wand Records later recounted how G-men showed up at their New York offices. "The FBI came to my studio. I swear. They sat there all day listening to Kingsmen's tapes. They never found nothing." Maybe not, but then again, they'd just gotten *started*. Over the next two years the investigation was actively pursued—Jerry Dennon was also interrogated at Jerden headquarters in Seattle, and both Richard Berry and Jack Ely were summoned to testify regarding the song's lyrical content. The new Kingsmen were also eventually grilled by the FBI while out touring in Massachusetts.

Twenty years later, the FBI's own internal files on the case—which had piled up to a stack of one hundred–plus pages—were pried loose by an astute researcher who invoked the Freedom of Information Act (FOIA) to get access. And those files make for some *hilarious* reading. Not only do they compile all of the letters (and nasty lyrics) mailed in by distraught parents, they also track the FBI's actions in chasing down this potential threat to America's decency. And if one reads "between the lines" in those FBI field investigation reports, there is some humor to be had in the realization that some hapless agents were stuck with an investigative process that required them and several of their forensic lab technicians to suffer through repeated spins of the Kingsmen's single at every possible speed, from 16 rpm to 78 rpm.

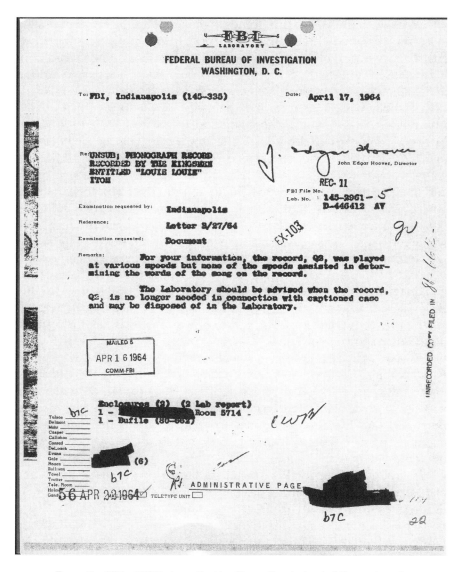

FEDERAL BUREAU OF INVESTIGATION
WASHINGTON, D. C.

To: FBI, Indianapolis (145-335)   Date: April 17, 1964

Re: UNSUB; PHONOGRAPH RECORD
RECORDED BY THE KINGSMEN
ENTITLED "LOUIE LOUIE"
ITOH

John Edgar Hoover, Director

REC- 11

FBI File No.
Lab. No.   145-2961 - 5
           D-446412 AV

Examination requested by: Indianapolis

Reference: Letter 3/27/64

Examination requested: Document

EX-103

Remarks: For your information, the record, Q2, was played
at various speeds but none of the speeds assisted in determining the words of the song on the record.

            The Laboratory should be advised when the record,
Q2, is no longer needed in connection with captioned case
and may be disposed of in the Laboratory.

MAILED 5
APR 1 6 1964
COMM-FBI

UNRECORDED COPY FILED IN 80-162-

Enclosures (2)   (2 Lab report)
1 -   Room 5714
1 - Bufile (80-332)

Tolson
Belmont
Mohr
Casper
Callahan
Conrad
DeLoach
Evans
Gale   (6)
Rosen
Sullivan
Tavel
Trotter
Tele. Room
Holmes
Gandy   56 APR 22 1964   TELETYPE UNIT   ADMINISTRATIVE PAGE

b7C

22

From the FBI's 1960s investigative file on "Louie Louie." Case closed!

Their final report, however, necessarily ended with a conclusion that basically echoed the one reached by the FCC's expert investigators: that the charges against the song were without merit. "As a matter of fact, we found the record to be unintelligible at any speed we played it." Newspapers carried articles with headlines like RECORD FOUND FREE OF OBSCENITIES, *Examiners* FAIL TO DECIPHER LYRICS. Well, *duh*. The fact is, *anyone* who had thought they heard streams of rudeness in the Kingsmen's record (beyond that nearly inaudible F-bomb at 54.5 seconds) was simply projecting their own dirty thoughts onto the poor innocent little 45. Far from being musical "pornography," the record instead was nothing less than a magical combination of a young band's energetic musical ineptitude, Ely's remarkably slurred vocals, and an epically muddied production job. In other words, a timeless rock 'n' roll classic that few bands would ever equal.

But meanwhile, the new Kingsmen played a series of dates in Southern California at the Cinnamon Cinders teen clubs, and they also appeared on

the *Murray the K Show* in New York City for two solid weeks. Following those high-profile gigs, the band set out on a major forty-day tour with the Beach Boys, performing for crowds of 10,000. Then there was poor Jack Ely. He was totally missing out on the rewards accruing to what was the biggest hit yet produced from the Northwest. Adding insult to injury, the single's B-side—his and Gallucci's composition, "Haunted House"—had *somehow* been miscredited on the label and showed the composer as "Lynn Easton."

But what was *especially* aggravating was the fact that every time Ely turned on the TV—to watch national musical variety shows like *Shindig*, *Shivaree*, *Hullabaloo*—there was *Easton* out front lip-synching to *his* vocals. And so Ely's bitterness grew: bitterness at the way Easton had bulldozed the band, bitterness about not getting any royalties, bitterness mainly that he was missing out on all the touring, all the fun, all the glory. But that's when a door of opportunity opened for him. It was about March '64 when Ely received a call from the Raiders' regional promoter, Pat Mason, who told him that the new Kingsmen were experiencing all sorts of problems on their road tours. Booking agents were getting reports that people had begun noticing that the Kingsmen's "singer" didn't sound anything like the voice on the record. Then Ken Chase soon chimed in with the suggestion that Ely should just record *another* "Louie Louie"–*type* song and try to chip away at Easton's band's momentum.

Ely was persuaded, and after convincing a Portland band called the Squires to play a few dances with him, they entered Northwestern studios and recorded a tune titled "Love That Louie," which RCA Records picked up but failed to make into a hit. Meanwhile, the new Kingsmen filed a lawsuit against Ely, who'd begun touring around with his own "Kingsmen." After a drawn-out court battle, a settlement was reached: Ely would refrain from using that band name, and Wand Records agreed to change the label credit on all future "Louie Louie" records to read "Jack Ely and the Kingsmen" or "The Kingsmen with vocals by Jack Ely." And they promised to get Ely his own gold record for the hit song. It only seems fitting that after spending all that time in courtrooms, the beleaguered singer would later surface with a Bang Records 45, "Louie Louie '66," cut by his new band, Jack Ely and the *Courtmen*. But Ely wasn't the only one who was still nuts for the song. In fact, other Northwest bands were also cutting namesake knockoffs, including H.B. and the Checkmates, with "Louie Louise," and the Raymarks, who had a song called "Louise." And then—when American radio suddenly began airing the Kingsmen's original recording around April 1966—Wand actually reissued the 45 under the title "Louie Louie 64-65-66" and the tune hit the *Billboard* charts yet again!

Meanwhile, the Kingsmen's first Wand LP had done well, becoming the No. 19 national best-seller for 1964—and then when the "Louie Louie" 45's sales passed the $1 million mark, Wand threw a big bash for the band at New York City's hot new discotheque, Arthur, where every band member (and Dennon) was awarded a shiny gold record award plaque. Well, everyone except the exiled Ely—who had also been ignored when city leaders honored the Kingsmen with their own float in the summer's annual Portland Rose Festival Parade. Lynn Easton and his crew were officially hometown heroes now, while their moping former leader—who never did receive his promised gold record—was about as visible as a ghost in a haunted house.

CHAPTER 22

That Sound
(A Slight Return)

The entire time span that the Kingsmen and Raiders' versions of "Louie Louie" fought it out across America was one also that saw an unprecedented uptick of activity all over the entire rock 'n' roll game board. In fact, just as the groups' twin singles were being recorded and released in 1963, a strong multiyear California-based muscial tidal wave known as surfer rock was just cresting. And then, as Jerry Dennon recalls, just as the Kingsmen appeared set to also conquer the United Kingdom . . . they were bumped aside by a band that few in the Northwest had even *heard* of. "The Beatles knocked us out of being No. 1 in England with the Kingsmen's 'Louie Louie.' We were on our way when that whole Beatle thing hit." And this sudden upset apparently caused the Kingsmen's big tour of England—which had been publicly announced for March—to be canceled.

Instead, the "British Invasion" was preparing to storm *our* shores. And although this region would have its fans of both surfer rock and British beat music, both forms initially faced big challenges in winning over local hearts. In fact, that uphill battle is perfectly represented by two incidents: the Beach Boys' live debut in Seattle, and the Beatles' radio debut on KJR—neither of which went over very well, because local ears were already acclimated to the hard-hitting, R&B-tinged Northwest Sound. It was Pat O'Day—who was then also operating the Party Line, a short-lived teen club—who learned all this the hard way when he brought the Beach Boys up here for a couple of gigs: "The Beach Boys had two hits then ["Surfin'" and "Surfin' Safari"]— but it's one thing to have a hit, and a whole 'nother to be a *dance* attraction. Well, we brought them up for the weekend to play the Spanish Castle, and then they played my club, the Party Line, Saturday and Sunday. And it was a *disaster*: The Beach Boys got booed off the stage their first time in Seattle!"

But O'Day and KJR kept at it, pushing surf sounds at—some have said—the expense of supporting the music that already had a natural audience locally. And even though a good number of new young Northwest bands would eventually arise to ride the surfer rock fad, that wave soon crashed. But it was in May of 1963 that KJR briefly—for one week, to be exact—showed a new tune titled "From Me to You" by some unknown entity called "the Beatles" on their Fab 50 chart. But because most Northwest rock 'n' roll fans at the time were staying true to the local teen R&B traditions, the station heard little positive feedback, and that Beatles single was dropped. More than six months would pass before the mop-topped lads from Liverpool would reappear on Seattle's airwaves.

Some indication of the loyalty that Northwest kids had toward their own groups was revealed in a protest letter sent to *Teen* magazine by a girl who simultaneously scolded the publisher as well as taunted those who failed to recognize the quality of our bands: "The hard, loud pulsating beat of the Northwest Sound rings in your ears. It burns in your soul and mind—but most of you don't even recognize that it comes from the Pacific Northwest. You say you love Paul Revere and the Raiders but you don't recognize that they're from the Northwest. Here in the Pacific Northwest, we salute the Wailers, the Sonics, Paul Bearer and the Hearsemen, Don and the Goodtimes, and the Kingsmen. We listen for their new records and play them over and over. It's not the soft show music of the English. It's the Northwest Sound. We're like Red China—not recognized by the U.S. One day it'll all change—and your hearts will be longing to visit Seattle or Tacoma, Wash., and Boise, Idaho. You'll want to know what's going on. And maybe, when that day comes, you'll be surprised to see we're not dead up here. We've been shut off, so we created our own sound. A sound that's wilder and groovier than the music you've been listening to for so long!"

And although all the great British bands would soon win over fans in this region, it would be a hard-fought battle. In 1964 one participant in the local scene—Dynamics guitarist (and University of Washington journalism student) Larry Coryell—shared his thoughts about the musical resistance shown by area musicians (and their fans) in a *UW Daily* essay titled "Why Did the Northwest Have a Different Sound?" In the piece, he wrote that "the Seattle bands have by and large stuck to the blues and have turned a deaf ear toward the Beatles, the Beach Boys, and Al Hirt. Hence, Seattle bands like Dave Lewis, and the Dynamics, have developed original and natural styles of playing that are welcome alternatives to the pop music that is packaged and peddled by Madison Avenue and shoved down the ears of gullible subteens as 'music of today'."

But the real reason that the Northwest Sound held its ground throughout that period was that it was both as valid as the southern R&B that had preceded it *and* as rich as the British pop that was receiving such a huge corporate push. "The rhythm-and-blues-based music of the dancehalls of the region was, in its own way," confirmed historian Warren Gill in the *Canadian Geographer* in 1993, "as fresh an interpretation of the African-American roots of rock and roll as that of the pioneers of the genre in the mid-1950s and the revival to come from the United Kingdom in the 1960s. In a period bereft of these elemental aspects of rock and roll, the Northwest Sound was not simply a return to a previously successful formula, but a different evolutionary direction in response to local conditions."

And those "local conditions" had resulted in a particular strain of teen R&B that was prized as the "Northwest Sound." Although the bands that were actively helping to forge that aesthetic would eventually produce a quantity of original songs, in the beginning they mainly relied on a canon of R&B hits that had been imported into the region. And it was those songs, really, that provided the young players with a vocabulary of riffs and rhythms that could serve as building blocks to create their own rather distinct mode of musical expression. And surely most notable within that emergent pool of favored tunes was Richard Berry's "Louie Louie."

But *that* song—while among the gems incorporated into the set lists of the greatest number of area bands—was hardly the most indicative of the greater wave upon which it crested. Far more prevalent were those included in the accepted pool of tunes that can best be categorized as "rude jazz" instrumentals along the lines of Bill Doggett's "Honky Tonk" (which was played by many and cut by the Dave Lewis Trio, the Raiders, and the Ventures) and Jimmy Forrest's "Night Train" (which was recorded by the Ventures, the Raiders, the Four Playboys, and the Kingsmen). But all that largely saxophone-driven music was about to be enriched by the next trend within Northwest music—the trend of adding an electric organ to the mix, which can be directly attributed to Dave Lewis and his influential switch from piano.

Following Lewis's move, bands including the Frantics, the Wailers, the Viceroys, and the Raiders all switched from pianos (or electric pianos) to

Promotional photo of Dave Lewis, circa 1963. (Photo by Odell Lee.)

organs. And thus another key component of the region's sound was formalized. But, the inquisitive reader may ask, "Wasn't the use of electric organs common amongst young bands *everywhere* by that point?" To answer that inquiry, let's rely on input from the guitarist of one of America's most-traveled, best-selling, bands of the 1960s, a fellow who'd been to every regional scene in the land and had seen and heard scores of top local bands open for his group: "First of all," explained the Kingsmen's lead guitarist, Mike Mitchell, "we incorporated the organ because of the influence of the guys from Seattle. And then, when we started travelin' around the country, we saw that everybody else was still in the Ventures mode! So they were pretty shocked with us comin' out there. We were the first rock 'n' roll band to really carry a double-manual Hammond out on the road. It was different.

It was a different period of time in music when a lot of things were still innovative. And you could take things out on the road and shock people in the Midwest who just didn't have much contact with that kind of thing."

So although teenage bands everywhere did play sets of rock 'n' roll hits they copied from records and the radio, the Northwest bands managed to add in some elements—like the swelling sounds of organs—that made our region's music stand out. Even three decades ago, Billy Miller, rock historian par excellence and editor of *Kicks* magazine, acknowledged this regional quirk: "As a tried and true East Coaster I can't tell downtown Seattle from uptown Tacoma—drop me off a bus in Portland and I may as well be on Mars. Despite my geographical shortcomings, however, I can spot a vintage Northwest disc at a hundred paces in a blizzard. It ain't all that hard mind you. There's a feel about the way they tend to pound a little harder and blast off faster than most rock & roll records." And what made the Northwest sounds stand out "in an era of especially thin sounding dance records," was that "these bands unleashed conspicuously explosive vehicles of thunder."

The Northwest's idiosyncratic sounds also stood out to the late California-based rock and garage rock historian Greg Shaw, who once affirmed that "not every region of the United States had its own distinctive sound in the Garage Band Era (prolific as they were, places like Florida, Pennsylvania, Wisconsin, New England and Ohio certainly didn't)—but everybody knows instantly what is meant by The Northwest Sound." Furthermore, as Shaw would note, "the 'frat bands' so common around the country would wither like pale slugs in the noonday sun before the onslaught of the least memorable at any Northwest high school"—and at least one British writer agreed, saying that "in regions as disparate as Texas, the Bay Area and the Southeast, white kids were playing black-styled R&B, but it would be safe to say that when it came to an unbridled fervour for rootsy rock and an accomplished reinterpretation of the same, the Pacific Northwest had everywhere else beat."

British rock historian Brian Hogg was also someone who appreciated our bands for their "storming instrumentals, exaggerated Little Richard riffs, pounding rhythms and honking saxophones." Ah, yes, those honking saxophone choirs—a presence within the Northwest Sound since the days of the Dave Lewis Combo, Clayton Watson and the Silhouettes, Little Bill and the Bluenotes, Ron Holden and the Thunderbirds, and the Velvetones. As Mike Mitchell also acknowledged, "There were some *great* bands out of Seattle. Bands like the Frantics, and Dynamics, and Counts that had horns.

I mean, they were really *way* ahead of their time." By this point, the Dynamics were in absolute peak form and had become probably the best and most respected band on the scene. And part of their increased appeal was the blazin' horn charts they'd arranged to showcase new trumpet ace Marcus "Mark" Doubleday—especially on tunes like their 1963 regional hit 45 for Bolo Records, the R&B gem "Genevieve." Doubleday, incidentally, represents a direct line to that later generation of horn bands: After playing with the Dynamics for a few years, he moved on and eventually resurfaced in such brassy '60s groups as Electric Flag and Janis Joplin's Full Tilt Boogie Band.

Another sax-led Bolo band, the Viceroys, scored a huge regional radio hit with the instrumental classic "Granny's Pad," which would eventually be recognized as the all-time (up to that point) best-selling 45 in the local marketplace. Originally formed as Vince Valley and the Chain Gang in '58 by guitarist Jim Valley and his pals, the Viceroys had written the tune—and named it after—the place where pianist Al Berry practiced: his grandmother's house. Cut at Fred Rasmussen's home studio, the 45 was quickly embraced by KZAM, KOL, and KAYO radio. Even without Pat O'Day and KJR's help, the 45 became a smash hit in the Puget Sound area for many months, which led to a national distribution deal with Dot Records in February 1963. In March, *Billboard* noted the record as a Regional Breakout Single—a status that indicated serious hope for impending national hit status. Finally, in early April, listeners to the regular *Battle of the New Sounds* segment of O'Day's afternoon show voted via telephone, and "Granny's Pad" was the clear victor. Still not all that enthusiastic, the station carelessly listed it on that week's Fab 50 chart as "Grandmothers Pad" (sic).

The good news is that the song's popularity soared. The bad news is that Dot fumbled their promotional efforts and the tune remained a strictly regional phenomenon, albeit one that led to a couple of subsequent Viceroys knockoffs: "Goin' Back to Granny's" and "Granny's Medley," which included stitched-together snippets of *everything*: "Granny's Pad," the KJR theme, "Goin' Back to Granny's"—and, of course, "Louie Louie."

Meanwhile, after Jimmy Hendrix had split town, his former Velvetones band mates—Luther Rabb (bari sax), Anthony Atherton (tenor sax), and Pernell Alexander (guitar)—carried on, surfacing in two different bands: the Nitesounds and the Boss Five. The Nitesounds formed in 1963 at Franklin High and featured a hot horn section comprised of Rabb and Jim Walters (trumpet). The band landed a regular gig at a new downtown room called the Tolo House. And the band's great dual-horn sound thrilled dancers and fans who heard their classic '64 Seafair Records 45 "Get Clean"—a disc that was ignored by every local station except the area's sole soul station, KZAM-FM.

Nineteen sixty-four would prove to be a year of upheaval for Seattle's R&B fans: For the past two years the Boss Five—which included Atherton and Alexander, along with former Gallahad Jimmy Pipkin—had held forth at the Birdland. But all that fun came to a crashing end when a winter snowstorm caved the roof in and the storied building, the cornerstone to a whole musical era, was bulldozed into a nondescript parking lot. Nineteen sixty-four also saw the premature demise of KZAM, and times became very tough once again for anyone trying to promote R&B records in Seattle. But then a new station, KYAC ("The Soul of the Northwest"), emerged and soon the Boss Five were enjoying a Top 10 hit with "Walkin' the Duck"— their funky combination of two prior dance fad hits: "Walkin' the Dog" and "the Duck"—which was one of the first 45s issued by a hip new Lynnwood-based label, Camelot Records.

But the biggest local radio hit that year was one scored by yet another group that made the most of their fine horn section, the Counts. Originally formed back in 1959 by a few Ballard High School pals, in 1964 the band added a trumpeter, Richard Person (who was later replaced by the Nite-sounds' Jim Walters), and worked with a few different local black singers, including Tiny Tony Smith, who was fronting them when they got their first chance to play the Birdland. The Counts recorded their horn-driven instrumental dance tune "Turn On Song" with Kearney Barton, and it was issued by a new label, Sea Crest Records, in the early summer. That's when the Counts' acting manager, KJR DJ Lan Roberts, gave it a listen and regrettably informed them that the 45 was "*way* too R&B for O'Day." But while KJR abstained, KYAC and a few other local stations pushed "Turn On Song" until Sea Crest suddenly had a regional best-seller on their hands. Sea Crest was amped up enough with that success that the label issued additional Counts recordings, including a couple of tasty Dave Lewis compositions, "Feel Alright" and "And Then I Cried."

Further changes were also in the wind that year. The Wailers lost Rich Dangel (who moved over to the Rooks); the Dynamics lost Larry Coryell (who split for New York in order to devote himself to jazz) and Jimmy Hanna (who stepped aside to focus on getting his grades up so as to fend off the military draft); and the Viceroys brought in a new bassist, Gary Snyder, and added sax man Kim Eggars (so that Mike Rogers could switch to Hammond organ). That's when things started getting rather interesting: The Wailers recruited the Bootmen's guitarist, Neil Andersson, and, after trying unsuccessfully to lure Hanna aboard as a singer, brought on the Bootmen's Ron Gardner instead. Then the Dynamics failed to persuade the Counts' awesome guitarist, Dan Olason, to join them and instead hired the Fabulous Casuals' ace guitarist, Harry Wilson. It was in September 1964 that Bolo Records issued the *Dynamics with Jimmy Hanna* LP (which had been cut at Parker's Ballroom; the record became an instant regional best-seller—then a few months later the band's "Busybody" 45 became a local standard adopted by scores of other bands, including the Kingsmen, who recorded a version of it. In May 1965 the Dynamics hit again with a cover of an obscure 1963 Motown number, "Leaving Here," which featured Hanna's most compelling vocals yet. Interestingly, three decades later, when Seattle's Pearl Jam cut the same tune, they—being wholly unaware of the song's local legacy—based their rendition on the Who's recording!

This time period also saw a hot new combo—Don and the Goodtimes—making a big splash in Portland. Formed by the Kingsmen's original pianist, Don Gallucci—who had also now switched to organ—the Goodtimes debuted in 1964 at the Chase, and after only a few gigs, they got a deal with Jerry Dennon. For their first recording session, the Goodtimes cut the Counts' "Turn On Song"—and their romp through the tune was hot enough that Wand Records bought in and issued it nationally. Although the 45 didn't do much outside of Portland, the band still showed enough promise that Wand issued a second one—this time a version of Big Jay McNeely's "There Is Something on Your Mind."

From the outset the Goodtimes had two main strengths, both of which would soon earn them a wide reputation as a band that earned their name anew at every dance. The first was an insanely action-packed live stage show, which had clearly been inspired by Paul Revere and the Raiders' wild and raucous stage act. Since 1963 the Raiders had been thrilling their crowds by wearing matching costumes—Revolutionary War uniforms featuring long coats, tall boots, and tri-corner hats—and the Goodtimes followed suit with matching sets of red velvet jackets with tails, English lace shirts, and top hats. But the Goodtimes' second strength—and their "secret weapon"—was that they unabashedly copped songs direct from the repertoires of their local forebears: the Dave Lewis Trio, the Wailers, the Raiders, the Kingsmen, and the Counts. So if their set lists weren't heavily weighted with

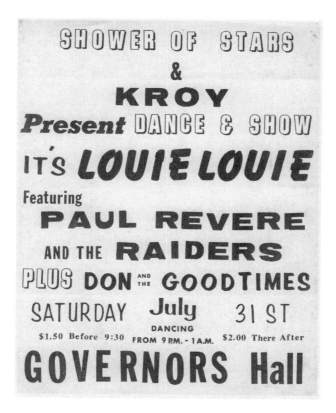

original tunes, they *were* fortified with proven winners. And just by giving those regional classics new life, Don and the Goodtimes were emphasizing the lasting value of the tunes, and bringing renewed focus to the Northwest Sound—a sound that was just about ready to gain additional power via a primitivistic back-to-the-garage movement led by a new band from Tacoma known as the Sonics.

CHAPTER 23

Psycho

When the extraordinary rock 'n' roll year of 1964 wound down there were probably many grown-ups who were vastly relieved. From the initial shock of the Kingsmen's "Louie Louie" scandal, through the outbreak of the Beatlemania contagion that swept the world, it must have seemed to the music's foes as if the signs of the Apocalypse were all lining up, prepping for Armageddon. But if those folks thought that "Louie Louie" was pornography, and that shaggy haircuts and lyrics like "She loves you yeah, yeah, yeah" portended doomsday, they should have dreaded what 1965 was holding in store.

As 1964 edged toward '65, the Northwest Sound was about to take a surprise sharp turn toward a radically harsher direction. That was the time frame within which nearly all of the Northwest's top bands took on a rougher garage rock aesthetic that would eventually be credited with fueling the '70s punk rock movement.

And the central source for much of the change was the Tacoma-based label Etiquette Records, whose young executives—especially Wailers bassist Buck Ormsby—were really on a roll. The commercial success of Rockin' Robin's "Louie Louie" and then the Wailers' *At the Castle* album had topped off their corporate coffers to the extent that Etiquette was able to produce a whole string of new releases by the Wailers, and various other bands that they discovered, including the Bootmen, the Rooks, the Galaxies, and Paul Bearer and the Hearsemen. Etiquette's *finest* hour, though, came was when it discovered—and had the balls to issue and promote—the Sonics, a combo that were the unholy practitioners of punk rock *long* before anyone knew what to call it. Which is not to say that certain parents in the Northwest didn't try to come up with a few choice words for the band and their primitive, brutally raucous sound—but the Sonics shrugged off their detractors and lived to have the last laugh when their music went on to receive approving global acknowledgment as some of the rawest and most savage rock *ever* achieved by humankind.

The saga of this fabled band began around 1961 when two brothers—Andy (bass) and Larry Parypa (guitar)—started holding weekend jams in their parents' living room with some of Larry's junior high pals, with the modest initial goal being that of attempting to play a rendition of Rockin' Robin and the Wailers' "Louie Louie."

Having already seen the Wailers' TV appearance on the *Dick Clark Show* back in June 1959, Andy Parypa remembered being very excited when it was announced that his heroes would be performing at his *Tacoma News Tribune* Paperboy Banquet. "The Wailers were the first rock and roll band that ever got me into a riotous mood. *All* of us were in total awe of the Wailers. I mean, they were *the* band from Tacoma—and the band that I and Larry had seen the most, and who had the most influence on us. All of us had a real reverence for the Wailers: This was pre-Beatles, and instrumental music was the thing. But I don't know that we gave that much serious thought to what we were gonna do . . . other than to try and sound as much like the Wailers as we could. I kinda learned how to play listening to the *Wailers at the Castle* album. I used to know every note on that album."

That would explain why Wailers songs like "Shanghied," "Wailin,'" "High Wall," "Wailers House Party," and "Dirty Robber" were central to their early set lists. But the boys kept adding to their repertoire—and because their saxophonist, Jay Mabin, was a black kid with a great collection of Ray Charles and other R&B records they could all learn from—the band soon had arrangements down for classics like Bill Doggett's "Honky Tonk" and "Leaps and Bounds" (which served for years as the band's "break song"), James Brown's "Please Please Please," and the Phil Upchurch Combo's "You Can't Sit Down." But it was the Northwest's own rock stars that really inspired the young band. "The Wailers, the Frantics, and the Dynamics—those people were kind of our idols," recalled Parypa. "On the local level, there were other influences, to be sure, but I used to listen to *everything* the Wailers did. And anytime the Frantics came out with a record, man, I bought that sucker quick! I always thought the Frantics were just gangbusters. They were heads and tails better than anybody else as far as being actual musicians, and so we thought *very* highly of them. To me they were the epitome. And the Wailers, for a different reason: I mean, they were balls-to-the-walls! I really liked them. And then the Ventures: We used to do them. *Everybody* played 'Walk—Don't Run.'

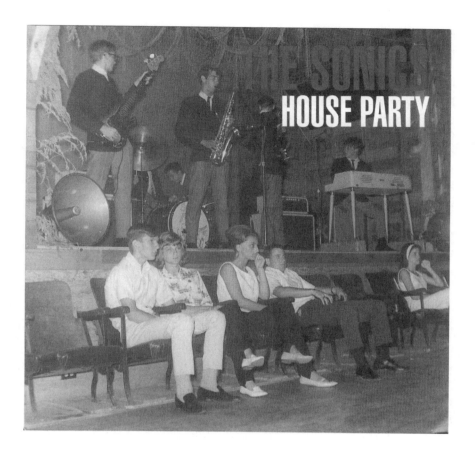

"It's real obvious, listening to our stuff, that we weren't even in the same ballpark with these people. So I don't think we thought we were gonna carve out a chunk and move these people aside; we just wanted to get in on the action. But as far as what material we played? We basically were R&B-oriented. We did kinda the same things everyone else was doing."

Well, uh, no, not *exactly*. Although their repertoire might have shared a common core of "standards" with many other Northwest bands, from day one these guys simply put their own unique stamp on anything they touched. Who else, for example, would have thought of naming their band after the frightening middle-of-the-night "sonic booms" that were a common disruption that plagued the neighborhoods around Tacoma's military bases? Yet it was perfectly apt that a phrase invented to describe the din a fighter jet makes while breaking the sound barrier would be adopted by a band destined to shatter the perceptions of how *hard* music could *rock*.

After adding a school buddy named Ray Michelson—who had already been in the Imperials—as their singer, the Sonics played their first gigs: a birthday party, and then a few teen sock hops and skating rink gigs, and the odd self-promoted dance, at rental rooms like St. Mary's Parish Hall (on Gravelly Lake Drive), the Tacoma Community Hall, and the Lake City Community Club. Before long, Michelson made the error of mentioning how great the Imperials' keyboardist/singer, Gerry Roslie, was—and, their curiosity piqued, the Sonics set up an audition. All it took was one jet-fueled roar from Roslie (who was by then in the Searchers) and the band realized that they'd found *the voice*: a larynx-shredding screamer whose ferocity was simply unprecedented. Prior to Roslie's emergence, it had been easy to think that maniacal singers like Little Richard or Screamin' Jay Hawkins had pushed rock 'n' roll vocalizing to the extreme edge. But the young singer from Tacoma was about to raise the stakes with his snarling demeanor, demented lyricism, and impossibly hoarse voice that recordings would ultimately document in all their admirably faltering and breaking glory.

The Sonics poached Rob Lind (sax) and Bob Bennett (drums) from the Searchers, completing the band's classic lineup. The Sonics rose through the ranks and, after gigging in rooms like the Midland Hall, the Lakewood Knights of Columbus Hall, the New Crescent, the Tacoma Armory, the Red Carpet teen club, and Olympia's Capitol Skateland, they attracted the interest of a few Tacoma radio DJ's—including Tom Coleman and Glenn Brooke from KTNT's weekly *Teen Time* show—who got involved in promoting dances. The band eventually worked their way up to bigger shows at Perl's Ballroom in Bremerton, the Evergreen Ballroom, and the Spanish Castle.

It was in the spring of 1964 that Etiquette Records got tipped off to the Sonics' existence—and eventually both Kent Morrill and Buck Ormsby dropped by Bennett's house to have a listen. "After we'd started the label," moaned Ormsby, "*a lotta* people started saying, 'Gosh, we'd sure like to get a record out too.' And that was a time when I used to go out and look at bands, and it got pretty tiring, because you'd see a lotta bands that we weren't really interested in. And then somebody called me one day and said, 'Go and see this band!' So I said, 'Okay, *one more time* [laughter].' And I made the arrangement and saw these guys practicing in Bob's garage. And *man*, I just thought, 'These guys are hot stuff.' I'd been looking for something that was different. Something that would rock my socks off. I went down and saw them, and I found it. In the back of my head, I always just

Teen Time newspaper ad, circa 1964.

wanted to find somebody that just *ground* it out. And [laughter] I walked into this place and these guys hit it and I went, 'Whoa!' It just *floored* me. I heard 'The Witch' and I went totally bazonkers."

"The Witch" was, lyrically speaking, within the long tradition of mildly misogynistic rock 'n' roll "put-down" songs. In it, Roslie warns the listener away from an evil chick who'll "make you itch / 'cause she's the witch." And it had *everything* going for it: a truly tuff one-and-a-half-chord interlocking guitar-and-bass riff, rhythmic punctuation via a Gatling-gun snare hook, and Roslie's ungodly shrieks. Though the individual Sonics had been weaned on fairly sophisticated R&B music, their own sound was one that simply rocked on a new scale of barbaric savagery. Garage rock historian Greg Shaw speculated that "maybe it was the presence since the late '50s of such regional instrumental giants as the Raiders, Wailers, Ventures and others that had taught area kids respect for a raunchy sax and powerhouse rhythm. Whatever the sociological explanation, the Northwest had a standard of sonic integrity dimensions beyond that which prevailed elsewhere. The best Northwest bands, like the Sonics, hit realms of intensity unmatched by anybody, anywhere, anytime."

At the time, Etiquette was just stunned by the band's primal power, and they signed the Sonics on the spot. It was July 1964, and, as producer for the project, Ormsby had been thinking about which of the handful of local studios would be the best fit for his new discovery. His main challenge would be to capture on tape, by whatever means necessary, the raw power and sinister essence of this unique quintet. And that would not be a simple matter. "I didn't really know *where* to take the Sonics," recalled Ormsby. "But we figured, 'What the heck?' and took 'em up to Commercial Recorders in Seattle, where the Wailers had cut a few. These engineers were more into the quiet acoustic bass, maybe a trap set, and maybe an acoustic guitar, acoustic piano, that kind of thing. *Not* loud. And so we showed up with this Wurlitzer electric piano, with Fender amps, and a guy that pounded his kick drum like there was no tomorrow."

With their gear all set up in Lyle Thompson's studio and the tape rolling, problems arose almost immediately. "We blew out some equipment in the studio doin' 'The Witch,' And I mean these engineers were like, 'Hey, we can't *do* this.' And we went, 'Yeah. Let's try it.' It was like these guys were *scared*. He says, 'Man you blew out this,' or 'You blew out that.' I said, 'Can't we just take it up to the edge?' I mean, 'Let's get some red lights happening here.' [laughter] These guys couldn't believe me. 'cause I'd say, 'You've gotta take the limiters off. You can't squish it. Let's try it. Let's just *try*.' Nobody'd done that. We had a hell of a time with the engineers. They just weren't used to the full-energy stuff. We kept saying we wanted to do this or that, and *they* kept saying, 'You can't do that.'"

Ormsby truly didn't care that the recording console's VU meters were redlining and limiter lights were blinking, and he proceeded to overload every tube in every old piece of the studio's ancient gear well past reasonable limits. So every time the Sonics' volume peaked enough to ping the meter, Thompson wanted to halt and start over. Technical perfection was not what Etiquette wanted, and a smidgen of distortion wasn't a problem—in fact, it might help convey the power of this band. At the end of the session—and after plenty of false starts, bickering, and the patching-up of failing gear—the Sonics had two songs in the can: "The Witch" and a take on Little Richard's rockin' "Keep A Knockin'." The latter tune was unusually hot—in part because at the very last second Lind asked the band to try playing the song one key higher than usual, a change request that caused Roslie to throw a little tantrum by singing it with extra aggression. Then, to cap the day off right, the Sonics spent the entire thirty-mile drive back to Tacoma engaged in a raging argument—and their only area of agreement was that the session had produced nothing but crap.

After a good night's sleep, Larry Parypa hauled his guitar (along with an old Magnatone electric piano amp) back to the studio in an effort to try and "fix" the recording. And so, with the addition of an overdubbed guitar riff (bolstered by a vibrato/Leslie rotating speaker–type effect that gives the track a spooky propulsion), "The Witch" was suddenly deemed acceptable to all concerned (except for Thompson, one would think), and Etiquette went ahead and issued the two songs as a single. Now, why any of these people thought that a record featuring the atomic tub-thumping of Bennett, the chaotic lead guitar spasms of Larry Parypa, the frenzied throb generated by Andy Parypa and Lind, and the bloody-murder screams of Roslie, would be commercially viable is beyond understanding.

The true miracle is that it ever got on the radio in the first place. Truth is, the song was really just not compatible with Top 40 radio. Hell, it made even the Rolling Stones and the Animals sound comparatively tame. But that was the point: The Sonics had taken rock 'n' roll to its next evolutionary plateau.

Goodness knows that Etiquette faced a daunting challenge in promoting the 45. After distributing promotional copies to all the stations that they typically did when the label had a new release, they patiently waited to see what level of response "The Witch" might get. The initial response was silence. Then, when the label reached out to those same stations again in order to talk the disc up a little, they found out that the major stations— KJR, KOL, and KING—collectively thought they were nuts and wouldn't even respond to them. Weeks were flying by and "The Witch" was consistently receiving the cold shoulder from the radio biz. In fact, Pat O'Day held the record, and apparently the band itself, in such minimal regard that he decided not to include them in the lineup for the biggest show he'd thus far produced.

Having been inspired by the success of the Beatles' August show at the Seattle Center, O'Day announced that a three-day Seattle Teenage Fair would take place there starting September 4, 1964. The fair would feature teen-oriented product display booths and concert—*no dancing allowed*— performances by imported acts like Annette Funicello and the Beach Boys, and local bands, including the Kingsmen, the Wailers, the Raiders, the Viceroys, and the Counts. The event was a such huge success, that Pat O'Day & Associates promoted quarterly Teen Fairs in Seattle, and similar shows in Spokane (in collaboration with KJRB) and Portland (with KISN and Pat Mason Associates) for the following five years.

By late October 1964, only Seattle's tiny KTW had given "The Witch" any airtime. While the Sonics would have loved it if KJR had embraced their record, after months went by with no response from the station's top two DJs, Pat O'Day and Dick Curtis, hopes were fading. "Pat O'Day and Dick Curtis used to do these record hops where they would go spin platters and throw out all the rejects to the kids in the audience," recalled Andy Parypa. "And so they did this record hop at Curtis High School, and all of a sudden they get all these kids comin' up sayin', 'Hey, play "The Witch"! Play "The Witch!"' The kids knew we had it out on record. And O'Day, who I'd given a couple copies to—but I doubt if he even listened to it—well, later he told me that somebody brought one up to him on the stage, they put it on the sound system, and the whole place went *nuts*. O'Day told me he knew right then and there that, 'Hey, we better get *on* this record!'"

It was on Christmas Day 1964 that KJR debuted "The Witch" in the No. 26 slot on their Fab 50 chart—and hearing it on that station was a huge thrill for the band. With all that exposure on KJR, retail sales of the 45 began skyrocketing—and that was the point when the young execs at Etiquette discovered a very important detail about the record biz: For every single sold, the label would need to shell out royalty payments to the owners of the song-publishing "copyrights" for both the A-side and B-side songs. Regardless of which one was the hit, both songs sold in the same quantity. So, for example, with "The Witch," this was pain-free—they just wrote a check to their own Valet Publishing firm, which contractually owned the Sonics' compositions. But for the B-side—"Keep A Knockin'"—they were stuck paying Little Richard's publishing company.

And it was that issue that forced a change of plan—and that soon saw the Sonics back in Seattle, this time working with Kearney Barton at Audio Recording. The goal was to cut another original composition that they could control the publishing on, and quickly reissue "The Witch" with a new B-side tune. The song that the Sonics came up with was another tour de force of manic rock 'n' roll dementia called "Psycho."

Quietly reissued, "The Witch" climbed toward the top of KJR's Fab 50 and looked to all observers poised to become an unstoppable chart-topper. But then the disc mysteriously stalled out at the No. 2 slot. It seemed that there had to be some explanation for that sudden loss of momentum. And there was: "Years later O'Day told me that sales-wise it was *easily* No. 1 for a long time," said Andy Parypa. "But they never charted it higher than No. 2.

And that's because their station format was that the No. 1 song would get played at all hours of the day and night—whereas I never ever heard 'The Witch' 'till after three o'clock in the afternoon."

That was certainly true. In order not to offend the sensibilities of KJR's morning and afternoon audience—which was then presumed to be middle-class housewives who enjoyed soft Top 40 pop—KJR apparently manipulated their own charts by restricting certain records from airplay until after school let out, at which point things started rocking somewhat harder well into the evening. Meanwhile, the Sonics' new B-side, "Psycho," also began rising on the local charts, and Etiquette suddenly had a two-sided hit on their hands. With regional sales of around 29,000 units "The Witch" / "Psycho" started to attract the eyes of the industry. The first to call Etiquette was Al Schmidt, a big-time staff producer at RCA, who said that he'd noticed the chart action over on KJR and then expressed interest in working with the band if the single showed that it had the mojo to do as well outside of the Northwest. And sure enough, "The Witch" did just that when stations in Vallejo and San Jose, California; Orlando, Florida; Pittsburgh; and Cleveland all began giving the hit heavy airplay. And along the way, "The Witch" became the all-time best-selling local single on a *local* label up to that point in Northwest history.

Etiquette was realizing just what a hot property they had, but rather than make any moves to pass the Sonics up to a major label, they instead redoubled their own efforts to promote the band. The Sonics were taken into Bill Wiley and Bill Griffith's tiny studio in Tacoma, where mainly country records were cut. Displeased by the flat sounds they were getting on tape, Ormsby and the Sonics began moving things around, even rearranging the egg cartons on the walls in an attempt to get a more "live" sound. The old cowboys parked near the recording console might not have been too pleased, but in the end Etiquette got enough tracks to fill out an album. *Here Are the Sonics* was a great introductory set of the knuckle-dragging garage R&B rock that the band had been dishing out at dances all over the state—ravers like Little Richard's "Good Golly Miss Molly" and the Wailers' "Dirty Robber." Additional originals included killer riffs and lyrical content that explored a full range of topics, from Andy's new Ford Mustang ("Boss Hoss"), to the sick joys of poison ("Strychnine"), to evil chicks ("The Witch"), to disturbed mental states ("Psycho"). Their follow-up LP, *The Sonics Boom*, would add satanic threats ("He's Waitin'") to the mix. And all *this* in the name of fun. *Loud* fun.

By mid-'65 the Sonics were a top teen-dance draw, and they also got chances to open shows for many touring stars, including the Beach Boys,

Jan and Dean, Jay and the Americans, Ray Stevens, Herman's Hermits, the Righteous Brothers, the Kinks, and the Lovin' Spoonful. They even landed an infamous show backing those "bad girls" from New York City, the Shangri-Las. But the band's true claim to fame is that, as the history of 1960s rock finally sorted itself out, they would come to hold a very revered place in the pantheon. The Sonics' savage sound and psychotic lyrical stance has in more recent decades come to be acknowledged by historians as a direct precursor to the rise of full-blown punk rock—and thus a critical contributor to the renewal of rock 'n' roll's original promise.

CHAPTER 24

Steppin' Out

By mid-decade the Northwest's teen scene had grown to such an extent that it could no longer be ignored. But while the fans of the music were proud of what had been created over the past half-decade since Dolton Records' shooting star–like blaze of glory began, others—industry skeptics, nervous parents, and grumpy squares in general—felt differently about it and dealt with it using various tactics. Those ranged from simply ignoring every positive development (which is what a few teen-oriented pop music magazines seemingly tried to do) to actively disparaging those same events as worthless achievements.

Of course, music fans in Seattle were long used to seeing the various editors at the *Seattle Times* openly deride and disparage any and everything having to do with rock 'n' roll or youth culture in general. As early as 1957, the paper's resident curmudgeon, arts and entertainment editor Louis R. Guzzo, seemed to be a man who obsessed with trying to single-handedly tamp down enthusiasm for anything that wasn't flat-out old-fashioned. And he would spend the next decades of his life publicly excoriating pretty much anyone and everything associated with rock 'n' roll.

In one of his many nasty screeds, Guzzo fretted that "with long-haired rock-'n'-roll singers in stovepipe pants and tight jackets setting the style, it's becoming increasingly difficult to tell which is a boy and which is a girl. Or, for that matter, which is the neighbor's sheepdog and which is his teen-age son. Like many adults, or 'Square Johns,' we presumed that the tight corduroy trousers, high-heeled Flamenco boots and whanging guitar were just a passing fad, something these teen-agers soon would outgrow. We couldn't have been more wrong, apparently. The thing gets bigger week by week. . . . In our neighborhood, there seems to be an amateur rock-'n'-roll group in every other block."

But again, that was a tradition at the *Times*, where one early and unforgettable published piece about a teen dance down at the Spanish Castle read like a passage from Dante's *Inferno* or the Bible's Book of Revelations: "We barely had stepped inside when we were met by a piercing blast of sound and nearly panicked for a moment. To the uninitiated, it sounded like the hounds of hell having one last big dogfight." Of course, to the *initiated* rock 'n' roll fan, that music was actually nothing more wicked than a typical dance set by the Wailers.

Then, at the absolute height of "Louie Louie" mania in the region, Guzzo teed off again—this time suggesting that our bands were all Johnny-one-notes who were pulling something over on their gullible teenage fans: "I think I have it figured out now. There really are only five young men with guitars and 1,000 batteries. All they do is walk off stage, change jackets and wigs and come back under another name. That must be the case because they play only one tune all night—the same one, over and over again, 1,468 times, not counting encores. At least, that's the way it all sounds." Well, Lou, just try telling that to the teens who were snapping up every new hit single—"Little Latin Lupe Lu," "Death of an Angel," "The Climb," "Annie Fanny," and "The Jolly Green Giant"—that the Kingsmen came up with. They didn't mind at all that the tunes had a certain similarity: It was the Northwest Sound, fool!

By this point, the suits upstairs at Columbia Records must have been ruing the day they'd ever signed the Raiders. Unlike the Kingsmen, the band hadn't really done a thing commercially since the "Louie Louie" debacle. Still smarting from having lost the hit to the Kingsmen, the Raiders somehow got the crazy idea in their heads that maybe Richard Berry had another gem like "Louie Louie" lying around that would make a good follow-up single. And that quest led to their pilgrimage to a ghetto dive in a Watts bowling alley where Berry was now stuck gigging.

The guys introduced themselves as fans and begged Berry for another winning tune, but the singer was less than impressed, and dismissively suggested that they just try doing his other '50s warhorse, "Have Love Will Travel"—which was a splendid idea, since that song was pretty much a direct knockoff of "Louie Louie." But Mark Lindsay reportedly felt slighted by Berry's attitude, and that very night he crafted his own musical response: "Louie—Go Home."

Columbia released the Raiders' "Louie—Go Home" / "Have Love Will Travel" 45 on March 17, 1964, to a complete lack of commercial action. But even if sales were slack, the tunes *were* noticed by rock 'n' roll fans who had a discerning ear for both songs' sub-"Louie" groove. Within a few months the Sonics and Counts (the latter with the Gallahads on vocals) had each recorded versions of "Have Love Will Travel." Meanwhile, over in Spokane, the Chambermen recorded a version of the A-side, and in June 1964 a British band, Davie Jones (later known as David Bowie) and the King Bees cut a rendition called "Louie Louie—Go Home," which was followed in 1965 by the Who and their own take, titled "Lubie, Come Home."

But in December 1965 the Los Angeles–based *KRLA Beat* magazine took notice of the Raiders' underachievement, noting that "they are on television more than practically every other American pop group, but they've

never had a number one record. . . . They've been on *Tonight, Hullabaloo, Lloyd Thaxton, American Bandstand, Shebang, 9th Street West, Hollywood A Go Go* . . . but still they haven't had a number one song. . . . How do Paul Revere and the Raiders persistently draw such huge crowds in their live shows and get so many TV spots without a top selling record? Maybe it's because they put on one of the wildest shows ever seen. The Raiders' performance can only be described as all-out chaos. All five of them have been known to climb all over a stage and everything on it, including themselves and their instruments."

As the hitless year of 1964 dragged into '65, Columbia must surely have been wondering again just exactly *why* they had ever signed this goofy Revere guy and his band, but things began looking up for the Raiders. Only weeks after replacing Holiday (who got married and stepped aside) with the Sir Winston Trio's bassist, Phil Volk, in January, the band was suddenly invited to do a pilot taping for a possible new CBS network show to be produced by Dick Clark. In hindsight, it is easy to see why Clark was eyeing this particular group for TV work—not only were they a good band with a very good stage show, and those flamboyant Colonial-era military uniforms, but each Raider was absolutely brimming with personality. Revere was the Groucho Marx of rock. The dreamily doe-eyed, ponytailed high-stepper, Lindsay; and Smitty, Levin, and the toothy Volk (who became known as "Fang") were all natural hams and immensely likable Joes. CBS, however, wasn't so impressed and passed on the deal. Luckily, though, ABC thought the pilot episode was great, bought in, and the Raiders were signed to a season of filming *Where the Action Is*. The show was a novel concept: Each episode the *Action* crew—Raiders, the Action Dancers, and a few guest acts—visited some "action spot" of the country. This format led to endless madcap mischief at various hot beaches, cool ski resorts, boating marinas, college campuses, et cetera—and a winning show.

But the ultimate significance of *Where the Action Is* was that it offered the Raiders a priceless opportunity to be the first band ever to have such wide exposure via television. And Columbia Records finally saw their path to successfully marketing this band. At that particular time the label was seeking ways to challenge Capitol Records' pair of blue-chip signings—the Beach Boys and the Beatles—and they settled on a plan that threw down the gauntlet to the British invaders. The Raiders would be pushed with a "Northwest retaliation" angle. The band's recordings were quickly cobbled together into the *Here They Come* LP, which came replete with this liner note blarney by manager Roger Hart: "In 1964, the British invaded America all over again. . . . Since history seemingly repeats itself, the United States is now marshalling its forces to protect the American Way of Music. Among the staunch defenders are five swingin' gentlemen known as Paul Revere & The Raiders." *Even* Time magazine chimed in with a prediction of victory: "Paul . . . and the colonially clad quintet may make whole regiments of fans waver from their British alignments."

Such silliness aside, the timing for all this was perfect: That album was released on May 24; June saw the debut of *Where the Action Is*, and by July 3, *Here They Come* had entered the *Billboard* LP charts, where it showed for forty-five weeks. Suddenly, and for the first time, the Raiders were paying off for the label. It was at about this point that Columbia considered working with the Sonics up in Tacoma.

"Somebody from Columbia records called the house—and *I* wasn't there, but my dad talked to them," recalled Andy Parypa. "I got ahold of Kent and Buck and said, 'Hey, these guys want to pick us up!' I was thinking that maybe they'd make a deal that would be beneficial to everybody. But Kent and Buck put the kibosh on that. Here was a major label that was genuinely interested in the group—and I just didn't think that Kent and Buck gave enough consideration to the prospects of just flat outright selling us. Or selling the master, or . . . *you know*? I mean, that was up to them—and they could be producers or whatever—but they just kinda flippantly put thumbs down on that *real* quick."

With the Sonics' "The Witch" and "Psycho" singles and *Introducing the Sonics* LP all selling extremely well, Etiquette Records had the first genuine moneymaker on their hands since the Wailers' *At the Castle* album three and a half years prior. And as a result, the label was able to settle into a new office suite with a staff that included a full-time promotions/PR man named Barrie Jackson. Then Morrill and Ormsby launched a new subsidiary label—Riverton Records—primarily so they could issue more and more product by more and more local acts and not fear wearing out Etiquette's welcome at radio stations. Needless to say, all this sudden corporate upgrading did not pass unnoticed by the Sonics.

But they were too busy performing and recording to raise much of a stink, and the Columbia connection was never consummated. But in February 1966 the Sonics' second LP, *The Sonics Boom*, was issued, and it contained classic originals like "Cinderella," "He's Waitin'," and "Shot Down," plus nine other blistering garage punk gems—including an absolutely killer version of "Louie Louie." Whereas other teen combos had cut renditions of the tune that ranged from soulful (Wailers) to funky (Little Bill) to sloppy

(Kingsmen) to electrifying (Raiders), it was the Sonics who had the punky temerity to actually *alter* the standard chord progression from a friendly I-IV-Vm to the sinister-sounding I-III-IV—to lay down a version that can only be described as fierce and threatening.

Robot A. Hull later noted in *Creem* magazine that by the mid-'60s the song had become "(thanks to the Kingsmen) the standard test of strength among thousands of aspiring punk bands. Through the Sonics, however, 'Louie Louie' was transformed from an expression of bumbling ineptitude into a frantic testament to the solidarity of teen bands everywhere." And the best of the following decades' punk pioneers—Iggy & the Stooges, the MC5, the New York Dolls, the Patti Smith Group, the Clash, and Black Flag—definitely paid homage to "Louie Louie." Over the years, countless non-Northwest bands—including the Syndicate of Sound, the Droogs, DMZ, the Cramps, the Fuzztones, the Flaming Lips, the Cynics, the Mummies, and Thee Headcoats—would bow to the Sonics by recording their toughest songs. And back on the Sonics' own turf, plenty of later Northwest bands, including the Moberlys, the Young Fresh Fellows, Screaming Trees, the Mono Men, the Kings of Rock, and the Fall-Outs—and even an all-Sonics tribute

combo, the New Strychnines, featuring members of grunge icons Mudhoney and others—would do the same.

But even back in the day, the Sonics' abrasive aural aesthetic and early snot-nosed lyrical stance definitely impacted loads of other Northwest bands. "These gritty bands," wrote Mark Shipper in the liner notes to *Explosives* (the 1973 reissue of Sonics recordings), "were a far cry from what the rest of the country was listening to in the early '60s, and were, without realizing it, conditioning their audience to a taste and acceptance of music that those outside of the Northwest simply would not be able to relate to. For this reason, major labels avoided the area. . . ." Well, all of the major labels except for RCA and Columbia, who had *tried* to reach out and help the band take their music to a wider audience. But if being locked into that contract with

Etiquette stunted the Sonics' progress, it was also true that the band's uncompromising aural assault—an acquired taste by any measure—would ultimately appeal only to a limited portion of the public. Their main strength—that gloriously crushing sound—was also their Achilles' heel.

This was a truth noted by D. Joseph Carducci in his 1990 book *Rock and the Pop Narcotic*: "Their music, though a dance music, typically had a psychotic male perspective and this led the sound toward a tougher, sardonic approach which competing with the softer in tone, tarted up English bands . . . frequently left them glowering in the lower reaches of the charts." Brad Morrell wrote in 1993 that "their sound was . . . heavier than anything from California or New York. As a result they were usually restricted to regional hits." That same year, Dave Marsh weighed in on the exact cause behind the Sonics' failure to ever really break out nationally: "The biggest reason Seattle rock wasn't mass merchandised stemmed from its content. Listening to the Wailers, the Sonics, the Frantics, and the rest involved direct and dangerous encounters with madness, poison, the edge of criminal lunacy. The best Seattle records sound like they were made by people involved in an occult ritual—in short, they appear as a prophecy of nineties grunge."

Although the Sonics' music would eventually have a widespread impact—one that other, later, founding fathers of punk rock like Iggy Pop and Joey Ramone (not to mention the saint of grunge, Kurt Cobain) would directly acknowledge—that influence was initially noticeable only in their own musical backyard. In fact, it was the presence of the Sonics that ultimately forced a big decision on other area bands: Either stick with the old tried-and-true jazz-tinged Northwest Sound, or leap into the future and start rocking as hard as possible. And four of the bands that reacted to the Sonics' shock therapy by taking that challenge head-on were the Wailers, the Kingsmen, the Raiders, and the Goodtimes.

So, for example, when the Wailers' new *Out of Our Tree* LP hit the racks in 1965, it revealed a *much* tougher overall sound—now the band's sax and keys were being downplayed in favor of grimy guitars and snotty vocals. Songs like the title track and "Hang Up"—and even a new version of their old "Dirty Robber"—came jacked up with punky screams and buzz-saw guitars. Don and the Goodtimes started toughening up too: After bringing in the Viceroys' guitarist, Jim Valley, to replace Pete Oulette, they recorded a naughty new tune that Valley brought along. Originally titled "Drive-in Movie Tease," the tune was retooled, recorded with Kearney Barton (whose Audio Recording Inc.—now at 2227 Fifth Avenue—had recently become

The Sonics rock a teen dance, circa 1966.

Seattle's first three-track stereo recording facility), and released by Jerden in July 1965 as "Little Sally Tease." And although the fun song was harder-edged than the band's previous outings, it didn't scare away radio stations. Perhaps they figured, "Well, better *this* than getting stuck with the Sonics!" The tune became a strong region-wide hit, adopted by garage bands far and wide—including the Kingsmen, who cut their own version. That and a new Wand single, "Give Her Lovin,'" both showed a tougher edge than prior recordings by the band.

It was at about this point that Kearney Barton's Audio Recording began gaining notoriety as *the* studio where the Northwest garage punk sound was being defined. Word spread that this was where the Sonics, Kingsmen, and Goodtimes were recording, and before long a number of hit-making bands—including California's Standells and New York's Knickerbockers—were making pilgrimages out to Seattle to record tracks here. Interestingly, the Standells' very next LP included a version of "Little Sally Tease." On a roll now, the Goodtimes made a national TV appearance in Los Angeles on the *Lloyd Thaxton Show*, and Jerry Dennon was soon able to get them a new contract with the big-time ABC-Dunhill Records. Following the national rerelease of "Little Sally Tease," the band's next 45—a rockin' version of the Drifters' old '61 hit "Sweets For My Sweet"—became another big regional

187

success. But once again, it failed to catch on nationally—perhaps in part because at that time Dunhill was a rather young company caught up in the massive success of the Mamas and the Papas and was unable to give their other acts as big a push.

So where in the hell were the Raiders? Sure, they starred on the *Where the Action Is* TV show. And yes, their Columbia LP had charted—but as of September 1965, it had been twenty-eight long months since they'd been signed, and they had yet to score a hit single. But that's when the promotional power of television became apparent: Immediately after they debuted "Steppin' Out" on their show, the new single entered the *Billboard* charts. Interestingly, that occurred right at the same time that the thirteen-week *Action* tour wound to an end. The show had been a breakthrough in the marketing of rock 'n' roll on TV, and Dick Clark was keyed up to carry on with taping for a proposed second season. But that's when the Raiders' management gently reminded Clark and ABC that their original contract was for the span of exactly *one* season, and that the network had neglected to pick up the option to renew the contract. And with "Steppin' Out" happening for the Raiders, negotiations for a second season with *Action* would, as a businessman like Clark surely understood, need to be more involved.

It didn't hurt the band's bargaining position one bit when—right in the midst of this negotiating process—Columbia issued a new Raiders' single, and it too rocketed up the charts. Suddenly this band looked unstoppable. "Just Like Me," too, had an interesting story: It had been written and recorded by another Northwest band, the Wilde Knights. But when the Raiders' cover version came out, the authorship credit for the tune had suddenly changed from the Knights' Rick Dey and Richard Brown to, well, the Raiders' manager's name, Roger Hart.

Regardless, the song itself was nothing less than a definitive Northwest garage punk classic that held the ideal pedigree of being based on an archetypical "Louie Louie"–type riff. And if that was something that would annoy Lou Guzzo and the *Seattle Times*, well, so be it—thousands of Northwest kids disagreed, hundreds of radio stations (including KJR) disagreed, and the general public disagreed. "Just Like Me" became Paul Revere and the Raiders' first Top 20 hit for Columbia Records—one that had been a long time in coming.

CHAPTER 25

Where the Action Is

By 1965 it was apparent to all observers that the Pacific Northwest teen scene had evolved into an unstoppable force: Locally based labels were at their most active level ever; several of the region's top bands were regularly scoring radio hits; the Raiders and the Goodtimes were rocking out on national television shows like *Where the Action Is, American Bandstand, Hullaballoo, Shebang, Shivaree,* and even *The Dating Game* with some frequency; and the quarterly Teen Fairs were regularly drawing thousands of teenybopper fans to Seattle's Center Arena.

None of this sat well with the old editors over at the *Seattle Times*. And because they couldn't attack *everybody* involved in the rock 'n' roll scene, they chose to focus their wrath and indignation upon the most visible target: KJR radio and Pat O'Day. Predicting the imminent collapse of Western civilization due to the evil scourge of rock 'n' roll was nothing new at this point, but Lou Guzzo's constant hand-wringing now began to have an edge of finger-pointing to it. It was as though he were seeking to establish a scapegoat for the crisis that was *certain* to occur: "Rock and roll stations grinding out their unmusical claptrap daily are the principal reasons for the continuing hold of the noisy drivel on young persons," bellowed Guzzo in reaction to a particularly fun O'Day-sponsored show in 1965. "They preach the nonsense that the rock-and-roll programs are all in good fun and help the youngsters 'let off steam.' Baloney. Last night's show was the third rock-and-roll show here in four months to come close to erupting into a riot. Who will accept the blame when the worst happens and the lights go up too late or the police are bowled aside?"

In Guzzo's wishful daydreams, KJR's powerful program director would ideally have an epiphany, reform himself, and switch to promoting classical ballet music or some such. "Pat O'Day is something of a Pied Piper . . . [so]

with all that coaxing power O'Day wields over the transistor set crowd these days, wouldn't it be something if he could be converted to the cause of good music and convert his flock in turn?" Oh yes, Lou, that really *would* be something, but KJR was highly unlikely at this point to disrupt their format—or to rein in O'Day, who managed to give *his* company's weekly dances numerous casual plugs throughout his every air shift. And the reason for that is simple: Business was *great*. Under O'Day's leadership the station was utterly dominating the whole region's radio market, regularly leaving others to peck at the remaining crumbs.

But if outside observers thought that O'Day had created a self-serving vortex of profiteering—a simple system whereby he might mention a particular band in his weekly *Seattle P-I* column (which he'd been writing since April 1964) or in KJR's own publication, *Disc A Go-Go*, and then maybe that same band's record got KJR airplay, and then that band "coincidentally" happened to be contracted to play his dances—well, all that was fine with KJR's upper management. And that's because they were well aware that he'd been fastidiously paying for each and every Teen Fair or weekend dance advertisement that aired. And that revenue stream was a significant one for the station. So the idea that O'Day should be brought to heel was a nonstarter—as was any hope that Pat O'Day & Associates might somehow walk away from the lucrative teen-dance circuit that they'd labored to establish.

By this point, Pat O'Day & Associates (which included former KJR jock Dick Curtis and former Wenatchee-based independent booker Terry Bassett) had managed to systematically take over most of the rock 'n' roll dance and concert promotions action throughout Washington and even in Oregon. The company had established themselves in the powerful position of being able to offer bands whole *seasons* of contracted work at the various dancehalls, high school gyms, skating rinks, and armories scattered from Aberdeen to Zenith. In sum, Pat O'Day & Associates' dance circuit reportedly became the biggest and most robust in the nation. "Eventually, during the summer, we had as many as *sixty* dances a week in the Northwest," O'Day proudly claimed, "'cause the Northwest was the *only* place where a group like Roy Orbison—or Bobby Vee, or Jan and Dean—could come and work seven, eight, ten straight nights at dances in the summer! It was the only place in the country where it was possible to get ten nights' work! Even L.A. did not have a dance scene as strong as the Puget Sound area. And there were no concert tours to speak of then. But even before we started doing concerts in '63, they could come up here and work. We gave them the opportunity.

Seattle had more successful bands than any city going in the United States. I mean *local* bands. There wasn't anything like this anywhere, you know, where there were bands that were actually selling records and performing."

Jerry Dennon agreed, and in a *Seattle P-I* essay titled "The Seattle Sound: What's Happening Is Pop," he suggested that O'Day's dance business was partially responsible for creating a milieu where a regional strain of music could be incubated. He wrote that one "vital ingredient in whatever contributes to the Seattle Sound would be the unique 'circuit' that groups and bands can work here in the Northwest. The 'tour' for an unknown group can mean working occasional school or neighborhood 'gigs' for $50 to $125 a night. Better than mowing lawns. If the group gains in popularity or attracts a promoter (who runs teen dances), then the price can go up. . . . And if the group is fortunate enough to break through with a record hit, even if it is nothing more than a local success, then their asking price can jump up to perhaps $400 a night or more. . . . The competition makes it tough to crack into this lucrative Northwest circuit. Thus the groups that do make it are usually good. And because the Northwest is unique in this regard, somehow the groups that then leave this area to tackle the world are a little bit better than those from anywhere else."

No doubt about it, O'Day's circuit was a tremendous opportunity for a good number of local bands, whose summer calendars might be booked up with thirty-five, forty dates. And *the* hottest new band to join the circuit was Merrilee Rush and the Turnabouts. The group formed in August 1965 when Neil Rush and his bride, Merrilee, split away from the Statics, who were intent on hanging tough with their raw teen R&B sound. The Turnabouts, however, would explore a more pop/rock sound that could break them into O'Day's empire—and a stage show that would focus more attention on Merrilee's obvious charms. The Turnabouts quickly became one of biggest live draws in the region, and Jerden Records quickly offered up a recording deal, but Neil was so sure of his band's talents that he declined, instead opting to form a couple of new labels, Ru-Ro Records and Merrilyn Records, on which they issued a series of energetic 45s (like "Party Song" and "Tell Me the Truth")—all of which, to the exasperation of the band, O'Day adamantly refused to play at KJR.

Although he'd failed in seducing the Turnabouts to sign on the dotted line, Dennon was a little more persuasive when he chatted up the Sonics. By 1966 they'd grown disgruntled with the way Etiquette Records had handled their career, especially the botched reactions to those nibbles by big-time labels like RCA and Columbia. But the band really figured that Etiquette

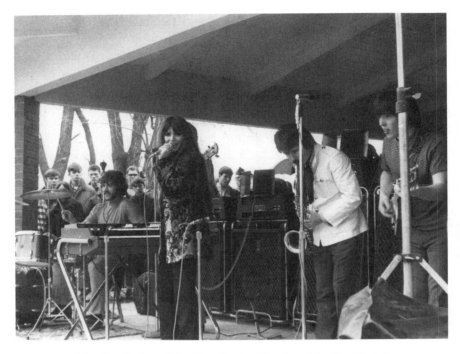

Merrilee Rush and the Turnabouts. (Courtesy Merrilee Rush.)

didn't "get it" when the label laughed off an offer by San Francisco's top DJ/ dance promoter Tom Donahue to have the Sonics play a huge concert at the gigantic Cow Palace. It seems that the Etiquette execs didn't like the stipulation that, to play the gig, the Sonics would have had to travel to the Bay Area at their own expense. Apparently failing to see the value of the exposure the gig would have given the band, Etiquette turned down Donahue's offer.

So when Dennon made a sneaky offer to take the band on (*and* immediately book them into a top-quality studio in Los Angeles for a new round of recording), the Sonics were swayed by his by now well-practiced sweet talk. But Dennon came though on his promise, and the band was soon ensconced in Hollywood's legendary Gold Star Studios.

The Sonics' work with famed hit-making engineer Larry Levine ultimately produced a whole batch of new tunes, including the punky "You've Got Your Head On Backwards." After Jerden issued that as a 45 in the early summer of 1966, Dennon cut a distribution deal with ABC Records, and the tune appeared at bubbling under" status on the *Billboard* singles charts. The Sonics were flown to Cleveland, where they'd been invited to make a TV appearance on Don Webster's syndicated *Upbeat* teen-dance show.

Although the Sonics still didn't have a national hit, things seemed to be looking up for them—until, that is, their bad-boy aura finally caught up with them on a few occasions. The band's aggressive music had often sparked drunken dance-floor brawls—which occasionally drew a band member or two into the fray—but one particular gig in Yakima took that rough-housing to a whole new level. It was the night of a record release party for Danny and the Seniors' new Dennon-produced 45, "Oh Devil" / "Wicked Girl," held at Yakima's Parker Heights area grange hall. In an effort to help ensure a good turnout, that little-known Yakima band hired the Sonics to open the show. Unfortunately, the town's fire department took notice of the large crowd of idle teens milling around outside the hall, which, having been oversold, was not legally compliant. Something, they figured, needed to be done before anything untoward happened. The answer came to these professional public servants: "What say we just shut down the whole dance? That ought to solve the problem."

So, on a hot night with a packed house—and just as the Sonics kicked off their opening number—the authorities cut the power and began barking orders to clear out and go home. The youth of Yakima were having none of that bullshit, and a full-scale teen riot ensued. When backup State Patrol troopers arrived, one officer was knocked down by young toughs, and his "Smokey the Bear" hat was stolen. Then kids tipped over and gutted the Coke machine and started heaving chairs through the windows and out into the street. Meanwhile, the Sonics—who were initially trapped in their dressing room—managed to escape, and were last seen fleeing out the back door with their instruments.

Then there were those fabled incidents involving the Sonics' hotel-related debacles: being banned from one in Spokane, and getting rudely rousted from their rooms in the tiny town of Ephrata during a raid led by a sheriff who was steamed that his own daughter and her girlfriends might be showing a bit too much "affection" for the band.

By this time, the Raiders' second Columbia LP, *Just Like Us*, had been hanging around the *Billboard* Top 10 long enough to earn a gold record award. Then, after Levin was drafted in March 1966, Jim Valley came over from the Goodtimes and soon became known to the national fan base as "Harpo." The Raiders' third Columbia LP, *Midnight Ride*, was released on May 9, and the first single off that album, "Kicks," entered the charts and peaked at No. 4 in *Billboard*. "Hungry" broke out in June and peaked at No. 6. At the same time, the second season of *Where the Action Is* brought the Raiders even more fame, which led to their first of endless major national tours, and more hit singles: Before the year was out, they'd scored two more Top 20 hits: "The Great Airplane Strike" and "Good Thing."

Put simply, the Raiders' string of hit singles and albums in 1965–'66 amounted to the most impressive streak since Dolton Records' opening run in 1959–'60. In 1973, *Phonograph Record Magazine* stated that the Raiders were "a group whose vast recording output turns out to be as solid a legacy of straight-forward exciting mid-sixties rock and roll as America produced in that illustrious era." Beyond even that, though, the Raiders can be credited with inspiring—every bit as much as the Beatles and Stones had—a nation of bored teens to pick up guitars and rock out in their garages. Liner notes to the *Highs of the Mid-Sixties Vol. 7* garage rock compilation LP nailed the matter in noting that "the massive success of Paul Revere and the Raiders, the Kingsmen and others encouraged local bands to seek the same, knowing it could be done without diminishing their raw style. Unlike commercially minded garage bands elsewhere . . . experience had shown them that all it took to succeed was a charismatic lead singer and a good hot riff."

CHAPTER 26

Louie—Go Home

The Pacific Northwest's "Louie Louie"–fueled universe—which had survived both the surfer rock tsunami and the British Invasion perhaps a bit bloody, but still unbowed—was soon confronted by additional musical trends that would now threaten to dilute and/or bury it. The American folk music revival arrived, which begat the folk rock fad, which begat the hippies' psychedelic sounds and acid rock experiments. Although plenty of local musicians would participate in those forms of music, it might be fair to say that the musical politics of the era were probably more interesting than the music itself.

Most of the folk, folk rock, and psychedelic songs and recordings produced in this region were so plainly derivative of styles forged elsewhere that even the finest of them seem—especially in hindsight—to be rootless, and even quaint period pieces. But the part of the history of those times that remains vibrant is the saga of the cultural tensions that all of this musical evolution brought to the surface. Consider the fact that while folk music would win a following in every American college town—where plenty of earnest, acoustic-guitar-strumming folkies would congregate to sing two-hundred-year-old British folk tunes—that music still did *not* make the grade for anyone who wanted to dance. Even though intellectual college kids might now be bored with dancing to "Louie Louie" at their local armory and instead prefer to sit and absorb the "meanings" and "authenticity" of "Michael Row the Boat Ashore," plenty of other teens felt otherwise.

That splintering of musical interests was good enough for rock 'n' roll's enemies to butt in and try and put a thumb on the scale when measuring the relative worth of the two factions. The *Seattle Times*, once again, couldn't resist weighing in in 1965—this time with a dual-purpose straw-man editorial that tried to simultaneously slam rockers (for wasting money by shifting over to acoustic guitars) and patronize them with a pat on the head (for finally seeing the light). "Most of these kids start with an inexpensive $25 acoustic guitar, then, about high school, graduate to a $100 electric guitar, and finally to a fancy $400—or $500 job—just the guitar, not the amplifying equipment . . . and by the time they are college age, they're back to the $25 guitar, the 'in' instrument for madrigal or folk singing, so popular with college students. Very often they end up with the same guitar they started out with. . . . Meanwhile, the parents have spent a small fortune on electric guitars and amplifying equipment—plus the nerve-shredding din of seemingly endless practice in the basement or rec room. It's the one consolation of rock 'n' roll, apparently. Eventually, the kids outgrow it. At least that's our fervent hope."

Not so fast, buster: Just because a few rockers might have switched over to folk didn't mean a major bugout from big-beat music was underway. In fact, the rise of the folk fad even fortified some rock bands' resolve to rock *harder*—just ask the Sonics: "We used to play in this little joint called the Red Carpet down on South Tacoma Way," said Andy Parypa. "And down the street, at the Tacoma Community Hall—this place'd just be jammed to the gunnels with all these young kids with their ten-dollar Sears & Roebuck guitars at what they called a 'hootenanny' in those days. Sittin' there singin' 'Puff the Magic Dragon' and all this *shit*. And, you know, we were just totally horror-stricken by this turn of events."

Luckily, the folk fad soon gave way to Lou Guzzo's worst nightmare (thus far): the West Coast hippie movement, which was largely brought to you by all those nice fresh-scrubbed folkie kids who'd discovered that they *did*, in fact, enjoy music with a beat. And by 1965 the world began to learn about such bands as the Byrds, the Grateful Dead, Big Brother and the Holding Company, Quicksilver Messenger Service, and the Jefferson Airplane—all of which were comprised of former folkies who had let their hair grow and their minds expand. And with San Francisco's Haight-Ashbury neighborhood pegged as the center of this new rock—the "New Liverpool"—that the town soon found itself in the glare of media spotlight.

The whole hippie style and ethos was something that quickly spread up and down the coast. In the Northwest, the first few hippie bands to emerge faced definite challenges—not the least of which was the issue of where to perform, since, by definition, their counterculture identities fairly well precluded the possibility that Pat O'Day & Associates would ever employ them at their "Louie Louie"–driven teenybopper shows. Conversely, the hippie bands did not want to play for O'Day—and nor did they ever want to even *hear* "Louie Louie" again. As far as they were concerned, those days were done and this was a new frontier. At the time, to refuse to play the region's long-standing signature song was still to assume a bit of a heretical position, but it was one way for bands to differentiate themselves from all the previous groups who'd used stage costumes, choreographed steps, and other "showbiz" trappings. Mainly, it was an honest choice to play their own brand of music and for hip people from the "new community" rather than trying to please drunken frat boys and power-drunk radio DJs. And among the earliest ringleaders on this uncharted path were Jack Horner and the Famous Plums, the Daily Flash, Thee Unusuals, and the Emergency Exit.

Perhaps because of their retro name and transitional bluesy, Hammond B3 organ–driven sound, the Famous Plums (who were comprised of four Nathan Hale and Roosevelt High guys) hit the scene and initially confounded some people—well, at least Pat O'Day, who actually let them (probably sight unseen) enter his 1966 Teenage Fair Band Championships. Despite their freaky music and hippie look (or maybe *because* of it!), the Plums proceeded to play for the assembled teenyboppers and actually made off with that year's prize. The *UW Daily* shed some light on why the Plums had been victorious: "Early this summer, an amateur band contest was held at the Seattle Teenage Fair. Ninety percent of the bands in the competition fell into two categories: poor imitations of Paul Revere and the Raiders, complete with their steps, routines and song list; or poor imitations of the Rolling Stones. Both types of bands work off the rather shaky assumption that the Raiders and Stones are worth emulating. But that, of course, is a personal prejudice. Anyway, somewhere between the 23rd version of 'Satisfaction' and a few versions of 'Kicks,' a most curious collection of musicians formed on the stage."

And that "curious collection" of players—with their mismatched apparel, which the paper went on to describe as "Contemporary American Funky"— wowed the Teen Fair crowd that day and were rewarded a record contract with Jerden Records. A session with Kearney Barton would produce a version of Bo Diddley's tribal stomper, "Who Do You Love?" which was then released on the *Battle of the Bands* sampler LP. But before O'Day could even think of saying no to airing the tune on KJR (because it rocked so damn hard), the Plums managed to give him a reasonable rational for blacklisting the band for good. O'Day had booked them at Parker's Ballroom for what would prove to be their first and *only* gig there. Mid-show, the Plum's keyboardist/leader, Dan Bonow, grew aggravated with some beery kid who kept bellowing for the band to play "Louie Louie" and who finally shouted, "Fuck you!" at the Plums. Unfortunately, instead of ignoring the lout, the hotheaded Bonow made the grave error of leaning into his microphone to respond with an amplified "FUCK YOU!" right back at him. Well, that led to an onstage scolding by a Seattle police officer, and ultimately a halt to the show—a turn of events that O'Day & Associates soon learned of. And, just as simple as that, the Famous Plums went from being *the* hot new Seattle band to a band who never got another job anywhere on the entire circuit.

Later, in hippie circles, that would have meant the attainment of a noble goal and a real badge of honor—but the hippie scene hadn't yet built itself up to a level that could support many bands. And there was no love lost on O'Day's end either: KJR kept on supporting selected local bands and their records, which explains why they overpromoted questionable records by harmless pop-oriented groups—like George Washington and the Cherry Bombs, the Dimensions, the Bards, the Springfield Rifle (ex-Dynamics), and the City Zu, who each scored Top 10 hits—while new hippie bands like the Time Machine or Brave New World saw their 45s shunted by the station. All the while, KJR got ever further behind the curve. . . .

Which is how the station *totally* missed out on the next great 45 to be cut in Seattle, by a band called the Daily Flash. Inspired by the Byrds, this band—formed in the early summer of '65 by folkie Steve Lalor (vocals/guitar), Don MacAllister (a bluegrass mandolinist–gone–electric bassist), talented frat-boy Doug Hastings (lead guitar), and Continentals drummer Don Stevenson—had just begun to jell when they lost Stevenson to the Frantics, who were headed to a gig at the Peppermint Tree nightclub in San Francisco. The Frantics also replaced guitarist Joe Johansen with ex-Searcher Jerry Miller; their former drummer, Jon Keliehor, jumped over to join the Flash, and the band's sound came together quickly. It was a fresh approach that featured a ringing twelve-string, eccentrically arty drumming, tasteful leads, and pure vocal harmonies. In other words, no "Louie Louie," and no more of the suddenly outdated Northwest Sound—which was just fine with their intended audience of hip UW students, U District beatniks, caffeine addicts, teenage runaways, and off-campus fringies. As the *UW Daily* noted in 1966, "The unique thing about their music is that it developed out of an area strongly entrenched in what tradespeople call the 'Northwest Sound'. Most locally based bands pattern their music after such groups as Merrilee and the Turnabouts, Don and the Goodtimes, and the earlier pieces by Paul Revere and the Raiders. Music with the 'Northwest Sound' generally has drums, bass, a lot of organ, and an occasional sax. The music they produce is often more rhythmically than melodiously oriented. The Flash, on the other hand, is made up of four musicians and singers who are well schooled in the melody-dominated folk style. Observers say their rapid success was due in part to their break with the traditional 'Northwest Sound.'"

Unwilling to get ensnared in O'Day's spiderwebs, the Daily Flash had to seek out alternative venues in which to perform—which was still a tough proposition, given the stranglehold that O'Day held on most of the area's venues. So out of sheer necessity the band resorted to guerrilla DIY marketing strategies, hand-inking their own posters and throwing their own dances at various rental halls like the Socialists' Freeway Hall and the Painters Union Hall. It was while playing a funky downtown room called The Door that a local record distributor discovered them and took them into Kearney Barton's Audio Recording to cut a cover of Bob Dylan's "Queen Jane Approximately" and a folk standard, "Jack Of Diamonds." Those two tunes were so strong that Parrot Records (a subsidiary of a major British label, London Records) signed the band and issued the disc. And although getting airplay in Seattle was problematic, a hot Hollywood-based management team, Greene & Stone—who also handled Sonny and Cher, Buffalo Springfield, and later, Iron Butterfly—courted and signed the band.

Named a "pick hit" by *Cash Box*, which declared that the band "should quickly and solidly establish itself as a group of some note with this power-packed debut," the record still failed to make the national charts. But in April 1966—and after enduring increasing harassment from the Seattle police at their Capitol Hill practice pad—the band loaded up their '48 Packard hearse and tripped off to Haight-Ashbury, where they played their first Avalon Ballroom show, and then went on to Los Angeles to share the stages at The Trip and the Whisky A Go Go with the scene's hippest groups, including the Byrds, Buffalo Springfield, Love, Sons of Adam, and the Doors. The Daily Flash would go on to do shows around the country with Jefferson Airplane, Sopwith Camel, Country Joe, Quicksilver, and the Yardbirds—but their finest achievement was "The French Girl," a single which was the debut for a major new label, UNI Records, and a beautifully baroque slice of folk rock that broke out in several radio markets in February 1967 before fading.

But the Daily Flash were not the only Northwest group who would join the great migration to San Francisco: Among the others were Portland's Hunger, Corvallis's Neighborhood Children, Butte, Montana's Initial Shock, and Bellingham's Thee Unusuals. The last band featured a full-throttle female singer named Kathi McDonald, and in '65 they were discovered and signed to a record deal in San Francisco. Their 45 "Summer Is Over" was issued by

Mainstream Records—the same label that would go on to release Janis Joplin and Big Brother and the Holding Company's debut discs. As for McDonald, she would go on to join Ike and Tina Turner, eventually replacing Janis Joplin in Big Brother and appearing on the Rolling Stones' classic *Exile on Main Street* LP.

Meanwhile, the Emergency Exit were now making their mark in Seattle. The group formed back in the spring of '65 from the ashes of the Nitesounds: Paul Goldsmith (guitar) and Luther Rabb (bass) joined up again and added Bill Leyritz (drums) and Jim Walters (formerly trumpeter, now on guitar), and they actually competed in that fall's Teen Fair Band Championship. But their freaky looks and nontraditional music—an exciting new blend of pop and psychedelia—was *not* going to cut it with O'Day. The band was wary of getting involved with Jerden Records, so they opted to work with Neil Rush's Ru-Ro Records, and the subsequent 45—"Maybe Too Late" / "Why Baby"—was a brilliant effort—albeit an A-side described simplistically by the *Seattle Times* as being "all about a chick who gets hooked on LSD and isn't nice anymore." Well, something like that anyway . . . What *was* nice was that ABC-Dunhill Records in Los Angeles liked the band and issued a second single so undeniably cool that even KJR took a chance with it: "It's Too Late Baby" rocketed right into the station's Top 10. In hindsight, what really made the Emergency Exit notable was the fact that that even though *all* of the band's members had once been fully invested participants in the earlier "Louie Louie" scene, they had individually been willing to move on and try new ways of making music.

And that was the crux of the situation facing most every local band— they could stagnate musically by playing "Louie Louie"–type music to a dwindling teen scene of dead-enders, or go with the progressive flow. The simple fact is, the Northwest's musical traditions were fraying with the passing of time, and those threads of R&B that had long been central to the "common stock" repertoire were fading. Soon, even the originators of the Northwest Sound were straying from their roots in an effort to stay current— for example, even the Wailers were feeling the strain of changing times. In March 1966, having sensed the seismic shifts in musical tastes that were occurring, Etiquette issued their new single, "It's You Alone," a waltz-time ballad with folky leanings that was a drastic departure from their usual sounds. The gentle and starkly arranged song not only bolted to No. 1 in Seattle and won a reissue deal with the big-time United Artists label, it also went Top 10 all down the coast, and charted in *Billboard* for four weeks. Too bad, I guess, that the band didn't have whole sets of such songs in their arsenal, because right after they performed a headlining gig at the Fillmore Auditorium in June (with Quicksilver opening), the hall's operator, Bill Graham, informed the Wailers that because they weren't *really* playing that town's preferred psychedelic music, "I don't know if we can have you back here"—and they never did!

The Frantics were also experiencing the discomfort of suddenly being considered old school. It was while booked into an extended engagement at the Peppermint Tree in San Francisco that the pain got to be unbearable: Here they were right in the middle of the hippest, most weed-worshipping and LSD-laced burg on planet Earth—a miserable band of short-haired, matching-suit-attired musicians stuck playing long hours of moldy oldies, show tunes, and Top 40 drivel to drunken tourists in a lousy titty bar. The poor Frantics had never had such cause to feel so downright *square* before. The final straw was when they got a chance to witness a couple psychedelic light show dances over at the Fillmore and Avalon ballrooms: Suddenly the idea of continuing to pound out "Louie Louie" seemed perfectly irrelevant. Nancy Claire was the first to bail out, followed by Chuck Schoning (who did resurface later as a *much* hairier keyboardist with Quicksilver); finally, Bob Hosko split for home. The only remaining Frantics, Jerry Miller and Don Stevenson, recruited new players—Bob Mosley (bass), guitarist Skip Spence (freshly booted as drummer from Jefferson Airplane), and Peter Lewis (guitar), and the group soon debuted as Moby Grape. The band were signed by Columbia, and their eponymous LP was simply amazing: *Rolling Stone* raved that it was no less than "a visionary concept of eclectic American music." With reviews like that—and the band's fine showing at the Monterey Pop Festival in June—*Moby Grape* sold a quick 200,000 copies and came to be regarded—along with *Sgt. Pepper, Surrealistic Pillow, Are You Experienced,* and *The Doors*—as one of the key albums in that Summer of Love.

Back in the Northwest, hippies were becoming increasing visible—and vocal—with their criticisms of mainstream popular culture, which included KJR and Pat O'Day. To be sure, it wasn't just those two entities who were proving to be anathema to the new scene—in fact, hippies naturally despised *all* Top 40 bubblegum boss jock DJs as ego-driven maniacs who pushed meaningless ear candy over the airwaves. Given O'Day's prominent role on the scene, he was an easy target for criticism. Seattle's first underground newspaper, the *Helix*, once published a piece by Tom Robbins which stated that "I used to think that O'Day and associates were a musical Mafia, but I've come to the conclusion that they aren't really dishonest—they're just dumb. When O'Day collapses into multiple orgasms over the City Zu (one of the lamest groups in the west), he probably really thinks the Zu is good. The man, like most DJs simply has no sense of aesthetics, no feeling for quality; he responds to music not in terms of profound sonar sensations that can tickle the innards and push back the wills of consciousness but only in terms of big-deal promo and dollars and cents."

Disgusted by O'Day (and the music he championed), one local hippie band, Fat Jack, even booked some gigs under the sarcastic name the City Puke—and another *Helix* staffer was quoted in *Seattle* magazine as saying that "our big complaint against KJR is that it exemplifies the whole disc jockey syndrome. Guys like O'Day have no awareness of the power of their own medium to influence culture. They just take plastic music produced on plastic discs and pump it out to the public."

The "new consciousness" demanded a more experimental listening experience than AM radio was providing, and thus arose an eclectic lefty nonprofit station, KRAB, and then KJR's long-standing competition—KOL-AM—saw an opening, and suddenly KOL-FM began broadcasting psychedelic album rock that was spun by the sort of hip, low-key DJs that a major mainstream AM station like KJR could never tolerate. Too, a growing number of kids had caught on to the fact that O'Day's Teen Fairs were really just a crassly commercialized forum for the hawking of teen-oriented corporate products that was staged around ritualistic—and unnecessarily *competitive*—band championship contests held in a cold concrete sports arena.

But finding a worthy alternative proved to be its own challenge. And anyone who even thought they might step forward to provide the kids a choice would, of course, still be facing all the red tape, rules, and teen-dance laws that O'Day or anyone else already was. But that didn't stop one nest of U District radicals from forming a "community services organization" called the Free University, which, as an "educational and charitable operation," would be able to throw concerts and hopefully skirt the in-city teen-dance restrictions. Renting the old Eagles Auditorium, the Free U succeeded in securing a city permit, and on January 14, 1967, more than six hundred happy people were immersed in the sounds of the Emergency Exit coupled with mind-boggling psychedelic light shows by two early local crews, the Union Light Co. and Lux Sit & Dance.

Inspired by that first blow against O'Day's monolithic empire, a number of other hip ad hoc organizations committed to finding new angles to finesse the long-standing anti-dance laws—such as producing "concerts" where dancing by minors was not, shall we say, effectively regulated. One of these organizations was a cooperative promotion firm called Trips-Lansing Inc.—which was comprised of members of the Emergency Exit, a few other musicians, and a couple of suits—and in announcing what they called a "Trips Festival," the Emergency Exit's Jim Walters sounded the clarion call to all freaks in a special essay in the *Seattle Times*: "TODAY, NOW, Sunday, March 19th is one of those proclaimed days of rest. And while The Establishment slumbers, the Now People will quietly climb out of their beds, creep out of their houses and congregate at the Eagles Auditorium for twelve solid hours. . . . They'll use the Sunday Silence to shout their message: Today is Sunday, March 19, 1967—Live it, feel it, participate in it—Now! While the mummies continue their permanent sleep, while the Establishment naps

1967 Seattle Trips Festival poster. (Courtesy Don Edge Collection.)

and the mausoleums are vacant, the Now People will have a Trips Festival. The Now People are using today . . . or any other day while they're alive to listen, experience and create."

And sure enough, on that day 6,000 "Now People" gathered to hear the Emergency Exit, the Daily Flash—plus the headliners the Seeds, from Los Angeles—and trip to a huge light show. This was all just too freaky for City Hall, however, and at 9:45 P.M.—and with a full house—the fire marshal (after having inspected the place *twice* earlier in the day and given his approval) showed up to issue a citation for violating city ordinances. And thus the pattern was set for the next couple seasons of cultural warfare. In the aftermath of the Trips Festival, the Free U submitted a permit application for another light-show "concert." This time, though, their application was stamped DENIED.

Then in early April the City Council's License Committee convened to consider an appeal filed by the Friends of the Free U—and that's where the government's angle was revealed. Rather than getting into the old dance-versus-concert debate, the police would assert that these "light dances" violated the city's 1929 ordinance outlawing "moonlight or shadow dances"—an old vaudeville-era entertainment mode where the shadowy silhouette of a naked woman is viewed by an audience as projected by backlighting upon a screen. Though perhaps visually interesting, that was clearly a different thing altogether than the hippie light shows of flashing and swirling colors, photographic images, film, smoke, and strobe lights, all synchronized to music by hand. The ever-helpful *Seattle Times* took the time to remind everyone that these light shows were a "simulated LSD trip experience"; police chief Frank Ramon advised the committee that "the light show has an avowed purpose, by reputation, of 'unhinging the mind,'" and that such shows were sponsored largely by outsiders: "A vanguard of . . . beatniks from the Berkeley–San Francisco area . . . is in Seattle and attempting to monopolize the presentation of these light shows at public dances for their profit."

But under threat of lawsuit by pro-dance agitators, the City Council finally saw the light, and on May 4 granted a permit to the Free U to throw "light dances." A "victory celebration light show/dance" ensued, featuring the Union Light Co. and performances by a few new bands: Crome Syrcus, Magic Fern, Blues Interchange, and Blues Feedback) performed. There was a great sense of joy in the air that the whole thing had been pulled off without any involvement by professional promoters, corporate advertising, or—*especially*—Pat O'Day. But any such wishes that KJR and O'Day would simply disappear were merely a pipe dream. In fact, the moment that light shows were finally deemed legal, Terry Bassett at Pat O'Day & Associates was on the phone suddenly wanting to work *with* the Union Light Co. One of their crew promptly informed the *Helix* as to how that interaction with O'Day's henchman went down. "Terry . . . let us know that he was a cool guy. He had been watching the whole light show thing and he knew it had to come to Seattle eventually. Of course most of the places they booked were filled every weekend [anyway] so it didn't pay to hire a good band even, let alone a light show, but they'd give us a try anyway to see if the kids dug it. And so we heard our name . . . broadcast on KJR—'Yes, kids, be there for a psychedelic show with Merrilee and the Turnabouts at the Target Ballroom in Burien.' The kids were not what you'd even call teenyboppers, couldn't dance, showed no visible response to the music, and were mystified by the light show. The boys, mostly drunk, rattled our scaffolding while the girls covered their eyes against the strobe and ran shrieking for the washroom. We had to straighten out our heads a little after that. We had experienced our first confrontation with commercial cooldom and the glittering money mind trap, and escaped only because it rejected us. We remembered that we wanted to do real shows for real people for real reasons."

But Pat O'Day & Associates had only *begun* to make their moves on the new scene. Next they hooked up with Trips-Lansing to cosponsor a second Trips Festival, on Memorial Day weekend. Only this time, instead of holding it at the hippies' Eagles hall, O'Day would herd his teenyboppers over to the arena via an ad blitz on KJR. The plan worked, and 10,000 kids attended a twelve-hour show featuring Don and the Goodtimes, the Emergency Exit, and Crome Syrcus, with headliners Jefferson Airplane, the Byrds, and the Electric Prunes—and a light show by Lux Sit & Dance.

Leaving aside the question of, "Just what in the hell were *Don and the Goodtimes* doing at a *psychedelic* Trips Festival?" there were plenty of other things that could be, and were, criticized about this show. One was the decidedly unhip, blaring corporate AM radio–style advertising KJR aired to promote it. Another, the *Helix* sniped, was the "outrageously priced" tickets, and yet another was that "throughout the day only a handful of persons dance. They're told to stop. Everyone else stands locked or seated." But the scorn went further, and one member of the Union Light Co. was later quoted in the *Helix* grumbling about how the "commercial promoters [who] yoked most of Seattle's creative community to the psychedelic bandwagon for their own profit was not where it's at. Recently we've gotten together with several rock and roll bands who have been through some of the same kinds of changes we have. We want to put on some dances, nice parties where people can come and do what they feel like doing. We want to just do it ourselves, without promoters or organizations or advertisements screaming it's a psychedelic happening the place to be there kids."

O'Day, however, was quite pleased to have made his first dollar off the hippie scene, and his mental gears were grinding out various scenarios by which he might weasel in on all the action that happened at the Eagles hall all through that Summer of Love. And that's about when Trips-Lansing

Counterculture concert king, Boyd Grafmyer, *Seattle Magazine*, February 1970.

Inc.'s festival coordinator, Boyd Grafmyre, broke off on his own and began promoting concerts there in the fall. But the big ex-military dude was *far* from being a laid-back hippie himself, and it rankled some folks when he played hardball with other potential entrepreneurs by striking an exclusive access deal with Jimmy DeCarro, the old-school boxing promoter who held the room's lease. But while some hippies were probably relieved that *somebody* had finally stepped up—and the long-haired Grafmyre was certainly no O'Day—they were also just plain tired of Seattle's draconian dance restrictions. The *Helix* would grouse that on the one night when Quicksilver and the Grateful Dead played—and Jerry Garcia encouraged the audience to "vote no on politics and dance"—Grafmyre told the band to ask the dancers to stop. Worse yet, when the band refused, he grabbed the mic and made the demand himself. Very uncool.

But it was the general consensus that paying Grafmyre for music was still vastly preferable to steering even one more red cent into O'Day's rich hands. And as the Eagles hall established itself as a haven for "new community," and Grafmyre brought hip bands (including Cream, Big Brother, the Doors, Fleetwood Mac, Jethro Tull, the MC5, Pink Floyd, and Steppenwolf) to town, it started to feel as if Pat O'Day and his evil empire had been successfully outmaneuvered once and for all. It seemed that the king had *finally* met his match in the form of Boyd Grafmyre.

CHAPTER 27

Guitar Freak-Out

The late 1960s was a time of accelerated cultural evolution, and by now even mainstream "Amerika" was being affected by all of this freaky countercultural stuff. Musicians everywhere were influenced by the developing fetishism for exotica: From psychedelic paisley apparel fashions to stoned noodling raga lead-guitar meditations—everything seemed to be changing at the speed of strobe lights. And so, here in the Northwest, while brand-new bands arose playing new music, even the remaining "old guard" bands of the once-grand "Louie Louie" teen scene were also showing that even they were not immune to the strong tidal pull of emerging trends.

Some of this activity was plain embarrassing—just consider what were surely the worst of all 250 different albums that the Ventures would ultimately record: *Guitar Freakout* and *Super Psychedelic*. Sheer dreck! Or ponder—but *please* never listen to—the Wailers' last recordings: bad faux-psychedelia "Bad Trip" and "You Can Fly." Similarly, the mighty Sonics also went out with a whimper, cutting a psychedelic folk rock mess called "Anyway the Wind Blows." One spin of that disc and we can guess why Bob Bennett opted to jump ship and go drum with Merrilee and the Turnabouts, why Gerry Roslie would up and storm out during a dance, permanently abandoning his PA system and effectively killing the group. Then there were the Viceroys, who—after completing a thirty-six-city *Where the Action Is* caravan tour along with the Raiders in April and May 1966—signed with Columbia, who promptly stuck them with a dreadful new name—the Surprise Package—and then made them revamp their last Bolo Records 45, "That Sound" as "Out of My Mind," replete with a mildly druggy production vibe.

The record-biz machine was doing Don and the Goodtimes and Paul Revere and the Raiders no better. Both bands used to rock out with

America's best but were now being systematically neutered. Nineteen sixty-seven saw the Goodtimes, which now had two new members—bassist Ron Overman (ex–Walla Walla's Gems) and singer Jeff Hawks (ex–Hawk & the Randelas)—scoring two national hits for Epic Records, "I Could Be So Good to You" and "Happy and Me"—and neither contained even one ounce of gritty Northwest rock *or* cutting-edge psychedelia. They were both just watered-down saccharine confections that earned the scorn of one critic, who nailed them (and their ilk) as purveyors of "personality rock." And that was a justifiable descriptor, too, for the current incarnation of the Raiders, whose sound had also begun to veer dangerously toward pure bubblegum. And while that approach might still sell records to teenyboppers, the old shtick was finally beginning to wear thin—even for the band members. It came as no surprise that in the spring of 1967 three key members—Jim Valley, Phil Volk, and Drake Levin—all exited. Rumors soon circulated that Revere's strict policy against marijuana smoking was one reason for this turnover—but fans never really knew. Decades later, the Raiders' tour mate, Brit singer Ian Whitcomb, sheepishly confessed to this writer that he'd once noted a smoky haze in a backstage dressing room and had actually gone and tattled to Revere.

Never pausing for a moment, Revere re-staffed his band with generic non-Northwest players, and suddenly the Raiders had neither their old ties to the Northwest Sound nor an "underground" hipness. It was now perfectly clear that they were, in fact, a corporate vehicle for selling dated pop rock. And even the new members were somewhat irritated that the band was scorned as mere teenybopper fodder by the new generation of powerful counterculture-oriented FM radio stations. Their angst over the matter reached such a point of desperation they even dumped their matching uniforms and, swallowing their pride, had their label publish large print advertisements that asked "How Do We Get an Audition With the Underground?" The group also made the quixotic plea for "all underground stations to take another look at the Raiders. No more funny costumes. And listen to their music."

But it was all too little, too late. The Raiders had already enjoyed their day in sun, and there was really *no* chance that the hippies would ever bother with their music. *If*, that is, those mean hippie DJs knew it was the Raiders music—or at least that was what the Raiders had convinced themselves. So, the band hatched a sneaky plan: What if they recorded some new material and got a friendly label rep to slip copies to various stations (along with a whispered tip that the mysterious new band—Pink Puzz—

was holed up in rehearsals and hadn't even played live yet)? What if those stations got intrigued by the tall tale and aired the record? Wouldn't that prove to the world that the Raiders' music was still cool and that it had been industry prejudices that had been holding them back?

Funny thing is . . . the scheme worked. And when a station or two began gushing over Pink Puzz and their hot new record, the Raiders felt vindicated and sprang their trap by announcing to the world what they'd just done. The victory was a minor one, however, because the burned stations dropped their support, and the Raiders' eventual *Alias: Pink Puzz* album yielded but one measly Top 20 AM radio hit, "Let Me!" But that was enough to keep the group touring—and it was for the fall '67 tour that they hired Merrilee Rush as an opening act, a move that led to her scoring her first national hit.

When the tour rolled into Memphis, the Raiders were scheduled to do some recordings, and somehow Rush ended up in a studio too. Given a new tune called "Angel of the Morning," Rush had a winner on her hands. Within months she was enjoying a smash No. 7 hit—one pushed along by Pat O'Day at KJR, who had finally heard a Rush record he liked. From there, Rush scored additional radio hits and bookings on big-time TV shows, including *American Bandstand, The Tonight Show with Johnny Carson,* and *Midnite Special.*

For his part, Paul Revere took additional steps to modernize the band's image: For a while they were booked as "the Raiders with Mark Lindsay," and then just as "the Raiders." But no matter—by this point, the world of showbiz had more to offer them than the rock 'n' roll realm, and Revere and Lindsay moved on from three seasons on the No. 1 daytime show *Where the Action Is* and popped up as cohosts of ABC-TV's prime-time musical variety show *Happening '68.* That show was great for publicity, but with its old-fashioned format and mainstream sensibilities, it basically served as the final nail in the coffin of their hopes for staying relevant.

Standing in stark contrast to that conservative approach were the changes that their protégés Don and the Goodtimes had embraced. Now called Touch, the band had reemerged in 1968 with an entirely new sound and image. And their sole album (whose L.A. sessions Jimi Hendrix visited and offered to help produce)—while hardly a commercial hit—would in time be praised as "perhaps the best of the early American progressive rock efforts." That same year also saw the Kingsmen finally abdicate their throne when Lynn Easton opted to host the *This Is It* teen-dance show on Portland's KGW-TV, and the other members skittered off to other gigs.

Meanwhile, new groups had cut some decent psychedelic records in the Northwest, including those by PH Phactor Jug Band, Magic Fern, Brave New World (whose masterwork, "It's Tomorrow," Jerry Dennon licensed up to Epic Records), and Locomotive (who recorded an LP of tunes like "Don't Cut Your Hair" for MGM); there was also the Natural Gas Co.'s "Hash Hish," the Phantoms' "Hallucinogenic Odyssey," and Zero End's song about copping a "Lid To Go."

At the same time, a number of veteran bands opted to update their old "straight" images by changing their names, growing their hair, and trading their Beatle boots and peg-leg pants for flower-power bell-bottoms and sandals. Along that stony path, the Bootmen became Cottonmouth, the Agents became the Crystal Sect, the Soul Searchers became Passion Flower Hotel, Phaze Six became the Sunday Morning Daze, Spectrum became the Electric Potato Chips, the Weeds became the Lollipop Shoppe, the Bards became Moses Lake (with their *insanely* psychedelic epic 45 "Oobleck"), and Tiny Tony and the Statics became International Brick (with their "You Should Be So High" / "Flower Children" 45).

And lastly, there was the supremely sad case of that long-lost Kingsman, Jack Ely, who'd finally reemerged, this time strung-out on heroin, in a bearded, shaggy-haired, and love bead–bedecked hippie band that boasted what was perhaps the most hopelessly unmarketable name of all time: Phleobus Union. Even sorrier was the fact that the 1960s drug scourge had also taken its toll on plenty of other Northwest musicians, with some of the finest players on the scene—including Dave Lewis, Larry Coryell, Rich Dangel, Mark Doubleday, and Joe Johansen—later admitting to having succumbed to the temptations of heroin before wising up and refocusing on their music.

CHAPTER 28

Sky River Rock

N ineteen sixty-seven's Summer of Love gave way to 1968's Days of Rage. The face of the Northwest's music scene had also been altered dramatically—to the extent that important cornerstones of the old scene didn't even exist anymore. Both of Seattle's best-loved teen-dance venues—the Spanish Castle Ballroom and Parker's Ballroom—had changed beyond recognition. The former was bulldozed in April 1968 after its owners tried to weather a couple of car wrecks out front on Highway 99 (in which teenage customers were killed) but eventually lost their spirit. The same year saw Parker's recast as a hippie joint, the Aquarius Tavern. Finally, another sign of the times was a last-ditch attempt by Pat O'Day to hang on by rebranding his Teen Fairs as Teenage Spectaculars.

Meanwhile, members of the "new community" felt proud that with the success of the Eagles shows: They had created what seemed like a viable alternative to O'Day's approach. But they also had some issues with Boyd Grafmyre. The *Helix* began publishing various disparaging reports—some true (like their claim that he'd announced raises in ticket prices), and others less so (that he'd pronounced smoking dope and "making out" to be forbidden activities). Those reports sparked an instantaneous response from a group of excitable high-schoolers, who formed the Eagles Liberation Front (ELF). The ELF announced a boycott of the Eagles shows, began to picket, and handed out their printed manifesto: "Rock music began in the alternative community, our community. Rock expresses the ethos of our community; its force is filled by our struggle. But over the years, the established entertainment industry—promoters, agents, record companies, media, and every name group—have gradually transformed our music into an increasingly expensive commodity. They have stolen our music. We are taking it back. This struggle will not end until Eagles and music have been completely returned to the community. This struggle will continue until the culture vultures who prey on our community have been eliminated."

The boycott had its desired effect, as Grafmyre was reportedly forced to humanize his operation: Staff got raises, fire improvements were made to the hall, shows were lengthened by a half hour, and those new admission prices were lowered from $3 down to $2.50. The Eagles hall remained the locus of great shows, including the "homecoming" concert by the Frantics' Jerry Miller and Don Stevenson and their new band, Moby Grape. Opening the show would be Crome Syrcus—a Seattle band that had formed back in 1966. At the time, Moby Grape were slated to compose music for the Joffrey Ballet's new piece, *Astarte*—but as it happened, Moby Grape backed out of the deal, and when Robert Joffrey happened to hear Crome Syrcus that night, he hired them instead for the ballet gig. *Astarte* made its stage debut at the Seattle Opera House in July 1968, and from there went on tour nationally. Eventually Crome Syrcus attracted a recording deal with a subsidiary label of ABC Records, which resulted in a unique album of dirgy aural collages like "Never Come Down" and "Crystals," and the seventeen-minute grand opus title track, "Love Cycle."

Crome Syrcus went on to play some great gigs, including shows with the Doors at the Eagles hall and New York's Fillmore East. They also played San Francisco's Avalon Ballroom with Pink Floyd, and gigged at the Eagles hall and the Fillmore West with such bands as Big Brother, Iron Butterfly, Vanilla Fudge, Canned Heat, the Strawberry Alarm Clock, and the Velvet Underground. But the most interesting gig Crome Syrcus did in that summer of '68 was at the first event to be billed as a "rock festival"—and this was fully a year *prior* to Woodstock.

On August 30, the Sky River Lighter Than Air Fair opened on a large raspberry farm located near the tiny old Skykomish River mining town of Sultan, just fifty miles north of Seattle. For a $10 admission charge, 15,000 attendees would get three glorious days of rain, mud, and music. Over forty acts performed—including Country Joe, Blues Image, Santana, the Youngbloods, the Flying Burrito Brothers, Muddy Waters, and the Grateful Dead. In addition to Crome Syrcus, a number of other Northwest bands (including Juggernaut, Easy Chair, and the Floating Bridge) also climbed the festival's stage. It was the *Helix* which noted that the last band featured the Frantics' Joe Johansen and the Wailers' Rich Dangel, who had paid their dues by having "done time on the O'Day circuit."

But it was at Sky River that the Floating Bridge were discovered by a talent scout from Los Angeles–based Vault Records. The band cut their sole

LP in California before settling into a regular gig at a Ballard neighborhood bar called Mr. P's—a far cry from the Eagles hall scene. Dismayed with their situation, the band whined to the *Helix* about how "drunks kept coming over and asking for 'Louie Louie.'" No doubt feeling a *serious* been-there-done-that sensation, Dangel moved on to another band, Sledgehammer, and the Floating Bridge replaced him with Denny McCleod, who elaborated to *Seattle* magazine about the group's disdain for the liquor-club scene: "Nothing I hate worse," sneered McCleod, "than those downtown air-conditioned cocktail lounges here. There's *no* atmosphere. The people are too hostile. We're an *underground* group. Our music is for people who want to be involved in it. . . ."

And there was no shortage of just such people. They had made the Sky River rock festival a success—and by the next spring they were looking forward to doing the same with the third annual Volunteer Park *Be-In* that was scheduled for April 13, 1969. But when six thousand peaceful young people swamped the park—*and* the upper-crust neighborhoods surrounding it— Seattle's reactionary new mayor, Floyd Miller, used the claim that he'd received a complaint petition with two hundred signatures to announce a clampdown on music making in the city's parks. When Miller made his capricious proclamation, the town's radical activists were naturally outraged, and the *Helix* lashed back in a scathing editorial: "The uptight honky park superintendent has officially banned all electronic amplification from all city parks indefinitely. The people's music has been turned off by the trembling hand of geriatrics ward-escapee, Mayor Floyd. No public hearings were held and none is planned. All 'authorized gatherings' will be under heavy surveillance by the police. 'All violations of the law will be prosecuted.' MUSIC BELONGS IN THE PARKS AND THE PARKS BELONG TO THE PEOPLE. Floyd Miller will melt under the sun of the people."

While everyone waited for the clouds to part and for the evil mayor to melt away like the Wizard of Oz's Wicked Witch of the West, Boyd Grafmyre announced his biggest feat yet, one that would have nothing to do with any park in town, but rather would bring a strong lineup of talent to a park just *outside* of Seattle, in the tiny town of Woodinville. The Seattle Pop Festival— held on July 25–27, 1969—featured stellar groups, including Led Zeppelin, the Doors, Santana, Delaney & Bonnie (with Eric Clapton), Ten Years After, the Byrds, the Flying Burrito Brothers (with Gram Parsons), the Youngbloods, Spirit, Ike and Tina Turner, and Chuck Berry, among others.

By most accounts, the three-day event had been a raging success—and probably Grafmyre's finest hour as a businessman—but when rumors began swirling that he'd taken in a personal profit of $125,000, hippies began grumbling. Still, what was the *alternative* to Grafmyre—Pat O'Day's teeny-bopper machine? Nobody seemed very happy with the situation. Although in time *Seattle* magazine would quote a Musicians Union Local 76 official as saying, "We had a lot of problems with O'Day a couple years ago; at one time he had a booking agent under his thumb, and he also got local groups to work at minimums by promising them promotion on KJR. But these days he's cleaned up his operation pretty well." But that latter assertion of progress was undermined in the same magazine when a member of Crome Syrcus scoffed, saying, "Maybe so, but the word is still out around here that if you don't work for O'Day, you don't work."

Meanwhile, news began breaking out that O'Day's karma might finally be catching up with him, when the *Helix* reported that "competing rock enterprises are having a tough time making it against O'Day's constant KJR plugging and against his organization's policy of keeping some of the better-known bands from working for anybody else in the area, in competition to his places. A local attorney is preparing to file papers in federal court against O'Day this week, in an attempt by some of the hurt competitors to get the Federal Communications Commission to clip his wings."

So Seattle's hippies weren't the only ones who despised O'Day, and, in fact, he was also earning the enmity of people in some most curious places around town. As the mainstream media began covering the story, a tidy narrative line took shape—that the Sherman Act antitrust legal action had been initiated by two moonlighting members of the Seattle Police Department (along with a real estate agent) who (back in April 1967) had decided to open a teen club, the Galaxie, in the Seattle suburb of Bellevue. Those parties had apparently been frustrated to discover that all of the area's top bands were already contractually bound by O'Day, who had monopolized their schedules with advance bookings via his control of a large number of dancehalls (including Bellevue's popular Lake Hills Roller Rink)—and thus came to the conclusion that independent dancehalls and other booking agents were being forced out of business by the wealthy DJ's hegemony.

Much of that was obviously true—and most of the bands that did cooperate with O'Day were damn glad to know how much work they could expect to have in the coming season. But there were, as ever, the disgruntled bands whom O'Day didn't favor, and it is conceivable that his long-standing dominance of the region's teen-dance circuit had placed potential competitors in dire straits. But the long and short of this legal action was that a $300,000 lawsuit (plus an additional figure of three times that for damages) was filed against O'Day with—as he put it in his memoir—a "laundry list of charges, including conspiracy to eliminate competition, coercion, restraint of trade, bribery and, to top it off, payola—a charge which by extension implicated KJR."

O'Day should have seen this trouble coming, because he already knew his accusers: One of the cops had actually worked as a security guard at his dances—and that's presumably where the pair's visions of riches had begun. But after leasing an old bowling alley—and then spending a fortune redecorating it as the Galaxie—the would-be dance promoters suddenly discovered that the best bands were unavailable, their dances were failing, and their financial losses were piling up. According to O'Day, the businessmen asked for a meeting, and he listened to them describe their predicament. But business is business, and the bands he'd already booked for his dance circuit were, well, *booked*. But that's when, O'Day wrote, "they opened a briefcase and produced a cashier's check made out to me personally in the amount of $10,000. . . . The money was all mine if I immediately dumped Lake Hills Roller Rink and moved my Bellevue dances to their building, where they would make us 50/50 partners." O'Day declined and wished the entrepreneurs well, but, as he later wrote: "Sometime after the lawsuit began, it occurred to me that my accusers likely were *already* planning legal action against me when they made their visit, and that the money they offered me was a clumsy attempt at entrapment."

What O'Day initially didn't know is that the guys who had sued him had a few "silent partners" in their scheme—local musicians who were, for varying reasons, disgruntled with O'Day and his empire. Far from being unhappy that his band had been ignored by O'Day, one conspirator was actually a player who had perhaps received the most work of any act on the circuit. Frustrated nevertheless with the whole system, Neil Rush played a significant role in trying to break up O'Day's stranglehold on the scene. As leader of Merrilee and the Turnabouts, he'd been contacted by the cops and invited to meet up and talk about gig opportunities at their new venue. As it happened, that meeting occurred during a highly improper joyride in a brand-new Seattle Police Department helicopter—and the two parties came to an agreement that they would set up O'Day by staging a scenario in which the Turnabouts would claim to want to play the Galaxie but be unable to due to their exclusive bookings with O'Day. And such claims were what the case hinged upon.

Regardless, O'Day moved to settle the case out of court for $55,000 in an effort to avoid a lengthy trial and hundreds of thousands in legal fees.

Nice try—but too late. By now the FCC had taken an interest in him. And then the FBI sent over investigators, who also grilled O'Day. All of this led to over a monthlong period of daily hearings at Seattle's old Federal Office Building, where scores of potential witnesses were subpoenaed to appear— including Paul Revere and Merrilee Rush (who truthfully testified that she personally liked O'Day and even exchanged Christmas gifts with him every year). The FCC's case finally closed with no charges made, and a final report that admitted they'd found "no evidence of any wrongdoing on the part of KJR or its manager, Pat O'Day." Still, O'Day did incur nearly a quarter million dollars in legal fees and other settlement costs.

But for O'Day, the biggest cost of the whole imbroglio was that he finally lost interest in conducting the teen-dance biz. By late '68, the thrill was gone, and O'Day sold off the business to a couple of his employees, Willie Leopold and Danny Fiala, who continued working it for the next several years under the name Seattle Mercer. But while members of the counterculture community must have been overjoyed at seeing O'Day finally being brought down a notch or two, there were still more surprises in store. Rumors broke out that Grafmyre had actually been working in cahoots with his supposed nemesis—that he'd launched Seattle's biggest "alternative" hall with money he'd solicited from none other than Pat O'Day. And if *that* were true, then the entire pretext of those two businessmen working in opposition to each other was a sham—a setup on the level of some professional wrestling match.

As things turned out, what had in fact seemed "too good to be true"— that Boyd Grafmyre's hippie haven over at the Eagles hall had been a righteous finger in the eye of O'Day's corporate ogre—was, well, a lie. O'Day had, it seems, bankrolled the entire thing from behind the scenes, and in his memoir he noted that the whole scam came about because of Pat O'Day *&* Associates' concerns that "music tastes were changing, and so was [the] audience." As attendance levels declined at his teenybopper dances in seemingly direct proportion to their increase at the Eagles events, evil wheels began turning in his brain. "There was a funny and kind of sinister side to our Seattle operation that was buffering us from losses during the transition." And O'Day's Machiavellian glee shone through when he recalled the ruse's context: "See, *I* was the commercial monster. Everything *I* did was considered very, very bad, but anything that happened at the Eagles Auditorium with Boyd Grafmyre was good. And Boyd was considered at that time to be a pleasant relief from me. The thing that I *enjoyed* (and that made me giggle)—and I'm sure [*Helix* editor] Paul Dorpat and [*Helix* writer] Tom Robbins and the rest would have had a heart attack if they'd known at that time—was that the Eagles was *my* business. Boyd Grafmyre was just the guy out there in front. And it was a new image. It was a new thing. We changed our *marketing* procedures."

Stung by this revelation, one of Grafmyre's disillusioned Eagles hall employees pointed out the blatant hypocrisy of the situation to *Seattle* magazine, saying, "[Here] we were passing out 'Pat O'Day is a Shuck' bumper stickers in front of the Eagles, when he practically owned the place." That same February 1970 article went on to add that "O'Day was unconcerned about the bumper stickers, but he was worried about the money the Eagles was losing. 'I dropped about $8,000 and then got out,' says O'Day." It was certainly true that the Eagles operation—a murky mix of Grafmyre's and Pat O'Day's interests—*was* having some financial troubles. The *Seattle P-I* noted that O'Day "got out of the acid-rock business for reasons that included the less-than-strict subculture's accounting work" and "that as a very public figure, he didn't want his name linked to a business in which people got paid in cash and tax forms weren't always submitted."

In fact, Grafmyre blamed O'Day's new company, Concerts West—which, with blue-chip clients like Jimi Hendrix, Led Zeppelin, Paul McCartney & Wings, and the Eagles, would go on to become one of the world's top concert production firms over the next years—for circling like a ravenous vulture right at the moment when he was most vulnerable. "I was going through a divorce, my bank account was frozen, and I suddenly couldn't afford to put deposits down to get bands," Grafmyre sighed. "It's a small community and they must have gotten wind of that—and that's when Concerts West stepped in. I became displeased with Pat because when I had personal issues, they came in and, in a sense, sabotaged me."

And so it was on the threshold of the 1970s that O'Day was—for the first time in over a decade—totally out of the Northwest's teen-dance picture. And while much of the void that his absence created would be filled up by Seattle Mercer—and a new strata of talent agencies that arose—the fact is, the scene had simply grown bigger than anything one man could fully control. O'Day's empire was destined to fall. But it's just as true that without one powerful man running everything like a well-oiled machine, some of the music scene's momentum was lost—and it would take a very long time for it to ever reach the simmering state that it had during the best days of the Pat O'Day era.

CHAPTER 29

Takin' Care of Business

As the 1970s dawned, the Pacific Northwest's music scene was in disarray—a state that also made it wide open to all comers who wanted to grab a piece of the action. Now that the longtime king-pin of the area's rock 'n' roll biz, Pat O'Day, had finally been dethroned, change and opportunity were seemingly *everywhere*. New record labels, new radio stations, new recording studios, and new talent agencies all emerged—and many of those were founded or staffed by former musicians who had come up through, and learned a lot from, the now-bygone Pat O'Day Era.

Although the Seattle Mercer company—which had arisen from the ashes of the Pat O'Day & Associates company—would have a head start in the effort to consolidate what they could of the old teen-dance circuit, times had truly changed, and with the aging of the baby-boom crowd, there was soon a great upsurge in the demand for rock bands to play in taverns and liquor bars rather than high school gyms, teen clubs, armories, and roller rinks. A whole new batch of booking agents and talent agencies—including Garrett Enterprises, Far West Entertainment, the Jack Belmont Agency, the Unicam Booking Agency, GEC, and William Stephan & Associates—formed to get in on this newly emerging tavern and nightclub scene. And just as that shift from weekly teen dances to the world of taverns represented sig-nificant changes in the structure of the local music biz, so too did it have a profound effect on the music itself. Under the "talent management" system that was developing, traits such as allegiance to Top 40 playlists—rather than musical creativity—would become highly valued by risk-averse tavern owners. And *that* factor alone would prove to have its own deleterious effect on the types of music that were rewarded.

In fact, that is how a place that now had more live music than ever soon saw its once-distinctive regional musical identity utterly lost. Instead of exhibiting a shared musical tradition, many new bands began manifesting a rootless sound that mirrored the splintering of the times. As in other regions of the nation, the Northwest scene soon became based around hyphenated-rock subgenres like country-rock (Lance Romance, the Skyboys, Rose and the Dirt Boys, the Cement City Cowboys, the Wasted Rangers), funk and disco (Cold, Bold and Together; Acapulco Gold; Seattle Pure Dynamite; Cookin' Bag; Robbie Hills' Family Affair; the Northwest Funk Factory; Onyx; Epicentre), jazz-rock (Crosswinds, Jeff Lorber Fusion), progressive pop (Providence, Gabriel, Bighorn, Sand), blues (Brian Butler Band, Isaac Scott Blues Band), and even Jesus-freak bands (the Last Call of Shiloh, Wilson-McKinley, the Sunpower Band).

But while a case could be made for the validity of most of those categories, there was at least one other that is difficult to find much merit in—and that was the creeping plague of nostalgia being wallowed in by a slew of 1950s revivalist bands. Rather than contribute something new to music—or even honor *local* traditions—numerous area bands realized that they could find regular employment by milking the golden oldies of days gone by. Which was how the taverns became glutted with such slicked-back-hair and black-leather-clad acts as Seattle-Tacoma's Johnny Saturn and his Lightning Fast Electricks, Cheeseburger Deluxe, Kid Chrysler and the Cruisers, Spike and the Continentals, and the Rock and Roll Allstars; Eugene's Happy Daze; Tacoma's Great Pretenders; and Port Angeles's Louie and the Rockets.

Of all the bands who were transfixed by gazing into the musical rearview mirror, only one—Jr. Cadillac—had a unique approach. Formed in 1970 by former members of the Frantics, the Wailers, and the Mark V, this band would become the area's archetypal "tavern band" by driving people to the dance floors with renditions of old rock favorites spiced up with tons of Northwest classics ranging from "Tall Cool One" to "There Is Something on Your Mind"—and of course, "Louie Louie." But even though the members of Jr. Cadillac made excellent incomes for over twenty years, they also serve as a fine example of the challenges faced by all Northwest bands of the era. And that's because even though they were scene veterans who were quite prolific in composing songs, reasonably skilled in recording studios, and the owners of their own label (the Great Northwest Music Company), they still couldn't scare up much interest from the local radio industry in their many records.

Because the nation's radio biz had also faced great changes—namely, rapid corporate consolidation that resulted in constricted playlists enforced by out-of-touch absentee owners running the show. Thus few stations had any incentive to care about hometown acts or their records, and abandoned local music altogether. AM stations largely stuck with their Top 40 formats, while the new FM stations—like both of Seattle's powerhouses, KZOK and KISW—quickly adopted narrow programming ruts that saw them stubbornly championing imported hard rock bands such as Led Zeppelin, Ten Years After, Foghat, and Bad Company, rather than supporting the best local bands.

Things had come full circle, back to the pre-Dolton days when all the disparate elements within a music scene fail to see the upside of synergistic cooperation. Another key problem locally was that by about 1969 *all* of the record labels that had originally helped to bring attention to the Northwest scene were extinct.

While new local labels were being formed, none of them had any clout, so Northwest musicians once again faced the same predicament as the region's first stars had decades prior—that of being at the mercy of outside companies. And that is why, even though the region harbored hundreds more bands than ever before, few of these groups would be lucky enough to score deals. In the 1970s, among the Northwest bands who did wrangle contracts were American Eagle (Decca Records), Ballin' Jack (CBS & Mercury), Bighorn (CBS), Calliope (Buddah), Fat (RCA), Fragile Lime (Warner Brothers), Gabriel (ABC), Kid Blast (Claridge), Magi (Claridge), Providence (London), Sand (MGM), Striker (Arista), TKO (Infinity), Johnny and the Distractions (A&M), and Kidd Afrika (Windham Hill). But few of those bands garnered much media attention—and only Ballin' Jack, with their 1971 Hot 100 tune, "Super Highway," scored a notable hit.

In fairness to these and other bands of the era, it should be pointed out that even though there were many more recording studios operating in the 1970s than ever before, most of the old two- and three-track hit-making studios were now defunct. The one exception was Kearney Barton's Audio Recording—and although Barton stayed busy (partly by running a recording school), the plain fact is that his old-fashioned techniques and sounds had fallen into disfavor.

The Seattle studio that came to dominate the era was the new Kaye-Smith Studios at 2212 Fourth Avenue, founded in 1972 by KJR and

KISW-FM's owners, Lester Smith and the Hollywood actor Danny Kaye, respectively—who also just happened to be O'Day's partners in Concerts West. Initially envisioned as a place to cut radio ad jingles for its owner's stations, Kaye-Smith soon gained recognition as the town's finest audio production facility, and local bands began eyeballing it. Unfortunately, Kaye-Smith's steep hourly rate was such that it prohibited most striving local bands from working there. And so the studio initially got attention for the sessions held there by outside artists who already had big-time corporate support. In fact, the first actual radio hit cut there was Bachman-Turner Overdrive's 1974 tune, "Takin' Care Of Business," but other established stars recorded there, including Tower of Power, the Spinners, Elton John, and the Steve Miller Band.

The recording biz was, of course, just one facet of the music scene in the early 1970s. A far more visible issue was the series of huge outdoor fests that were produced locally in the wake of the trailblazing 1968 Sky River rock festival and 1969 Seattle Pop Festival. These events ranged from the Sunshine Freedom Festival, to the Sunrise to Sunset Rock Festival, to Vancouver, B.C.'s Strawberry Mountain Fair, to Oregon's Banana Fest, Vortex 1, and Bullfrog Festival.

Attendees of these gatherings of countercultural tribes loved the rock festivals for providing a momentary respite from the turbulent times, a chance to experience a utopian glimmer of what might be possible in a more peaceful future, and a here-and-now chance to share food, drugs, free love, and music (performed by local as well as nationally prominent bands) with their fellow freaks. Conversely, the Establishment media was unrelenting in its negative coverage, and various city, county, and state politicians quickly proceeded to enact numerous restrictive laws designed to halt any further such events. In response, the ever-resourceful hippies concocted many different sorts of ploys to attempt to sidestep those new rules. One of the cleverest of their tactics was the formation of a series of new front organizations: the Buffalos and Dinosaurs

The former was the name bestowed by its founders on a new political organization, the Buffalo Party, which they figured would have constitutional protection under the First Amendment. The idea was to hold annual "conventions," just like the Republican and Democratic parties do—only instead of renting a big hotel ballroom, this new party would have its event in open fields, with entertainment provided by rock bands. For a while, this ploy worked—thus inspiring the founding of another group, the Dinosaur Club, which had its origins in the tiny rural town of Roy, Washington.

That's where a particularly nasty local sheriff had been making a crusade out of harassing every long-haired patron who exited a hippie tavern called Judge Roy Bean's. In order to escape this persecution, the Dinosaurs were founded in May 1972, and they proceeded to plan for their own organizational meeting—one that would also be held outdoors and feature rock bands and plenty of unbridled Dionysian revelry. But when county officials attempted to intervene and halt the event, a bright fellow named Ken Kinnear stepped up and filed a lawsuit against the government—a legal offensive that was later upheld in the courts. So the Buffalo Party and the Dinosaurs both managed to keep the rock festival form alive for a while, but in the end—sometime after the *fourth* Sky River festival in '72—the weight of new laws, liability insurance issues, and continuous negative media coverage became too great, and the Sky River blowout proved to be the last major noncorporate festival for decades.

Kinnear, however, had only just begun to have an effect on the fortunes of Northwest rock. He next surfaced as the Seattle-based promo man for the biggest band to emerge from the region in years: Vancouver, B.C.'s Bachman-Turner Overdrive. It was while working with BTO that Kinnear really figured out how the biz worked—and also spotted a promising Seattle group who was then working in Canada, a band that would become the most successful Northwest one of their generation—Heart. The group traced its origins back to 1967, when Roger Fisher (guitar) and Steve Fossen (bass) formed the Army, which they renamed Whiteheart in '68. The following year, the band added a latter-day member of the Turnabouts and became Carl Wilson and Heart. They broke up, and Fisher and Fossen began auditioning new members, including a singer named Ann Wilson, whom they had met at a gig down at Bellevue's Lake Hills Roller Rink. Wilson had been inspired by dances featuring Merrilee Rush and the Turnabouts. She'd formed the Viewpoints with her guitarist sister, Nancy, before moving on to the Daybreaks, a band that cut a pair of acid-folk 45s for the old Topaz label that Kearney Barton now owned.

By 1971 the group were named Hocus Pocus and had fully integrated Wilson's powerful voice into their hard rock sound. Under the moniker Heart, they fled northward to Vancouver, seeking haven from the Vietnam draft. Then, around 1974, Heart added sister Nancy and the band really began to forge a great sound. It was while honing their act in a Vancouver nightclub that the group caught the ear of Mike Flicker, the A&R head at Canada's tiny Mushroom Records; recording sessions soon began at Vancouver's new (and first) sixteen-track studio, Can-Base. When a couple of local studio players—Howard Leese (guitar) and Mike Derosier (drums)—were brought in to help, they clicked, the band's lineup was revamped again, and Heart was on its way to establishing itself as the hottest act on the Vancouver-Seattle-Portland tavern circuit.

Their debut single, "How Deep It Goes," was issued in the fall of 1975 to no great response from radio. Undaunted, Heart carried on (with the help of Kinnear's new management firm, Albatross Productions), snagging a few helpful gigs like opening for Jefferson Starship, Rod Stewart, and Supertramp—and then opportunity really knocked. When Supertramp suddenly had to cancel their March '76 Portland appearance, Heart was given the opportunity to headline their first big-time concert. Meanwhile, their debut LP, *Dreamboat Annie*, was issued in Vancouver (and then in the Seattle and Portland markets), and the hard-rockin' single "Crazy On You" exploded, first as a regional hit, catching fire throughout the rest of the country and then the world. By April it had hit the *Billboard* chart's Top 40, and was soon followed by "Magic Man" and "Dreamboat Annie." And just like that, Heart was in the big leagues, touring the globe with other hard-rock and heavy metal groups, including Led Zeppelin, Nazareth, April Wine, and ZZ Top.

Soon word began spreading that San Francisco's Steve Miller Band was holed up at Kaye-Smith Studios and the sessions were producing some outstanding material. In December 1976 KZOK and KISW began airing the new single "Fly Like an Eagle"—a record that blazed its way to the *Billboard* chart's No. 2 slot. The excitement in Seattle was palpable—with BTO, Heart, and now Steve Miller all scoring with recordings cut at Kaye-Smith, perhaps the Northwest had finally emerged from its lean years. In January 1977, *Seattle P-I* music critic George Arthur was as giddy as anybody, writing an essay titled "1976: A Very Good Year for the Local Rock Scene," which stated in part that as the year "ended, the hope or fear that Seattle was about to go 'big league' in the music biz was in the air. Long a favorite 'test market' for labels and national promoters, Seattle's music may soon catch their attention."

Ah, but if *only* that vision could have been true! Instead—except for those lucky few bands with big recording budgets working at Kaye-Smith—the long slog toward reestablishing the Northwest as an exciting music center would continue. For the time being, Heart was the *only* local band making any news. In May 1977, "Barracuda" hit and was followed by a string of hits like "Kick It Out," "Heartless," "Straight On," and "Even It Up," and classic LPs, including 1977's *Little Queen* (which was recorded at Kaye-

NANCY WILSON   ANN WILSON   STEVE FOSSEN

HOWARD LEESE   MICHAEL DEROSIER

Smith Studios), 1978's *Magazine*—an album that included tunes that had been recorded live at Seattle's Aquarius Tavern (formerly the old Parker's Ballroom)—and *Dog and Butterfly* (which was recorded and mixed at Seattle's new studio, Sea-West). Meanwhile, *Dreamboat Annie* reached the six-million-unit sales point. *So* successful was the band that in 1991 they were—in partnership with a former KING radio personality, Steve Lawson—able to acquire Kaye-Smith's former facilities and revamp the place into their own world-class recording studio, Bad Animals.

By now, Northwest's tavern rock scene was quite active, and a handful of bands—including Jr. Cadillac, Annie Rose and the Thrillers, and the Dynamic Logs—worked hard to make a living playing the area's best rooms like Seattle's Aquarius, G-Note Tavern, and Rainbow Tavern; Bellingham's Dos Padres; Olympia's Captain Coyote's; Spokane's Washboard Willies; and Portland's Springers, Last Hurrah, Earth, and Euphoria. But getting record deals just wasn't in the cards for these groups. In fact, only two bands on that circuit would ever manage to break out of it and go on to wider success and big-time hits: Seafood Mama, and the Robert Cray Band. Portland's regrettably named Seafood Mama featured a female singer/saxophonist named Rindy Ross and a polished smooth pop sound. After working the tavern circuit for a couple years, the band independently released their "Harden My Heart" 45 and were discovered by the Los Angeles music industry mogul David Geffen and signed to his new Geffen Records in 1981. Fortunately, the band changed their name—to Quarterflash—and went on to score a few national hits, including "Harden My Heart" (No. 3), and the Top 20 winner "Find Another Fool."

Meanwhile, Tacoma's black blues guitarist Robert Cray was coming up on the same circuit—and his career arc was to be an amazing one. Cray would eventually release some fine albums—especially 1986's Grammy Award–winning *Strong Persuader*, which contained the huge MTV hit "Smoking Gun" and became the biggest-selling blues album by anyone in years. In fact, Cray would soon be established as perhaps the finest young bluesman of his generation, a man who would be credited by a critic as the person who "more than any other individual was responsible for the revival of guitar-based blues that began in the 1980s."

But Cray's journey began humbly enough in a couple nearly forgotten local bands, Steakface and Foghorn Leghorn, before he formed the Robert Cray Band in 1974. It was while gigging in Eugene that the largely unknown player got his first big break. A Hollywood film crew was in town to shoot an upcoming feature to be called *Animal House*, and one of that film's stars, the actor/comedian John Belushi, saw the band play and dug their sound. Cray ended up appearing in the 1978 movie as a player a fictitious frat-party band, Otis Day and the Knights. And so began his journey to the world's stage. But *Animal House* also had another tie to the ongoing saga of Northwest music—it was the movie that revived the song "Louie Louie." No one who has ever seen Belushi and his fellow frat-rat toga party characters slobbering their soused way through the song will likely ever forget it. The massive popularity of *Animal House* (not to mention the Who's 1979 movie *Quadrophenia*, which also included the Kingsmen's recording on its soundtrack) can be credited (or blamed) with firmly, and probably permanently, establishing the Northwest's signature rock 'n' roll song as an icon of "frat rock"—a tune that fun lovers far and wide have enshrined as the Party Song of the Universe.

Consequently, "Louie Louie"—the same song that has been variously cited by *Rolling Stone* as "one of the fifty most important recordings in the

twentieth century," and "the No. 4 most influential recording of all time"—
also became a song that a subsequent generation or two of Northwest rock
bands shied away from performing. Perhaps this was a simple case of famil-
iarity breeding contempt, but no matter the cause, the once-beloved song
was so shunned that just about the *only* recording of "Louie Louie" to be
issued locally for many years was a mocking, dirgelike mess by Pink Chunk
that was released in 1979 on a speckled, vomit-colored vinyl 45.

CHAPTER 30

So Long to the '60s

The final nails in the coffin of the original Northwest Sound came in the 1970s with the rise of two concurrent, and oppositional, rock 'n' roll movements—heavy metal and punk rock—neither of which cared much about looking backward. Nor did the participants within those aesthetically disparate scenes care much for each other—in fact, the punk and metal camps were separated by an ideological chasm so wide that no one could ever have believed it might one day be bridged.

Because the metal scene was mainly based in the comfortable upper-middle-class Seattle suburbs of Bellevue and Redmond, there existed a palpable resentment amongst early street punks toward those overprivileged ex–football jock headbangers. To a punk's ears, heavy metal was—like the equally dreaded disco sound—largely a result of production smoke and mirrors. Metal lyrics were disdained for their horribly clichéd fantasist themes of Dungeons & Dragons, enchanted swords, and macho posturing. And metal music was derided as self-indulgent—epic guitar solos layered over ponderous Teutonic drum rhythms designed to fill out inexcusably elaborate song arrangements. In short, a form of music that is marketed as a rebellious entity while in reality it's a comparatively conservative and safe commodity—an idea that would seem to have some basis in reality given metal's acceptance by the mainstream music biz, as opposed to punk's struggle to gain a foothold.

But there are two sides to any argument—and the metalheads also had their critique of punk "culture." While metal players and fans considered their music to be very progressive—virtuosic solos coupled with headbanging rhythms and *fun* lyrics—they typically viewed punks as unkempt, angry, short-haired losers whose primitive musical "skills" couldn't attract big enough crowds to make a difference. What is true in that critique is that the earliest '70s punks were basically misfits—but often by choice. They rejected everything they despised about mainstream (and *especially* heavy metal) culture, preferring torn clothes and black leather motorcycle jackets to metal's spandex and fishnet tank tops; crew cuts (or even Mohawks) to poofy and overly sprayed ringlets; lyrics that addressed sociocultural topics or pointed a finger (usually the middle one) at right-wing politicians rather than singing about Gollum or Mordor; and minimal stage gear to metal's ostentatious use of high-end instruments, fog machines, and elaborate lighting systems

Metal and punk seemed to have *nothing* in common. One major difference was that the metal crowd was able to gain access to halls where they could develop their scene while punk pioneers literally faced a united front by area club owners, who refused to book any such bands. From 1976 up through about 1979, most punk shows occurred only because some of Seattle's old community halls were still available for rental. Facing that uphill challenge, Seattle's punks just burrowed in and created a small underground scene for their own enjoyment. But in 1977 one of that scene's pioneering bands, the Feelings, stepped out by submitting a recording for possible (but highly unlikely) inclusion on a new compilation album being organized by KYYX-FM. And thus it came to pass that the town's first punk tune—"Destroy Destruction"—saw the light of day as part of the *Seattle Grown* LP, which was promoted as featuring the best and brightest crop of current Seattle bands.

The *Seattle Times'* rock editor, Patrick MacDonald, lent his enthusiastic support—albeit by misstating the area's actual musical history just a bit. "KYYX's album couldn't come at a better time," he began, before steering off course. "The Northwest music scene is booming as it never has before, with national attention being focused on Seattle as an area rich in untapped talent. Thanks to the success of Heart and the emergence of Seattle as a major recording scene, the area is finally being taken seriously by the music industry." Well, yes *and* no. Certainly there was loads of "untapped talent" in the Northwest, but the scene's level of activity in 1977 was nowhere near that of, say, 1965—and the day when it would be "taken seriously by the music industry" was, alas, still a *long* ways off. Nevertheless, while the production of this *Seattle Grown* album was a worthy endeavor, very little of the music it contained was interesting—although a *Seattle P-I* music critic, George Arthur, provided some upbeat liner notes that served perfectly as a state-of-the-scene report: "There may not be a 'Pacific Northwest sound' on this disc, but the diversity of music on it is what makes this a worthwhile documentary of Pacific Northwest music, 1977."

The *first* half of Arthur's statement is a flatly stated acknowledgment that the Northwest region had already frittered away our hard-won uniqueness. The second clause seemed to merely be an attempt to put a happy face on a sad situation, and while it's certainly true that diversity goes a long way, for some music fans the new album was a painful reminder of what had been lost. *Seattle Grown* purported to represent the Northwest's finest talents—and yet what was offered up was not especially promising: one disco crew (Epicentre), a Rolling Stones clone (Shyanne), a pop-metal group (Rail), a twelve-bar-blues band (Blueseye), and an overabundance of safe and passionless lite rock club acts (Breeze, Pilot, the Ozone Street Band, and the Lane James band). Truly, there was very little that merited any attention by the outside music industry—unless your eye caught the odd-man-out track amongst all that boring tripe.

"Destroy Destruction" by the Feelings was a gnarly, angry-sounding song that owed nothing to the country rock, pop, or blues music common to the area's taverns. Instead, it reflected the tastes of a growing portion of young rockers who realized that a lot of the fun and vitality had been bled from rock 'n' roll. These kids saw that many of the era's top bands had gone soft and their music was too safe. In fact, the music that excited them had much more in common with that made a decade prior by the Sonics—and the entire '70s crop of American and British bands like the MC5, Iggy & the Stooges, T. Rex, Alice Cooper, the New York Dolls, David Bowie, and the Patti Smith Group who'd descended from that point. It was that music which had inspired a few Roosevelt High School kids to start the era's first rock publication, the *District Diary* (soon to be *Chatterbox*); the town's first glam rockers (Ze Whiz Kidz); and then the first batch of punk bands like the Tupperwares, the Telepaths, the Meyce, the S'nots, the Knobs, the Idiots, the Mentors, and the Feelings.

Ze Whiz Kidz were a theatrical troupe that was comprised of a shifting cast of flamboyant gays and other campy thespians, including Tomata du Plenty, Melba Toast, Rio de Janeiro, and Satin Sheets—who were backed by a band, the Fabulous Pickle Sisters. After making their debut at the 1970 Sky River rock festival, the *Berkeley Barb* raved, saying they were "the real stars" of the whole fest and deemed them "THE WORLD'S FIRST ACID ROCK FREAK SHOW EXTRAVAGANZA." In the wake of their 1972 gig at Bellingham's Western Washington State College, a newspaper article (headlined THRASH THEATER—IT CAN'T HAPPEN HERE? IT DID) mentioned the band's "X-rated" performance that included "nudity and coarse language."

Yet even after that, the band bookers at Far West Entertainment still gave the Kidz a shot at playing on the local high school dance circuit. But that was to be a short-lived relationship, as their very first school booking won Far West an irate letter from an outraged principal who decried the band's attitude, looks, and debauched lyrics—their songs included "Lay Me Down and Knock Me Up" and "Swastika Sweethearts." So maybe playing for schoolkids wasn't the correct route for these guys. But they carried on, winning fans in Seattle's gay dives and eventually working their way up to opening for Alice Cooper at Vancouver's Commodore Ballroom and Seattle's Paramount Theater in '72, and at the Moore Egyptian Theater opening for the New York Dolls in '74.

In 1975, du Plenty headed off to New York City and Ze Whiz Kidz broke up. But in their wake arose a few young bands who'd attended those New York Dolls and Alice Cooper shows, and Seattle was about to have its first real punk bands. The Luvaboys performed at a riotous Roosevelt High School talent show where they were pelted with fruit, called "faggots," and beaten up afterward by schoolmates who hated their glam tendencies. After playing a few more house parties, Jim Basnight (vocals, guitar) helped form the Meyce, while two other ex-Luvaboys—Geoff Cade (bass) and Dean Hegleson (drums)—helped form the Telepaths.

In time, du Plenty returned from New York with wild tales of having hung out with the Ramones, Blondie, and all the rockers at fabled punk mecca CBGB's. Reenergized, he hooked back up a couple Whiz Kidz and formed the Tupperwares with new recruits—including drummer Eldon Hoke—and some provocative new tunes like "Instamatic Fanatic," "I'm Going Steady With Twiggy," and "Eva Braun." And then history was made when the Tupperwares, Meyce, and Telepaths organized a cooperative gig— the now-legendary "TMT Show" at Capitol Hill's IOOF Oddfellows Hall at Ninth Avenue and Pine Street. That event, which took place on May 1, 1976, has been credited as one of first punk shows ever mounted on the West Coast, and some historians have even placed it chronologically as occurring two months *before* the first punk show in London.

But since the vast majority of music fans in Seattle hadn't even been aware of the show, it was like a tree falling in the forest with no one to hear it. Except, of course, for the few dozen kids who were thrilled to see such radical rock music emerging locally. After doing a few more shows here, the Tupperwares found that the small size of the scene didn't meet up with their greater vision, and they relocated to Los Angeles. Renamed the Screamers, the guys quickly became key members of the nascent Hollywood punk scene.

Meanwhile, the Meyce scored the opening slot for the Seattle debut by New York's top punk band, the Ramones. But while that March 1977 show at the grand old Olympic Hotel's plush Georgian Room proved to be a watershed punk event for Seattle, it was also to be the Meyce's final gig. That's about when a punk named J. Satz Baret—who had performed as Satin Sheets with Ze Whiz Kidz—resurfaced with the Knobs, who opened for the Feelings at an IOOF hall gig in May '77. By June, Baret was fronting the Lewd, who opened for the Ramones in Vancouver (and again in '78 at Seattle's Paramount Theater). Then a few former Knobs formed the S'nots, who issued Seattle's first punk 45, "So Long to the Sixties," in January 1978—and from there more and more new local punk 45s spewed forth, including "She Got Fucked" by Jim Basnight (with help from the Telepaths and the S'nots) and "Must I Perform" by the Telepaths. Then, in '79, the Lewd (who had just added bassist Kurt Vanderhoof) issued "Kill Yourself," which was followed by Clone's "Jacuzzi Floozi," Chinas Comidas' "Peasant/ Slave," and other singles by the Frazz, the Cheaters, the Vains, and the Fastbacks. Of all the '70s punk singles, though, none received any radio support, save one, "Kill the Bee Gees" by the Accident—which was used by KISW radio for their weekly *Disco Destruction* hard rock show.

Nineteen seventy-eight also saw a couple of new local punk fanzines— *Snot Rag* and *Stelazine*—pop up, along with the band that would become the era's most visible: the Enemy. Formed from the ashes of a hippie group, the Fruitland Famine Band, who'd converted after seeing the Sex Pistols perform, the band initially asked a Bellevue kid, Penelope Houston, to be their singer, but she declined in order to attend school in San Francisco. It wasn't long before that town's rising punk scene pulled her in, and soon she was fronting one of the best of America's '70s punk bands, the Avengers.

The Enemy's lineup solidified around vocalist Suzanne Grant, but the problem they faced was getting booked anywhere. Their manager determined that the solution was for the band to launch their own venue. Seattle's first punk club, the Bird, opened March 4, 1978, at First Avenue and Spring Street. The lineup that night was the Enemy, the Telepaths, and the Mentors—and of those three bands, it would be the last (formed by ex-Tupperware drummer Eldon "El Duce" Hoke, along with bassist Steve "Dr. Heathen Scum" Broy and guitarist Eric "Sicky Wifebeater" Carlson) that would cause the biggest commotion. Wearing scary black executioners' hoods, the Mentors employed all sorts of stagecraft tricks—like bringing their morbidly obese (and impossibly endowed) "Whipping Girl" onstage so they could degrade her while performing their uniquely vile brand of debauched songs like "Outhouse Sex" and "Macho Package." The *UW Daily* was the first entity to object to the band's violent musical misogyny—but not the last. In 1985, Tipper Gore and her PMRC pro–music censorship organization targeted the Mentors and famously undercut their own position by actually reading aloud—live on national TV—the gross, urine-centric lyrics to "Golden Showers." Hoke—who had long since moved the band to Los Angeles—must have reveled in the high-profile attention. By all accounts a rather sick puppy, Hoke experienced his finest (and final) moment when he was flattened by a speeding locomotive while drunkenly flipping off its traumatized engineers in 1997.

All of the activity at the Bird was starting to catch the attention of the Establishment—and City Hall. And sure enough, one night the Seattle Police Department found a reason to raid the Bird—an invasion that resulted in members of the Enemy and a number of other punks being battered and broken in a full-scale police riot. Interestingly, a tape recorder was running that night, and an audio portion of the police riot was later included on the Enemy's "Trendy Violence" 45. Local newspapers covered that raid—but in terms not at all sympathetic to the punks—and in the end the Bird was squeezed out of its location. The Enemy carried on, though, and by May "The Bird in Exile" was promoting shows at the rentable Carpenters Hall with bands including the Screamers, the Enemy, and the Telepaths—and then at the IOOF hall, where they began throwing weekly shows by visiting punk bands like the Weirdos, Subhumans, DOA, Negative Trend, and new local bands—the Cheaters, Fast Food, and the Refuzors.

By this point the pop fringe of Seattle's punk scene was seeing larger crowds of the curious turning out to shows—a result of positive coverage that the *Seattle Times* and *Seattle P-I* were both suddenly awarding to bands who had a poppier edge to them. The biggest beneficiaries of the papers' attempts to steer readers *away* from hardcore punk and *toward* new-wavey "power pop" were the Moberlys and the Heaters. The Moberlys came together when Jim Basnight recruited a bassist, Steve Grindle (ex–Ze Whiz Kidz); a drummer; and a series of guitarists, including Steve Pearson, Don Short, and finally, Ernie Sapiro—and they debuted at the Ethnic Cultural Center, opening for the Mentors. Meanwhile, the Heaters (soon to be the Heats) formed when Pearson and Short added a rhythm section; they debuted by opening at the Moberlys' third gig.

Although the Moberlys had the head start—and their classic 1980 LP would please many with its fresh pop sheen (*Trouser Press* magazine named it their No. 3 Underground Record of the Year, and their *Trouser Press Record Guide* would eventually describe Basnight as a "startlingly talented power-pop titan")—the Heats quickly overtook them in popularity, becoming the most commercially successful (as measured by column inches of fawning media coverage and the resultant gate receipts at area taverns) Northwest band of their generation. A lot of their success can be directly attributed to the legacy of Heart. By this point in time, Heart had done it *all*—the band members had enjoyed access to various world-class recording facilities; they'd sold many millions of records and toured the world; they'd dealt with big-time record labels, built up a staff and crew of professionals, and developed a long-term relationship with Ken Kinnear's Albatross Productions management firm.

And all that collective knowledge and experience would now be lent to the new kids on the block. The Heats were set up with an Albatross manager (and former KZAM DJ), Jon Kertzer, who worked quickly to help establish them as *the* top new local act—one with a charmingly snotty debut 45, "I Don't Like Your Face." Regional radio—likely impressed as much by the Heats' association with Heart's sphere of managerial pros as the tune itself—lined up to support the band, and strong airplay helped them sell a fast 18,000 copies.

Reentering the studio, the Heats were accompanied by their producer, Heart guitarist Howard Leese, and the resultant *Have an Idea* album sold an initial 15,000 copies and was eventually cited by *Goldmine* magazine as "one of the top 50 power-pop albums of all time." Albatross arranged for the band to head out touring with Heart—including one huge gig at the Radio City Music Hall in New York—and also a tour with the Knack, but the band just never got their big national hit. Still, they ruled the Northwest's new wave clubs for the following few years and were only challenged in popularity by their rivals the Cowboys, who counted among their ranks alumni from the Feelings and Moberlys.

Along the way, the Seattle scene began to feel an energy that had been lacking locally for a decade. Things were getting stirred up by new participants, and good things were happening everywhere: Bellevue-based KZAM radio shifted their programming focus away from an eclectic mix and toward a "New Modern Music" format, and DJ Steve Rabow's *Music for Moderns* show became particularly influential. Then, too, a new local music publication, *The Rocket*, sprang into being with a fund-raising benefit gig held in

September 1979, at the Showbox Theater. Promoted by Modern Productions, the gig featured the Enemy, the Look, the Macs Band, and the Dish Rags, and in October *The Rocket* made its debut with a feature essay about the punk/new wave explosion and a cover image of Triangle Studios— Seattle's first studio to embrace punk culture. This was the beginning of the *Rocket's* twenty-year odyssey of covering original local music.

But even though KZAM and *The Rocket* were now both heralding new music, Seattle's taverns and nightclubs still generally shunned punk bands. But the bands carried on producing increasingly crowded shows—in rental rooms like the IOGT hall, the Socialist Hall, and an outsider art house called Rosco Louie Gallery. Before long, a few daring businessmen took a chance and brought a few punk bands into rooms like the Funhole and Showbox Theater, faltering gay dives now recast as punk joints like Wrex and the Gorilla Room, the odd liquor bar like the Bahamas Underground, and even the Golden Crown Chinese restaurant.

In Portland, among the earliest punk rooms were the Revenge Club and Urban Noize—and the most impressive Portland band of the era was the Wipers. Formed in 1977—by Greg Sage (guitar/vocals), Sam Henry (drums), and Doug Koupal (bass)—this iconoclastic band's goal from the outset was, according to Sage, to record music "without touring or promotion of any type. My thoughts were that the mystique built from not playing the traditional rock & roll promotion game would make people listen to our recordings much deeper, with only their imagination to go by." And though the band played plenty of live gigs, it was the Wipers' early records— like 1978's self-recorded "Better Off Dead" 45 on Sage's Trap label, and *Is This Real?* (1979) and *Youth of America* (1989, both on Portland's Park Avenue Records)—which drew rave reviews and offers to tour England and Europe.

But even as the Wipers influence grew in the punk underground, Sage's stubborn resolve not to cooperate with the demands of the biz resulted in those opportunities being squandered. Conversely, that punky attitude would endear Sage to his fans all the more.

In Seattle, a few former Telepaths (Bill Reiflen, Erich Werner, and Mike Davidson) recruited Roland Barker (synths), formed the Blackouts, and began carving out their very own brand of off-kilter and enigmatic rock music as featured on their 1979 single, "Make No Mistake" / The Underpass." The following year's excellent *Men In Motion* EP showed an altered lineup—Barker had switched to saxophone, and his brother, Paul, replaced

Davidson—and an evolved sound that had become even more dissonant. There was simply nothing else like this music being played in Seattle at the time, and between their sounds and arrogance, the Blackouts made a firm impression. But they weren't satisfied with the high level of awe that the town's punks were offering them, and after a final IOOF hall show in August 1982, they split for the East Coast seeking a breakthrough. But having left their comfort zone as the top band on Seattle's underground scene— a stature which they characterized in an interview as being the "big fish in a small pond"—the band went on to discover that the Big Apple wasn't so easy to conquer, and they soon straggled back to the West Coast. However, one connection they'd made—that with their Boston producer, Al Jourgenson—eventually paid off when he asked Reiflen and the Barker brothers to work with him in his '90s industrial rock band, Ministry.

Also swimming in the Seattle's "small pond" were a number of interesting new wave groups (Student Nurse, Red Dress, the Debbies, Visible Targets, the Beakers) and punk bands (the Fartz, the Rejectors, the Pudz, the Refuzors, Maggot Brains, X-15, 10 Minute Warning, the Accüsed, the Dehumanizers). Meanwhile, sixty miles south in Olympia, the action was picking up with bands like the Wimps, the Young Pioneers, and Tiny Holes, the last comprising a pair of students at Evergreen State College—Steve Fisk (synthesizers) and Bruce Pavitt (vocals)—who would both go on to play central roles in the resurgence of the Northwest scene.

Pavitt would—through his radio show on KAOS (and later, Seattle's KCMU), his featured column in *The Rocket*, and his *Subterranean Pop* cassette 'zine—ultimately go on to be the single most influential tastemaker on the scene. Fisk—who formed his own label, Mr. Brown, and issued a handful of new wave 45s by area groups including Olympia's Westside Lockers, Seattle's Macs Band, and his own solo endeavor, Anonymous—would eventually go on to engineer sessions for many top local bands over the next decades. At that point in time, Evergreen College was a nexus for bright kids who had a keen sense of the possibilities inherent in a new grassroots rock subculture. Even the name of Pavitt's 'zine—*Subterranean Pop*—signalled his fascination with a clash between the seemingly oxymoronic notions of "underground" and "popular," and each issue showcased obscure cutting-edge new wave bands who would likely have been otherwise ignored by the music biz and effectively "lost."

Calvin Johnson (also a KAOS DJ) was among those who got caught up in the excitement and founded his own influential label, K Records. But Mr.

Brown and K Records were far from the only labels that were now firing up locally. The realization that big Hollywood or New York labels were never going to come to the rescue and sign up every good band had, at long last, finally sunk in. *And so* the only apparent solution was the DIY one. So many bands—punk, new wave, metal—had begun entering studios that the June 1982 issue of *The Rocket* actually hyped all the activity in a cover feature essay titled "Seattle Record Boom!"

But having a pallet-load of your new record on hand is one thing—selling it without radio airplay is another. And radio support for local records was already shaky when KZAM suddenly folded and the airways remained virtually free of "New Music" for a spell. But eyeing an opening, who of all people should reappear, but Pat O'Day.

This time the former king of the scene popped back up as an owner of a new wave–oriented pop station, KYYX. Then, when another station, KJET, also began broadcasting that music, there was suddenly some good, healthy competition in town, and eventually a few local records finally made a little stir nationally. The first was "Hello," a tune by Bellevue metal band Rail, which became such a strong hit on KZOK—whose listeners would for three years vote them "Seattle's Best Local Band"—that it helped their *Arrival* album (which featured a guest vocal by Ann Wilson and was produced by Heart's soundman, Mike Fisher) move 200,000 units. Subsequently, the music video for "Hello" beat out 40,000 other entries and won MTV's national *Basement Tapes* contest in 1983—which earned the band the grand prize of a new big-time record deal with EMI and led to their popular *Rail* EP and the opening slot on gigs with Heart, Blue Oyster Cult, Nazareth—and even a forty-seven-date tour with Van Halen.

The following year a video for "Emma Peel"—a single by Seattle power-pop band the Allies—made it into the semifinals of MTV's 1984 *Basement Tapes* competition. That year also saw *Rolling Stone* magazine salute as "perfect" the *Sounds of the Pacific Northwest* album debut (on the new label PopLlama Records) by Seattle pop band the Young Fresh Fellows. Then in 1988 Bellingham's power-pop champions the Posies gained some serious attention with their *Failure* album—a success that ultimately attracted an offer from Geffen Records' new subsidiary imprint, DGC Records, which led to "Golden Blunders," a single that hit the modern rock chart's Top 20, and "Suddenly Mary," and "Dream All Day," which became alternative radio and MTV hits.

But while radio lavished attention on the accessible sounds of such bands, the media remained deaf and blind to most of the other interesting records being issued locally. And in doing so, they *totally* missed out on fun Northwest punk era groups like the Wipers, the U-Men, and the Silly Killers, whose records would be recognized as some of the earliest murmurs of a musical movement that would soon rise up from the Northwest and conquer the world.

CHAPTER 31

Rage for Order

While punk and new wave bands struggled in the Northwest's major urban centers, out in the suburbs the heavy metal hordes had created their own ecosystem. Initially taking their cue from the Led Zeppelin–inspired music of Heart, an entire metal scene had arisen by the early 1980s—one that by now included scores of bands, professional management firms, regularly scheduled shows, and before long even a few dedicated record labels.

And while the massive success of Heart served as these bands' guiding light, the band was not the only one to define a proto-metal sound back in the early 1970s. Among the other local pioneers of the genre were Iron Maiden (an all-girl band that began in 1969), Valhalla, Juggernaut, Amethist, Mildstone, Cypress, Oz, Tyrant, Smack, Rick Shaw, Wraith, and Rail.

It was Craig Cooke—the Unicam Booking Agency pro who'd helped Rail rise through the ranks—who would play the central role in the growth of a distinct suburban metal scene. By 1978 he was already expanding his reach, exiting Unicam to form his Craig Cooke Entertainment agency and promoting regular Battles of the Bands for suburban teens and imposing some organizational structure on the east-side metal scene. Later the *Belle-vue Journal-American* would report that the next big step occurred in the summer of 1982 when the owner of the Crossroads Skate Center "decided rock 'n' roll was a good bet to supplement roller skating revenue. Apparently he was right. Since then Seattle-based promoters Craig Cooke and Jim McHale have been staging battles of the bands every Saturday night—and the Skate Center has helped establish Bellevue as the Heavy Metal center of the universe."

Well, yes, that roller rink was ground zero for local metal—but credit must really be given to one particularly talented band whose participation on the scene clearly caused the metal "universe" to take notice of all the heavy rock 'n' roll emanating from Bellevue. And that band was Queensrÿche, whose roots trace back to 1980, when Michael Wilton (guitar) and Scott Rockenfield (drums) met up while hanging out at Bellevue's Easy Street Records shop. After adding Chris DeGarmo (guitar)—and later Eddie Jackson (bass)—the band became the Mob, and they found their dream vocalist, Geoff Tate, performing with Tyrant at one of the battles. The Mob's rehearsals quickly led to some great new songs, and the band cut a four-song demo cassette—featuring "Queen of the Reich," "Nightrider," "Blinded," and "The Lady Wore Black"—at Triad Studios. Seeking a second opinion, Rockenfeld's brother handed the demo over to his pals, Kim and Diane Harris, who owned Easy Street. And while those two older retailers may not have been the universe's biggest metal fans, their shop had become an unofficial crossroads for the town's burgeoning headbanger scene. Having met plenty of young metalheads—from bands like Arson, Culprit, Hammerhead, Mistrust, Overlord, Prophecy, Syre, Titan, and Werhmacht—they could tell that the Mob had a sense of discipline and pragmatism about their career goals that was most rare among their peers. And then there was that demo tape chock-full of killer originals that showed an instrumental virtuosity and compositional maturity that completely belied the fact that the band had only just formed.

The Mob changed their name to Queensrÿche at the very last minute, and the Harrises formed the 206 Records label. They had 3,500 cassettes made and in November 1982 made an audacious quick trip to London solely to deliver a review tape to the offices of the world's biggest weekly metal magazine, *Kerrang!* Upon their return, they offered the demo to KISW, KZOK, and Portland's KGON, and all three stations instantly latched onto "Queen of the Reich" and "The Lady Wore Black." That's when the new issue of *Kerrang!* hit the racks, and their initial review was a unqualified rave: "Something's happening in Washington. . . . We have an absolute monster of a band in Queensrÿche. . . . Very few genuine heavy metal bands write material as classy as this, and very few writers of classy songs can get as utterly vicious as this; the successful blend that Queensrÿche have created puts them at the forefront of a small field that's previously been almost exclusively British."

And as simply as that, Queensrÿche—a band that had made exactly *zero* public appearances to date—was effectively introduced to the worldwide metal audience as the "next big thing." 206 Records quickly pressed a vinyl EP of the tape, and when 60,000 raced out of the warehouse, a deal

QUEENSRŸCHE

was struck with Capitol/EMI. The disc was promptly reissued, and with all that major label muscle behind it, *Queensrÿche* quickly moved about 350,000 units, and the band's popularity skyrocketed. After making their official live debut (on June 29, 1983, at Portland's Paramount Theater), Queensrÿche began touring major stadiums and arenas with other top metal bands, including Quiet Riot, Twisted Sister, and Kiss. From that point on there was no stopping this Bellevue band. Further accolades would roll in for subsequent LP's like 1984's *The Warning*, 1986's *Rage for Order*—and especially for 1988's ambitious concept album, *Operation: Mindcrime*—which led to a Grammy Award nomination and Queensrÿche being tagged the "thinking man's metal group." But the band's *real* breakthrough would be 1990's *Empire*, with the massive international smash single "Silent Lucidity," a song that garnered them a second Grammy nomination.

All told, many hundreds of hard-rock and metal bands played in the Northwest, and a good number went on to score deals, including Striker (Arista), TKO (Combat, Roadrunner), Widow (CBS), Black 'N Blue (Geffen), Russia (Warner Brothers), Q5 (Polygram), Fifth Angel (Epic), Coven (Medusa), Lethal Dose (Ever Rat), MACE (Restless), and Culprit (Shrapnel). All of that activity had generated a potent image in the minds of the outside music biz that the Northwest was a veritable hotbed of metal music. Metal music—Heart, Rail, Queensrÿche, and all rest of the headbanging hordes—*was* what the region had become known for. However, unbeknownst to anyone, hovering just over history's horizon was a major turning point for the entire Northwest music scene—a musical reconciliation of the punk and metal hordes that would take the form of an entirely new hybrid strain of music. A sludgy and grimy sound that would be soon be tagged "grunge rock."

CHAPTER 32

Ain't Nothin' to Do

By the mid-1980s the Northwest's punk/new wave subculture had been plugging along for a full decade. And while it had grown exponentially in size—hundreds of bands playing regularly in scores of rooms and supported by several fanzines—the scene had failed to produce any bands that had an impact on the level that so many London, New York, and Los Angeles bands had. There had been no major-label signings, no hit records, no national tours, and no big flashy national magazine spreads about Seattle's energetic scene.

For its part, the local mainstream media dependably offered up negative news coverage to aspects of the scene that caught their attention. Conversely, there was plenty of positive coverage given to politicians and their supporters who were behind new efforts to outlaw public postering and an ordinance aimed at further tightening teen-dance regulations. Both of these do-goody initiatives were considered to be daggers pointed at the heart of the scene—free postering on publicly owned telephone poles was a nearly hundred-year-old tradition in Seattle, and it accounted for the entire publicity efforts made by most bands. The proposed requirement that any potential dance sponsor post a million-dollar insurance bond was absurd.

Yet the Teen Dance Ordinance was passed with fervor by the Seattle City Council, along with the anti-postering law. Thanks to these two directives, all the dire predictions made by scene advocates would, over the following few years, come true. Dances for underage kids declined dramatically, some bands moved away, and poster wars erupted all over town, with guerilla posterers even going so far as to slap up faux reelection campaign posters for City Councilwoman Jane Noland (replete with her office's telephone number and street address on them) in an effort to demonstrate how difficult it was going to be to enforce the new rule, which basically stated that punitive fines could be levied against whatever nightclub's name or address was on any poster.

It was a time of discontent. But the *king* of discontent was the ever-grumpy Lou Guzzo. By this time his scowly mug could been seen regularly on Seattle's most conservative station, KIRO-TV, and as their editorial commentator, the veteran rock-hater loved to use his bully pulpit to issue vitriolic attacks aimed at youth culture. But for once the old sport met his match with the Dehumanizers, a punk band that responded to Guzzo's fulminations by issuing the tongue-in-cheek 45 "Kill Lou Guzzo." While clearly a harmless counter-jab to earlier provocations, the record did, understandably, end up causing trouble for the band when Guzzo's lawyers drew up threatening cease-and-desist letters—copies of which were quickly included as sleeve graphics on two subsequent, truly "underground," reissues of the targeted disc.

With such ongoing clashes—and the aforementioned talent drain—going on, the scene kind of drifted into the doldrums. Yet at least one local DJ, KCMU's Jonathan Poneman, somehow spotted what he thought was a silver lining to all the gathering clouds. In the December 1986 issue of *The Rocket*, he shared his optimistic sense about a newly creative undercurrent in Seattle. "The town right now is in a musical state where there is an acknowledgment of a certain consciousness. A lot has to do with our geographic isolation: for once that's paying off in that the bands here are developing with their intentions staying pure. In bigger cities, that all gets diluted because so much is going on . . . Something's gonna happen." *Hmmm.* What an interesting theory—that the Northwest bands getting no attention from the greater music biz was a positive thing. That having given up on getting approval from outsiders, local rockers were forging a "pure" new sound geared toward satisfying their own muses. But where could that sort of insular approach *ever* possibly lead?

That inquiry was about to addressed by a seemingly left-field answer—the overnight global success of a local hip-hop MC named Sir Mix-A-Lot. A Roosevelt High grad by the name of Anthony Ray, Mix began producing songs (including "My Kick Ass Drum") with a Commodore 64 computer, an early digital drum machine, and Moog and Korg synthesizers, which were stacked up in an apartment bedroom "studio." His mechanized beats and funny challenges to other sucker DJs apparently hit a real nerve, because when the *Rocket* published a feature titled "The Hip-Hop Debate: The Northwest Hottest Funk DJs Square Off" in May 1985, Portland's pioneering rapper, Chris "VitaMix" Blanchard, lashed out in response.

Claiming primacy, he spat back that "everyone else is trying to do it now, but I was first. Mix-A-Lot has all the equipment, but let's get people back into it. Forget the machines." This dissing continued with VitaMix's assessment that Mix's music "sucks" and that "there's no street feel to it . . . just all these synthesizers. Well, anyone can spend $4,000 on synthesizers and be the best DJ in town. But where's the talent? I'm for rawness; this is supposed to be street music." Luckily, Mix's raw talent was appreciated by other rap fans—including Seattle's K-FOX radio, who aired his early works and even commissioned him to record an intro theme song for their hip-hop show, *Fresh Tracks*.

It was in 1986 that Mix's self-recorded single "Square Dance Rap" was issued by the new Nastymix Records—a label he cofounded with his friend Nasty Nes (Rodriguez), who was also the DJ host of KCMU's *Rap Attack* show. While the novelty nature of that single led some to believe that Mix might not having the staying power to score again, he did just that with 1987's "Posse on Broadway," a song that recounts a day in the life of Mix and his homeboys cruisin' their hooptie up and down the main drag on Seattle's Capitol Hill neighborhood. Breaking out onto the national charts and on MTV, the tune ended up selling more than a million copies—but perhaps even more importantly, as local historian Clark Humphrey noted, "it also proved that you don't have to pretend not to be from Seattle, that you could sing honestly about your life here and people across America could identify with it." Mix had actually managed to make the Northwest seem cool to the hip-hop kids in the Bronx and Compton!

Nastymix would become the biggest music-biz success story that the town had seen in almost three decades—in other words, since Dolton Records' reign. The label opened lavish downtown offices, hired a large staff, and moved forward issuing Mix's debut album, 1988's *SWASS* (aka "Some Wise Ass Silly Shit"), and then 1989's *Seminar* album, which contained three hit singles—"I Got Game," "Beepers," and "My Hooptie"—all of which scored well on the rap charts. Both *SWASS* and *Seminar* earned platinum record awards. Nastymix also began broadening their aim by issuing recordings by other local rappers and hip-hop crews, including Kid Sensation, High Performance, Criminal Nation—and even a popular thrash-metal band, the Accüsed. And for a season or two there it really began to feel as if Seattle might be entering a great golden era where its music scene would perhaps once again be taken seriously. But then Nastymix began experiencing its own internal problems, and far too soon the label closed up shop. Mix moved on to a deal with the mighty New York–based hip-hop label Def American, where in '92 he scored again with the Top 10 *Mack Daddy* album's "Baby Got Back," a No. 1 hit that sold over two million units and won a Grammy Award for that year's Best Rap Solo Performance. Meanwhile, the last anyone ever heard from his former archrival was an Internet posting in which the now-obscure VitaMix confessed to Googling his own name and then whined about how he was finding it "especially irritating to hear that 'big butts' song every now and then."

Mix's other notable act of defying expectations was recording a cover, with Aberdeen's Metal Church, of the old Black Sabbath metal classic "Iron Man." While the surprise collaboration was rewarded with Top 20 hit status on the R&B charts, it failed to score on the pop chart's Hot 100, as Run-DMC

and Aerosmith's take on "Walk This Way" had famously done back in 1986. But on the upside, that collaborative spirit did serve as a fine example of the kind of "out-of-the-box" sort of risk taking that would ultimately help the Northwest's rock scene to finally break out in a big way. And the biggest risk of all was one that very few Northwest bands—including Culprit, Overlord, Crisis Party, Heir Apparent, Sanctuary, and Metal Church—took on: that of embracing the various aspects of metal and punk that they liked and merging the two aesthetics into something new. By playing a transitional form of rock music, such bands took the chance of alienating both camps and satisfying neither.

The first sign that something new was beginning to boil was the 1984 release of the *Northwest Metalfest* compilation album, produced by the region's new metal-oriented label, Ground Zero Records. While much of the music contained on the disc could be considered straight-ahead metal, one song—"Death Wish," by a band whose name alone (Metal Church) offered no clue that they might be harbingers of a new muscial path—had something different about it. That is, it was a unique amalgam of those previously irreconcilable schools of rock: metal *and* punk. And that musical miscegenation only occurred because the Aberdeen-based band had been formed by a metal-loving veteran of Seattle's pioneering punk band, the Lewd: guitarist Kurt Vanderhoof. After '70s punk peaked, he returned to his hometown and recruited four other guys who began playing music that reflected their diverse interests.

Metal Church were not alone in helping this new music take shape—in fact, their debut gig back on May 4, 1984, at Aberdeen's D&R Theater also featured their pals the Melvins, a Montesano-based band mockingly named after a despised clerk at the local Thriftway grocery store and whose sub-Sabbath sludge rock would also help signal a new cross-pollinating of the metal and post-punk scenes. While the Melvins—Buzz Osbourne (guitar), Matt Lukin (bass), and Dale Crover (drums)—might not have seemed to display much commercial potential to most ears, the power trio's slow-paced and extremely distorted guitar-heavy stoner rock sound and playful punk-ass attitude (the same factors that years later got them dumped from a major-label deal with Atlantic Records, who refused to release their *Prick* LP) would make a hugely positive impression on their fans—*especially* those local hangers-on Kurt Cobain and Krist Novoselic.

After playing a few out-of-town gigs in Olympia, Tacoma, and Seattle, luck struck when the Melvins were selected by Daniel House to appear on a compilation album, released by his new C/Z Records, which would feature some of the area's heaviest new groups. Issued in 1986, *Deep Six* proved to be a landmark record that highlighted tunes by six bands that were beginning to turn heads: the Melvins, the U-Men, Malfunkshun, Skin Yard, Green River, and Soundgarden. Of those bands, the first to make any waves was the U-Men, who formed in Seattle in 1981 and impressed local crowds with a harsh sound that shared at least a strand of garage-demon DNA with the long-gone Sonics. While their tune "They" was a definite highlight, the release of *Deep Six* also impressed everyone with the fact that the U-Men were not by any means alone in exploring a new dark form of rock music. And that maybe that Poneman guy was correct. Perhaps something *was* actually "gonna happen" in Seattle.

At the time, House was an employee at Bruce Pavitt's new Sub Pop label, which had moved on from merely issuing the *Subterranean Pop* cassette 'zines. It was in July 1986 that the label released their first record, *Sub Pop 100*—a compilation LP that featured recordings by thirteen bands from all around the world, including the U-Men from Seattle and the Wipers from Portland. At the time, Pavitt was spinning discs as a DJ on KCMU—the godsend University of Washington–based alternative radio station that had won a sizable audience by supporting music, local and otherwise, that no other area station would bother with. While at KCMU, Pavitt realized that he and fellow DJ Jon Poneman shared a keen eye for cultural shifts—and they'd both noticed that the latest crop of Seattle rock bands were quite special. The music being created of late, they thought, indicated that old barriers were being breached and a new sound was developing—a form of rock music that merged skillful metalesque musicianship with socially conscious, literate, post-punk lyrical themes. While the duo pondered where it all might lead, Pavitt moved ahead by issuing Sub Pop's next record, 1987's *Dry as a Bone* EP, by that promising new band, Green River.

This group was fronted by a guitarist, Mark Arm, who had gotten his start in rock 'n' roll through a prank. Arm and some bored high school pals in Kirkland figured it would be amusing to publicize a nonexistent band— Mr. Epp and the Calculations—that they'd mockingly named after a math teacher. Posters were pasted up announcing gigs, graffiti was scrawled, and Arm even nominated the "band" for a contest in Seattle's new punk magazine, *Desperate Times*, as the town's "most overrated band." But, significantly, it was the specific, and seemingly prescient, *terminology* that Arm—a future English major at UW—employed in his reverse-psy-ops tactic to draw attention to the "band." In that nominating letter (which was published), he wrote in part, "I hate Mr. Epp and the Calculations! Pure grunge! Pure noise!

Pure shit! Everyone I know loves them. I don't know why. . . ." Well, 'nuff said. Who in their right mind would ever want to hear a band described as having a "grunge" sound?!

With such great publicity it was inevitable that Arm would eventually form an actual Mr. Epp band. He also began performing with Limp Richerds, which included another grungy guitarist, Steve Turner. Along the way, Turner also spent some time with the Ducky Boys, a band that included bassist Jeff Ament (ex–Deranged Diction). That group was quite limited, as Turner once noted: "We learned two songs, basically: 'Dr. Love' by Kiss and 'Louie Louie.'" With that development, Seattle began to see the potential start of a reconciliation phase in the Northwest's ongoing relationship with "Louie Louie"—but further rapprochement was obviously still necessary.

In 1984, Arm and Turner would form Green River by recruiting Ament and drummer Alex Vincent. In '85, the band added Stone Gossard (guitar), and they cut the *Come On Down* EP, issued by the Boston-based Homestead Records. Then the group's personnel shifted again—Turner bowed out in disgust over Ament and Gossard's obsession with scoring a major-label deal and was replaced by Bruce Fairweather (ex–Deranged Diction)—and the band carried on winning new fans with every show. Then in 1986 the group worked with a producer/engineer at Reciprocal Studios named Jack Endino—who also played guitar in the band Skin Yard—and the result was their "Ain't Nothin to Do" 45. Reciprocal was the latest incarnation of the Fremont/Ballard neighborhood facility formerly known as Triangle Recording—a shabby but affordable studio that had been the birthplace of darn near every punk and new wave disc cut in Seattle since '77. Under Endino's watch, the place would soon go on to greatness, and he would rightfully come to be associated with the birth of the "grunge rock" sound.

At that point, Seattle's scene was still struggling under the weight of various forces that were trying to keep a lid on all the action. The local authorities were enforcing their poster ban and Teen Dance Ordinance, but they also had other tricks up their sleeves, including sending in the fire department for surprise inspections, or sending police out to halls with their volume meters to enforce noise ordinances. It was in his liner notes to another local compilation LP, *Secretions*, that Endino attempted to explain the connection between this restrictive sociocultural environment and the resultant eruption of great music that was occurring: "Well, when you have a city exploding with musical talent but a lack of clubs to play in and a repressive atmosphere of cops, liquor board agents, and general paranoid fear of everyone under 21, what do musicians put their energy into? They record, and then record some more. When they get tired of playing in bars, they make a record."

Yup. That's *exactly* what was occurring, and the flow of records from the Northwest was about to turn into a veritable gusher. One of the first discs to raise a few eyebrows was the Screaming Trees' *Even If and Especially When*, an LP issued in August 1987 by the revered Los Angeles–based independent hardcore punk label SST Records. The Trees—which featured neopsychedelic guitars and the smoky baritone vocals of Mark Lanegan—had formed back in 1984, and it was just their luck that Steve Fisk (former KAOS DJ and owner of Olympia's Mr. Brown Records) had moved to their small hometown of Ellensburg in order to work at the upstart Velvetone Studios. After producing their remarkable no-budget debut cassette, *Other Worlds*, and the stunning 1986 LP, *Clairvoyance*, the Trees struggled to catch hold in Seattle—but that finally occurred with the release of *Even If* . . . and the band was now on the path to greatness.

Meanwhile, Poneman had seen one of the *Deep Six* Seattle bands, Soundgarden, perform on a "new music" night at the old Rainbow Tavern and, duly impressed, offered to help them produce a record. Interested in his offer, the band mentioned that maybe he should hook up with Pavitt over at Sub Pop and then it might make sense. Well, Pavitt wasn't so hot on the band, but after further discussions it was agreed that Poneman—and the $20,000 of investment funds he happened to have on hand—would come into Sub Pop as a partner and Soundgarden would get their record.

Initially formed in 1984 around drummer/vocalist Chris Cornell—plus Kim Thayil (guitar) and Hiro Yamamoto (bass)—Soundgarden altered their lineup after Cornell's amazing vocal skills became fully evident. By 1986 they'd added a drummer, who was replaced shortly after *Deep Six*, when they poached Skin Yard's drummer, Matt Cameron. Now working with Sub Pop, Soundgarden entered the studio with Endino and emerged with two amazing tracks—"Hunted Down" / "Nothing To Say"—which revealed the band's true strengths: a punky attitude merged with a deep streak of Zeppelin-esque metal. Upon releasing the 45, Sub Pop began a hype campaign that quickly led to a bidding war between two Los Angeles–based majors, Warner Brothers and A&M.

But the band—under the savvy guidance of their new manager, Susan Silver (formerly the lowly door person at the Central Tavern)—played their hand deftly by deferring those offers and choosing to take their time, cutting another indie record with Sub Pop before rushing to sign up with the big boys. But after the *Screaming Life* EP was issued in November 1987, all of the trendsetting UK rock magazines went absolutely nuts over the band, as did New York's *Village Voice*. The result of these unanimous accolades was that a dozen big-time labels descended on the group. Epic and A&M were particularly aggressive. Soundgarden, however, were still more interested in playing a role in the underground world than in becoming the flavor-of-the-month act for some huge corporation. At least with smaller independent labels they knew that they wouldn't get steamrolled into grotesque commercialism, as so many rockers had in the past.

On April Fools' Day, 1988, Pavitt and Poneman did what perhaps no one else had done for many years in Seattle—they committed themselves to making their record label a full-time profession. The twosome had formulated a very shrewd marketing plan. Sub Pop would master the use of tongue-in-cheek hype as a way to mock major-label sins of the past. The little upstart company, backed by minimal funds and no great successes to its credit, would go for the Big Lie, trumpeting itself to the world with such wishful hype as "The new thing, the big thing, the God thing: A multi-national conglomerate based in the Pacific Northwest." But if Sub Pop was "new," it certainly was not yet "multi-national," or a "conglomerate," or "big," or a "God thing." *That* would all come later.

CHAPTER 33

Singles

S ub Pop ramped up their efforts in 1988, issuing a three-disc box-set compilation called *Sub Pop 200* and launching an initially laughable concept called the Sub Pop Singles Club. The box-set featured songs by nineteen promising talents—including Soundgarden and Green River—and it won instantaneous accolades from as far away as England, where the legendary and taste-making Radio One DJ John Peel raved in the *London Observer* that "it is going to take something special to stop *Sub Pop 200* being the set by which all others are judged."

Around the same time, Soundgarden signed with the midsize indie label SST and released their first LP, *Ultramega OK*. The record made enough of an impact that Soundgarden set off on their debut UK concert tour, but upon their return Yamamoto quit and was eventually replaced by Ben Shepherd. Tours opening for Sonic Youth and Soul Asylum followed, and *Ultramega OK*—an album without a hit single—went on to earn a gold record, and was nominated for a Grammy Award in the Best Metal Performance category—a designation that became a source of considerable mirth on the grunge scene. Finally ready to take the plunge into the big leagues, Soundgarden signed with A&M, and their next album, *Louder Than Love*, was released in '89. They were immediately sent out to tour with the big-hair L.A. glam metal band that punk rockers *loved* to hate: Guns N' Roses. But, as Thayil later explained to *Guitar Player* magazine, "In the beginning, our fans came from the punk rock crowd. They abandoned us when they thought we had sold out the punk tenets, getting on a major label and touring with Guns N' Roses. There were fashion issues and social issues, and people thought we no longer belonged to their scene—to their particular sub-culture."

Sub Pop's audacious Singles Club—which flew in the face of conventional wisdom by attempting to (at a point five years into the new compact disc era) convince fans to commit in advance (via a subscription) to buy a series of vinyl 45s, sight unseen, and containing *whatever* bands and songs Pavitt and Poneman chose to release—proved to be a magical success, for both Sub Pop and those who took a chance and joined up. Early subscribers would be the lucky recipients of limited-edition two-dollar 45s that contained awesome music and would also, over time, prove to be worth quite a bit on the international collectors' market. The club debuted in October 1988 with the release of the limited-edition 45 "Love Buzz" / "Big Cheese" by an Aberdeen band called Nirvana. This was a group formed by those early Melvins disciples Kurt Cobain (guitar), Krist Novoselic (bass)— and a series of drummers. The guys played their first gig at a house kegger in another nearby depressed logging town, Raymond. Luckily for their future fans, the fact that the straggly, inept band were promptly "invited" to pack up and leave didn't discourage the boys from carrying on.

Nirvana eventually moved up to Olympia, added a new drummer, Chad Channing, and drew the attention of Sub Pop. Poneman somehow heard something intriguing lurking amidst the din of their Endino-recorded demo

Nirvana, 1989, Bainbridge Island, WA. (Photo by Charles Peterson.)

tape, and he got the band their first Seattle gig at the Vogue dance club. Though that gig was poorly attended, Poneman was able to study them closer, and a deal was cut. From the beginning, Cobain was cynical about Poneman's studied low-key label-exec shtick—their "Big Cheese" was actually a jab at their new benefactor. And though it was far from their best song, the 1,000 Singles Club 45s sold out so quickly that the band was actually angry because their family and friends couldn't get copies.

Luckily, KCMU had a copy. While returning to Olympia from Seattle one day, Cobain asked his girlfriend to pull off the freeway so he could get to a telephone and call in a request for "Love Buzz." And when the station followed through, Cobain was overcome: "It was amazing . . . more than I ever wanted. But once I got a taste of it . . . I thought I would definitely like to hear my future recordings on the radio."

Cobain also was getting wound up over thoughts of impending fame (and various issues of concern to the scene for instance), and he personally penned the sarcastically over-the-top text to his band's first Sub Pop press release, which in part was a pimp-slap to careerist, old-school, music-biz hacks: "SOON we will do encores of 'GLORIA' and 'LOUIE LOUIE' at benefit concerts with all our celebrity friends." Adding to that idea, Cobain (we would later learn) also jotted a related thought into his personal journal: "Nirvana has never jammed on GLORIA, or LOUIE LOUIE. Nor have they ever had to rewrite these songs & call them their own." Interestingly enough, Cobain's palpable distaste for those two über-classic garage rock tunes was likely just calculated posturing: In fact, the Northwest's signature tune, "Louie Louie," was reportedly the very *first* song he ever learned on guitar. Maybe the guy was just a little fonder of the old three-chord wonder than he was letting on. . . .

Regardless, the cumulative effect of their single and the "Spank Thru" track on *Sub Pop 200* had the desired impact, and in February 1989 Nirvana began their first West Coast punk club tour. When their *Bleach* album was issued on June 15, they embarked on their first national tour. Sub Pop surprised even themselves by moving a quick 35,000 units—and early fans got a chance to marvel at Nirvana's magical blend of thunderous drums, interlocking guitar and bass hooks, washes of gnarly distortion and feedback, lyrical melodies, and Cobain's mysterious and scratchy vocalizing. To those who were in on this secret, every song seemed to be a dead-on classic. Nirvana were clear contenders for greatness.

CHAPTER 34

Superfuzz

oon after Green River's 1988 Sub Pop LP *Rehab Doll* was released, the band was gigging in Los Angeles with Jane's Addiction when disagreements over musical directions (and all the usual rock band tiffs) finally caused the group to fold. That parting of ways would, however, have its upside in that it fathered two other bands that would have an even greater impact: Mudhoney and Mother Love Bone. Mudhoney was formed by Arm and Turner—who recruited former Melvins bassist Matt Lukin and drummer Dan Peters—and after signing with Sub Pop, their fuzz-drenched single "Touch Me I'm Sick" became an instant Northwest classic right up there in the pantheon with the Sonics' "The Witch" and the Kingsmen's "Louie Louie."

The song was a rock 'n' roll head-kick that was felt around the world. British music magazines (including *NME, Melody Maker,* and *Sounds*) all dropped their standard reticence to applaud modern American rock and surrendered to Mudhoney's bratty charms. When the band's 1988 Sub Pop EP, *Superfuzz Bigmuff,* was issued, the dam burst: New York's Sonic Youth took the band along on a 1989 tour through England, and that's all it took for the disc to enter Britain's indie charts. Back in Seattle, Pavitt and Poneman sensed that the time to strike was *now,* and they brashly contacted *Melody Maker* magazine—perhaps the publication with the most clout at the time—and offered to pick up the tab if they'd send a reporter over to check out the action in Seattle.

Melody Maker was intrigued and sent along rock journalist Everett True, who was knocked out by the vitality of the scene he witnessed. The March 1989 *Melody Maker* had a splashy cover feature on Mudhoney, and True gushed about the peculiar punk-metal hybrid present in the clubs, concluding that Seattle—albeit "one small, insignificant, West Coast American city"

Mudhoney at the Motorsports Garage, Seattle, 1987. (Photo by Charles Peterson.)

had "the most vibrant, kicking scene, encompassed in one city for at least 10 years." And with that grand pronouncement—and subsequent statements that pegged the Seattle sound as "grunge rock"—a powerful image was introduced to the international consciousness.

In Seattle the momentum gained strength. It was on the night of June 9 that Sub Pop held an ambitious showcase concert downtown at the grand Moore Theater. Once again employing their thus-far-successful marketing tool of faux-grandiosity, they billed the show with the self-mocking name the Lame Fest. Featuring performances by their top three bands, Mudhoney, TAD, and Nirvana, it was a great success—the sold-out crowd of more than 1,000 was the largest audience any of the bands had yet drawn— and while the subsequent mainstream media coverage was negative, it *actually* suited Sub Pop's purposes perfectly.

For unknowable reasons, the *Seattle Times* assigned their otherwise astute *jazz* critic, Paul de Barros, to cover the event and his review really made one wonder if the spirit of ol' Lou Guzzo wasn't being channeled that night—especially when he wrote that "the whole point of this show seemed to be based on the perverse, reverse notion that grungy, foul-mouthed, self-despising meatheads who grind out undifferentiated noise and swing around

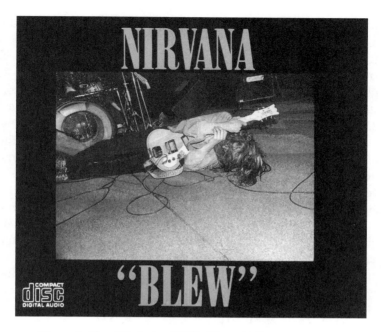

Nirvana's *Blew* CD-single, 1990. (Photo by Tracy Marander.)

their long hair are good—and 'honest'—by virtue of their not being 'rock stars.' How confounded this primitivism is. . . . If this is the future of rock n' roll, I hope I die before I get much older."

But it *was*, in fact, Sub Pop who were helping to shape "the future of rock n' roll." Part of Sub Pop's overall marketing strategy was to define an image for Northwest rock that stood in stark contrast to everything else that was then being pushed by the corporate music biz in Hollywood. Instead of the slick, pretty, faux-rebellious "hair metal" bands then being favored by record labels and MTV, Sub Pop honed a rougher, sweatier, more primitive look and sound for their bands and their product. And with that goal in mind the label occasionally went overboard—it might be one thing to brazenly brag about leading Northwest rock to eventual "World Domination," or to flagrantly fantasize about being a "multi-national conglomerate" when they decidedly weren't. Or even to produce promotional T-shirts emblazoned with the word *Loser*. But still, it was quite another to go so far as issuing a record jacket (and accompanying video) for TAD that showed the guys in plaid flannel logging shirts and wielding lethal-looking chainsaws.

Not subtle, but apparently effective, as the public and international media picked up on the meme and the flannel-clad, Doc Marten–booted, shaggy-haired, stage-diving, grunge loser cliché took hold. But there was a method to Sub Pop's madness—in fact, it was a masterful case, as Clark Humphrey has noted, of playing "up an image of the label's acts that exploited British stereotypes about non-Manhattan Americans as ugly and stupid." The Brits ate it up. Sub Pop produced a follow-up Lame Festival in London, and the same three bands were shipped overseas in October to spread the grunge contagion to France, Belgium, Austria, Germany, the Netherlands, Hungary, Switzerland, and Italy.

Meanwhile, Green River's Ament, Gossard, and Fairweather recruited a charismatic vocalist, Andrew Wood (ex-Malfunkshun), and drummer Greg Gilmore (ex–10 Minute Warning and Skin Yard), and resurfaced as Mother Love Bone. In a radio interview, Woods slyly explained to listeners that the inspiration for the band's name came from his two biggest loves—his mother and his bone. From its inception, this group had street cred galore in Seattle—and an exciting arena rock sound that caught the ears of a manager, Kelly Curtis, who was deeply versed in the ways of the rock biz. As a high school kid in Bellevue he'd befriended Ann and Nancy Wilson—in fact, he'd once taken guitar lessons from Nancy. Then, in 1974 (and at age seventeen), he hired on as a roadie for Heart. Within a few years he'd toured widely with them, and by age twenty-five he was working out of Albatross Productions' office as the band's spokesperson and publicist. Now, once again, the Heart machine was about to extend a hand to a young band in need of some help. Taking on the manager role, Curtis proceeded to solicit offers and then negotiate a deal with the big-time Polygram label, who issued Mother Love Bone's debut five-song *Shine* EP in March 1989—making the group the first band of the grunge generation to score a major label contract. Mother Love Bone played a number of local gigs to warm up, then headed out on a short promo tour, and with *Shine* selling well, the buzz was that Seattle was about to see another band break out big. Later in the year the band completed tracks for a new LP, and anticipation was so keen that fans were literally counting off the days till the disc's release.

But then, on March 19, 1990—on the very eve of their first big national tour (and just a matter of days before the scheduled release of their *Apple* album)—Wood died of a heroin overdose. Seattle was stunned. Polygram delayed the release of the record for a couple of months, and the scene fell into a dazed hush. But, despite the loss of such a promising talent, the community rebounded—partially because there was an unstoppable level of creative energy being generated by the scene in general—and because many within our music community could sense that all that hard work over the years was finally leading to a truly vibrant scene, one that even the international music media was beginning to salute for its undeniable "teen spirit."

CHAPTER 35

Teen Spirit

With England's *Melody Maker* and *Sounds* magazines competing to out-hype one another in promoting the tidal wave of heavy rock that was rolling out of the Pacific Northwest, the collective antennae of the corporate music biz were all suddenly tuned in. But just because those rags and Seattle's Sub Pop Records were bandying the term *grunge* to describe the music didn't necessarily mean that everyone understood exactly what they were referring to. Point of fact: The Los Angeles music industry had always been confused about rock music from up north. They never got the appeal of anything coming out of Seattle, ranging from the Fleetwoods to "Louie Louie"—and since its emergence in the mid-1970s, they had ignored our punk rock nearly to death.

And so, when grunge broke, at least a few of those companies jumped to the incorrect conclusion that this music—which *was*, after all, emanating from the heavy metal heart of the Northwest—was just some new variation of that genre. Which—because they had practice in dealing with *that* stuff— was comfortable for them. Thus, if "grunge" was to be the "next big thing," well, by golly, corporate America was *not* going to miss out on this new gravy train. They just needed to bone up a bit on what this "next big thing" actually was! But that's how the Great Grunge Rock Rush began—and over the next season or two, droves of hapless A&R reps from out-of-town labels descended on Seattle in a feeding frenzy to sign anything that was hairy and not yet nailed down by some other label. And that indiscriminate greed led to the hilarious spectacle of numerous flat-out *metal* bands who were decidedly *not* any part of the emerging grunge scene scoring deals: Among these were Bitter End (Metal Blade Records), Forced Entry (Relativity), Panic (Metal Blade), My Sister's Machine (Caroline), and War Babies (CBS).

But as none of these bands were supported by the growing ranks of grunge fans, each was unceremoniously dumped after issuing one measly underpromoted record. While that was unpleasant, further joy could be had in knowing that in their haste some befuddled labels signed bands that they accidentally *thought* were metal but instead were actually quite punky! Three of these—Crisis Party (Restless), Apple Maggot Quarantine Area (Medusa), and SGM (Medusa)—would prove to be quite a handful for their label bosses. One prime example was Crisis Party, who were *so* unmanageable that the band was sacked by their label after engaging in a drunken and riotous food fight at their record-release party!

The one label that—whether they really knew what they were getting or not—landed a worthwhile act, was Columbia (Epic) Records. The former longtime home of Paul Revere and the Raiders had obviously come a long way over the years and was now all set to partner up with what was easily Seattle's most metal-oriented of the top grunge bands—Alice in Chains. Originally formed back in late 1987 as a standard issue glam-metal band called Diamond Lie, they had come up playing the roller rinks of the Bellevue metal scene. But, much to their credit, they also had an understanding of the merits of punk rock—and they of *all* the bands who would be lumped together as "grunge" probably represented the most musically successful merging of those two opposing schools of rock. And that was no mean feat— even Seattle's premier music magazine, the *Rocket*, struggled to understand the band and ultimately confessed to having "confused eardrums" over their sound.

The crossover appeal between the metal and punk camps came through Layne Staley's enigmatic vocals, the taut vocal harmonies and brilliant guitar work of Jerry Cantrell, and a stellar rhythm section. As Diamond Lie progressed—if nothing else by toning down their spandex quotient—their audience expanded in kind. Soon they'd taken on the name Alice N' Chainz and eventually attracted the services of Kelly Curtis's Silver-Curtis Management firm—a partnership with Soundgarden's manager, Susan Silver. Finally renamed Alice in Chains, the band's debut EP, *We Die Young*, was issued in June 1990. Perhaps because people didn't know how to categorize it—it seemed like heavy metal, yet those lyrics were uncommonly introspective— the music took a while to catch on, but eventually "We Die Young" became a moderate radio hit on *metal*-oriented stations. Then, in August, *Facelift* was issued, and the band scored an opening slot on tour with one of the era's heaviest metal acts: the Los Angeles–based Megadeth.

In the days following Andrew Wood's death, his grieving roommate, Chris Cornell, penned two sweet tunes in his memory—"Reach Down" and "Say Hello 2 Heaven." And since neither song seemed to be in the Soundgarden oeuvre, he contacted Ament and Gossard about recording the songs together in a one-shot deal. By this time the two former Mother Love Bone members were cutting some instrumental demos of their own with a hot young metal guitarist, Mike McCready, who had played with Shadow—and they had already passed a demo tape out to a few people in the quest for a new singer. One of those cassettes made it all the way down to a San Diego–based surfer dude named Eddie Vedder, and after listening to it a few times he overdubbed some lyrics onto three of the tunes—songs that would become eventually become classics that we know today as "Alive," "Footsteps," and "Once." After hearing his contributions to their tunes, the band invited Vedder to come up and audition (along with a new drummer, Dave Krusen), and one week later he was in Seattle, and the band—who would soon be known worldwide as Pearl Jam—played their first gig.

As the Northwest music scene looked ahead at the new year of 1991, no one could really have known what was in store. What was about to unfold over the next few years was, in fact, just about the greatest run of success for any regional rock scene imaginable. The whirlwind of action was to be so fast and furious that it would have made the executives at Dolton, Seafair, Jerden, and Etiquette Records' heads spin—due to the growth of the rock marketplace alone, the modern era saw an exponentially greater number of units sold, and the sheer amount of accompanying publicity that would be bestowed upon the new bands was on a scale that would have been unthinkable to the pioneering acts and their labels.

In January 1991 alone, Alice in Chains' *Facelift* yielded a huge radio and MTV hit, "Man in the Box," which was followed by "Sea of Sorrow." Then the Screaming Trees' major-label debut, *Uncle Anesthesia*, was issued by Epic Records. In March, Pearl Jam entered Seattle's new London Bridge Studios to begin recording their debut album, and Epic stepped up and closed the deal; in April the Andrew Wood tribute sessions—in which Vedder joined Ament, Gossard, McCready, and Soundgarden's Cornell and Cameron—were released by A&M as Temple of the Dog, and the beautiful "Hunger Strike" single broke out as a hit. That same month—after being courted by majors including Capitol, Columbia, and MCA—Nirvana (who'd just added an amazing new drummer, Dave Grohl) signed with DGC for the whopping advance of $297,000 in a deal that also gave Sub Pop $75,000 and a percentage of any future DGC sales.

In May, Sub Pop issued Mudhoney's *Every Good Boy Deserves Fudge* album, which hit No. 37 in the UK and sold over 60,000 copies, establishing it as the label's biggest seller since *Bleach*. On July 1, Hole—an up-and-coming band that featured Cobain's girlfriend, Courtney Love—saw release of their first album, *Pretty on the Inside*. Nirvana headed off to tour Europe opening for Sonic Youth, while Alice in Chains hit the road with Van Halen. August brought Seattle a new radio station, KNDD, which immediately began broadcasting the most concentrated playlist of Northwest music ever heard.

Meanwhile, from August 20 to 25 a remarkable event occurred when the International Pop Underground Convention brought many of the world's coolest underground bands to Olympia, where throngs of hip Generation X alt rock music fans listened to great music and networked. The insanely ambitious festival had been organized by Calvin Johnson, the founder of K Records, a label that pushed a contrarian, lo-fi, DIY, *anti*-grunge aesthetic.

Johnson had long before developed his own theory of the joy of rock 'n' roll. It was a full dozen years prior—way back in November 1979—that Calvin "the Teenage Radio Star" Johnson had written a letter to the editor of *New York Rocker* magazine expounding on his ideas. "Now, I'm not just your average 'I know all the punk bands' kid. After fifteen months at the good radio station (KAOS-FM in Olympia, Washington) playing great teenage music, I feel that I know rock 'n' roll. I mean, I know it. And I know the secret: Rock n' roll is a teenage sport, meant to be played by teenagers of all ages—they could be 15, 25, or 35. It all boils down to whether they've got the love in their hearts, that beautiful teenage spirit."

Bingo! That, in point of fact, is the force that motivated more and more musicians to get active. And in Olympia, Johnson became such a guru to the burgeoning scene there that his followers became known as "Calvinists." K Records' slogan and stated goal ("exploding the teenage underground into passionate revolt against the corporate ogre") found resonance with legions of disaffected youth—including Cobain, who got a tattoo of the label's K logo. Olympia's teen underground grew to include a good number of interesting bands who recorded for K, including Beat Happening and Heavens to Betsy—one of the town's hard-core militant feminist punk bands who came to be collectively known worldwide as instigators of the Riot Grrl movement, which operated parallel to the grunge movement, and went on to make its own impact on the world via media coverage in the *Washington Post, Newsweek,* and even *Seventeen* magazine.

But Johnson and K's highest-profile achievement was that International Pop event in August 1991, which garnered international media attention that hailed it as a sort of bellwether indictor of the mood of the entire alt rock realm. An essay by J. Serpico asserted that "Olympia was largely responsible for the national proliferation of bands who merged punk, pop, and DIY aesthetics into new, exciting conflagrations. Olympia had a thriving music scene, a cozy college-town vibe, and two tiny record label start-ups— K Records and Kill Rock Stars—all of which provided for a hothouse atmosphere, rife with inspirations, cooperative visions, and built-in enthusiastic audiences. K Records and Kill Rock Stars eagerly nurtured budding and wannabe musicians and artists, all fortunately and mutually in search of artistic fulfillment and self-expression with little or no interest in financial rewards or profits."

Well, given that the two labels *must* have raked in plenty selling discs they marketed by bands including the Melvins, Nirvana, Bikini Kill, and Bratmobile . . . that last bit seems to have been little more than utopian fantasy. However, K and Kill Rock Stars' profits were small potatoes compared to the action that erupted a mere two weeks after the International Pop fest wound down.

On September 10, DGC lobbed Nirvana's new single, "Smells Like Teen Spirit," out onto an unsuspecting world, and the thing hit like a megabomb. Rarely in the entire arc of rock 'n' roll history has one song exploded into the public consciousness with such dramatic impact. In addition to endless airings on MTV, there were many good reasons why the song met with immediate acceptance—not the least of which were its beat, or pulse— which some observers were quick to point out bore an uncanny resemblance to, of all damn things, "Louie Louie." In fact, some DJs reportedly began referring to "Teen Spirit" as "the 'Louie Louie' of the nineties." Too, there were Cobain's easily misunderstood lyrics, and guttural vocalizing, which in combination had the same effect as, well, the Kingsmen's "Louie Louie." Pop critic Dave Marsh wrote that "like 'Louie,' only more so, 'Teen Spirit' reveals its secrets reluctantly and then often incoherently." But if anyone might think that all that was taking things too far, Cobain himself would settle the matter when he confessed to *Rolling Stone* that the tune's main chord progression "was such a clichéd riff. It was so close to a Boston riff or 'Louie Louie.'"

271

On September 20 Nirvana headed out on a North American tour, with the Melvins in tow. *Nevermind* hit the streets on September 24 and immediately entered the *Billboard* charts at No. 144. By mid-October the album's massive sales were certified with a gold record; then "Teen Spirit" went gold. On November 27, *Nevermind*—which had also yielded the strong hits "Come as You Are," "Lithium," and "In Bloom"—was declared platinum. On January 7, 1992, the album's two millionth sale earned it double-platinum status—and on January 11, the very day that Nirvana made their national TV debut on NBC's *Saturday Night Live*, *Nevermind* hit No. 1 on *Billboard*, sold a quick ten million copies, and was critically acclaimed as one of the best rock records *ever*.

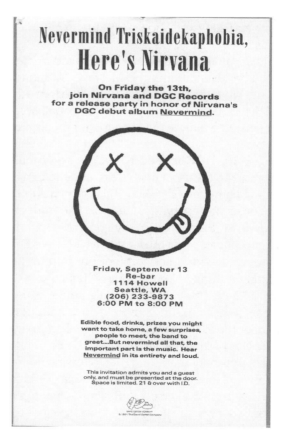

Original invitational card for Nirvana's *Nevermind* record release party, 1991.

CHAPTER 36

Sweet Oblivion

In January 1992, Pearl Jam's "Alive" single (from their debut album, *Ten*, which Epic had issued back on August 27) finally broke out as an MTV hit, and the band set out on their triumphant first concert tour of the UK; then "Hunger Strike"—the nearly *year*-old single from the Temple of the Dog project—was resurrected by MTV as a major hit, and Pearl Jam's "Even Flow" and "Jeremy" both scored. In March, Soundgarden's "Rusty Cage" followed "Outshined" as the second hit from the *Badmotorfinger* album—which upon its release back in October had been, well, *outshined* by the

Soundgarden at the Vogue Tavern, Seattle, 1987. (Photo by Charles Peterson.)

Nevermind juggernaut. In August, *Ten* peaked at No. 2; in September the Screaming Trees' *Sweet Oblivion* (which yielded the band's first genuine radio and MTV hits, "Nearly Lost You" and "Dollar Bill") was issued, selling a quick half-million units; and that same month, Alice in Chains' *Dirt* (with the hits "Would?" and "Them Bones") was issued and raced up to the No. 6 slot.

"Would?"—*another* musical tribute to Andrew Wood—was also included on the soundtrack to a new feature-length Hollywood movie, *Singles*, which was filmed in Seattle and featured acting roles for members of Pearl Jam, as well as music by bands including Mother Love Bone, Soundgarden, Mudhoney, and the Screaming Trees. In November, *Singles* began its successful run in theaters nationwide and brought about further public awareness—and an opening wave of mythologizing of the grunge scene. By December, *Spin* magazine would declare that "Seattle is currently to the rock 'n' roll world what Bethlehem was to Christianity."

The whole grunge uprising was suddenly being acknowledged by the mainstream media as the biggest rock 'n' roll phenomenon since Liverpool 1964 or San Francisco 1967: "Seattle became known as the rock capital of the world," wrote author Gina Arnold in her 1993 book, On the *Road to Nirvana*. "And the world took note." And thus, incredibly, Bruce Pavitt and Jon Poneman's once-laughable goal of taking grunge rock to a state of "World Domination" now seemed within reach.

CHAPTER 37

Overblown

The global appetite for grunge was seemingly insatiable, and the successes racked up by Seattle's best bands continued in a blur. In December 1992, Nirvana's *Incesticide* was issued, and then Alice in Chains scored the international hits "Hate to Feel," "Down in a Hole," and "Rooster" (with backing vocals by Ann and Nancy Wilson of Heart); 1993 brought Pearl Jam's next hit, "Black," and in September their "Jeremy" video won four MTV Video Music Awards, including Video of the Year, while Nirvana's "In Bloom" won the Best Alternative Video award; that same month, Nirvana's *In Utero* actually *debuted* at the *Billboard* chart's No. 1 slot and yielded the hits "Heart Shaped Box," "Dumb," and "All Apologies." In October, Pearl Jam's *Vs.* was issued with the hit singles "Daughter," "Dissident," "Spin the Black Circle," and "Tremor Christ." In November, Nirvana performed acoustically on *MTV Unplugged,* and a year later the CD of that show hit No. 1, ultimately winning a Grammy Award for Best Alternative Music Performance.

But the Northwest's youth culture was impacting the world in ways that went way beyond musical influence—*Rolling Stone, Entertainment Weekly,* the *New Yorker, Time,* and *Newsweek* all ran one or more features on the Seattle scene. As Gina Arnold pointed out, "By October 1992, fashion runways of Milan, Paris, and New York featured 'the grunge look' as their theme." And then the December 1992 issue of *Vogue* magazine ran a ridiculous "Grunge and Glory" fashion spread that highlighted $500–$1,400 "grunge outfits" by Ralph Lauren and Calvin Klein, supposedly representing a style that had "broken out of the clubs, garages, and thrift shops of Seattle." Then, too, the *Wall Street Journal* and *Village Voice* were now commenting on—and *Mademoiselle* joined *Women's Wear Daily* in touting—the "new Seattle look" haute couture designer fashions. And thus, all to soon, the joy began dissipating when it became painfully evident that what had originally begun as a local reaction against silly corporate entertainment trends—a regional preference for low-key thrift shop apparel versus Los Angeles's glam-metal excess—had already become just another silly corporate-entertainment trend.

The corporate ogre's appetite for destruction was only just revving up—the culture vultures would go on to produce hundreds of music magazines adorned with cover images of Northwest bands; Kmart started running ads for kids' back-to-school grunge fashions (i.e., plain old-fashioned flannel shirts); various opportunistic companies began selling such crass abominations as "Pearl Jam air-fresheners" and "grunge pencil sets," and there was even a grunge issue of the *Archie & Veronica* comic book. Not only was all this commodified Grungemania overwhelming, some fans viewed it as standing in the way of a desired return to punk's social-protest roots. Kurt Cobain was one who fought back against the idiocy—by wearing a "Grunge Is Dead" T-shirt.

Epilogue

N ow that the Northwest's cozy, insular music scene—which had taken a decade and a half to nurture—had been discovered in a big way, a strange sense of disenchantment with this newfound fame began settling in. And several of the best bands—the very ones who were benefiting the most from all the publicity—were among the most pained.

It had been a hallmark of the scene's ethos to resist any careerist impulses, just as it had always been a Northwestern social characteristic to downplay one's ambition and/or wealth. But grunge's breakout saw our scene blown all out of proportion by the media, and milked for everything it was worth by corporate ogres.

For a while it was Seattle this, Seattle that. Seattle. *Seattle*. SEATTLE! Having that international media spotlight glaring on all things Seattle annoyed the locals—just as it, apparently, had bothered others. Two non-Northwest bands responded to the media overkill with their own Seattle-themed rock songs—"I Left My Flannel in Seattle" by Butt Trumpet, and "Sick of Seattle" by the Smithereens. But grunge had already become a powerful cultural magnet, and every week it seemed that more and more musicians and/or their bands from outside the area—including Silkworm, the Supersuckers, the Best Kissers in the World, the Gits, 7 Year Bitch, and Alcohol Funny Car—were all doing what another band, the Cogs, sang about on their 45, "I'm Moving To Seattle." Mudhoney responded to this invasion by recording "Overblown," which said in part: "Everybody loves our town / That's why I'm thinkin' lately / The time for leavin' it's now / . . . It's so overblown."

Still, Northwest bands continued to rack up the hits. In 1994, Alice in Chains' hit-laden *Jar of Flies* was released. In March, Soundgarden's

Superunknown debuted at No. 1—the same month Nirvana began sessions for their eagerly awaited follow-up to 1993's *In Utero*. Meanwhile, fans were already anticipating the release of Hole's next album. Only three months in and 1994 was already looking as if it would be yet another stellar year for Northwest rock.

When news of Kurt Cobain's suicide broke on the morning of April 8, a pall fell over the whole community. Pearl Jam reacted by quietly announcing the cancellation of their entire tour while they mourned. Conversely, Hole trudged on, just days later releasing an amended version of their *Live Through This*, whose song "Rock Star" was deleted at the last second by DGC—reportedly due to the now-untimely lyrics: "How would you like to be Nirvana? / So much fun to be Nirvana / Barrel of laughs to be Nirvana / I'd rather die."

Meanwhile, all sorts of dire predictions about the imminent collapse of the Seattle scene were being published, some written with obvious glee—but that was not to be the case. In fact, Pearl Jam's next album, *Vitalogy*, debuted at No. 1, as did the eponymous debut album by Seattle's newest hit makers, Candlebox. In May, Portland's Everclear saw "Santa Monica" from their *Sparkle and Fade* album hit No. 1, and additional new bands—including Mad Season, Pond, Sunny Day Real Estate, Mono Men, and the Presidents of the USA—kept local sounds on the radio and/or MTV.

As a capper to the era, a documentary film chronicling the rise of the grunge—the appropriately titled *Hype!*—debuted in the nation's theaters in October 1996, and, as the *All Music Guide* so succinctly noted, it took the "unusual position that the grunge explosion of the mid-1990s was the worst thing to happen to rock music in the Pacific Northwest. *Hype!* depicts Seattle as a town where a fertile musical community with a distinctive sound and style grew largely because it was ignored by the rest of the world."

For a local music scene to reach the boiling point that Seattle's finally did—one that resulted in the sale of many millions of records as well as the dissemination of a set of ideas and ideals about the role of individuals within a creative community—requires many things, the first being some space—both physical and philosophical—to create within. And then there is the energy, commitment, and dedication of a network of individuals and organizations. Regardless of geography—from Memphis to Motown, Liverpool to St. Louis, Harlem to Haight-Ashbury, Athens to Austin—a productive music scene *only* develops in the presence of community spirit.

Today—in the post-grunge era, and for the first time ever—the Northwest music scene *finally* has the necessary music-biz infrastructure in place to sustain a living, breathing, music industry, one that has produced such additional talents as Death Cab for Cutie, Girl Trouble (who issued the 1990's only recording of "Louie Louie"), the Walkabouts, Sleater-Kinney, Harvey Danger, Modest Mouse, Murder City Devils, the Shins, Blue Scholars, Fleet Foxes, Grand Archives, and many more. We created a fresh art movement—one fueled by "Louie Louie" and sparked by an electrifying bolt of "teen spirit"—and the result rocked the world like a sky-cracking sonic boom.

Discography

This is a discography of select—and highly recommended—Pacific Northwest music that is, in particular, accessible on compact disc. As dedicated collectors well know, many significant Northwest recordings remain unavailable on CD and survive today only in the form of old and dusty vinyl records held in private collections. But a considerable amount of the *best* stuff—as noted below—*has* successfully jumped to the modern sound-carrier format and is widely available.

This information is arranged in roughly chronological order, and listed by artist—with a subsection of worthy multi-artist compilation discs included at the end. Because the region's more recent musical outpourings are probably familiar to most folks, this listing—which is merely the "tip of the iceberg" of the region's truly seminal recordings, and is limited due to space restrictions—also has a decided emphasis on the formative years of the original Northwest Sound and the Grunge Era.

Bonnie Guitar

* *Dark Moon* (Bear Family; BCD 15531) A twenty-nine-song collection that includes her big late-1950s hits, "Dark Moon" and "Mister Fire Eyes," along with many other interesting tunes that reveal the Seattle star's grasp of pop—and even the collector's rarity, "Love Is Over, Love Is Done," whose rockabilly vibe hints at her future as a producer of spirited teenage rock.

The Fleetwoods

* *Come Softly to Me: The Very Best of the Fleetwoods* (EMI USA) This is absolutely the best collection of the group's recordings ever compiled. Twenty-eight tracks include all of their notable hits plus five previously unissued tunes—including a cappella takes on their two biggest ("Come Softly . . ." and "Mr. Blue") and even a promotional radio jingle! *Great* booklet and fine liner notes by David Dasch.

The Frantics

- *The Complete Frantics on Dolton* (Collector's Choice Music; CCM-463-2) Wow! The four-decade wait for this was truly worth it! Not only do we get all of the Frantics sides originally issued as Dolton Records 45s in 1959–1961, but we are treated to a total of twenty-six tracks, including fourteen previously unreleased tunes like the Wailers' "Dirty Robber" and a Northwest band fave, Bill Doggett's "Hold It." Nice booklet with good pix and largely accurate liners by Richie Unterberger.

The Wailers

- *The Original Golden Crest Masters* (Ace; CDCHD 675) The band's groundbreaking 1959 album with the hits "Tall Cool One" and "Mau Mau," along with bonuses: single versions of several tunes and four previously unreleased gems, including the legendary "Snakepit."
- *At the Castle / Wailers & Co.* (Big Beat CDWIKD 228) This awesome 2003 release combined the Etiquette label's first two LPs and topped of the set with six bonus tracks compiled from various stray singles from 1961 to 1964. Issued by England's Ace Records, this fun package features rare photos and excellent liner notes by Alec Palao.
- *Livewire!!!* (Norton; NW 904) A sixteen-track roundup of the Wailers' best work from the mid-1960s. The disc shows the band at their punkiest, includes previously unissued demos and rare singles—and, thankfully, also features the Wailers' final radio hit, 1966's folk-rock winner, "It's You Alone."

Little Bill and the Bluenotes

- *Retrospectively Yours* (Monkey Hat; LB 020) A seventeen-song set that spans much of Bill Engelhart's career—with an emphasis on gathering his earliest works, including 1959's "I Love an Angel," 1960's "Sweet Cucumber" (with the Frantics), 1961's Louie Louie" (with the Adventurers), Ray Charles' "I Got A Woman," and other rarities.

Ron Holden

- *Love You So . . .* (Del-Fi; DFCD 72111-2) This is a straight reissue of Holden's 1960 LP with its meager original eleven tunes—but among them are several of Holden's singles, including the hits "Love You So" and "My Babe."

The Ventures

- *The Best of the Ventures* (EMI America; CDP 7 446600 2) A solid overview of the band's, well, best. Memorable hits ranging from 1960's "Walk—Don't Run," to their No. 1 smash, 1969's "Hawaii Five-O"— plus a couple tasty live tracks.

Dave Lewis Trio

- *The Godfather of Northwest Rock & the King of Northwest R&B* (Jerden; JRCD 7026) Despite the clumsy title and horrible graphic design, this is the only Dave Lewis CD marketed thus far, and it does include a good array of twenty-four tunes representing the trio's best studio and live tracks including the essentials: "David's Mood," "Lip Service," "Little Green Thing," and "Feel Alright."

The Viceroys

- *At Granny's Pad* (Seafair-Bolo; BSCD 8006-2) The band's classic 1964 regional best-selling album includes the hit "Granny's Pad," a version of Dave Lewis's "David's Mood," "Louie Louie," and a dozen previously unreleased winners like "Buckin' the Wind," "Jerkin' Around," and "Comin' Home Baby."

The Dynamics

- TBD (Seafair-Bolo; TBD) As one of the Northwest's most highly regarded bands of the 1960s, the release of two vinyl albums by Seafair-Bolo Records—1983's *Memory Bank of Northwest Sounds* and 1985's *Leaving Here*—was joyously welcomed. However, it has been a point of frustration for fans that since the dawning of the compact disc era way back in 1982, the Dynamics awesome music was never made available in digital format. All that changes in 2009 when the label will finally cut loose with an as-yet-untitled set to highlight the band's formidable contributions to the region's unique sounds.

The Kingsmen

- *The Best of the Kingsmen* (Rhino; R2 70745) All of the band's important tracks are complied here—a disc that Bruce Eder credited in the *All Music Guide* as "the album that helped restore the group to modern record collections . . . and Peter Blecha's essay is still the definitive account of the band's history." Dave Marsh concurred, saluting it in 1994 for having one of the "25 Best Liner Notes" ever!.

Paul Revere and the Raiders

- *Mojo Workout!* (Sundazed; SC 11097) To hear all the band's mighty Top 40 hits look elsewhere. What this stunning 2-CD set offers is forty-four tracks cut at Columbia Studios in September 1964. The tunes are split between a live session with a captive teen audience and regular studio cuts (including the original "Louie Louie")—but there are too many special bonus tracks (including sixteen previously unissued songs) to mention beyond live versions of Ray Charles' "What's I Say," "Louie—Go Home," and alternate studio takes on "Have Love, Will Travel," and "Louie—Go Home."

The Sonics

- *The Savage Young Sonics* (Norton; CNW 909) A wonderful aural chronicle of the band's earliest years: home recordings from 1961, a high school dance in '62, a teen club bash in '63, and more rehearsal tapes from '64. All told, a magical glimpse back at the band prior to their breakout in 1964.

- *Busy Body!!! Live in Tacoma 1964* (Norton; NW 913) A testament to the rabid demand for anything and everything Sonics—this disc features the band's performances for a live broadcast radio show—KTNT's *Teen Time*—that were recorded over a radio by a fan and discovered in 2006. Definitely *not* "high-def," but the disc provides the thrill of hearing the band in full power mode just on the cusp of their hit (included here) "The Witch" breaking out. Cool graphics, and liners by Peter Blecha.

- *Here Are the Sonics* (Norton; NW 903) This is the complete original 1965 album—with classics like "The Witch," "Boss Hoss," "Have Love Will Travel," and "Strychnine"—plus the bonus tracks of 45 B-side, "Keep A Knockin'" and the three Sonics tracks from Etiquette Records' ill-fated *Northwest Christmas* album: "Don't Believe in Christmas," "Santa Claus," and "The Village Idiot." Cool packaging and great liners by Norton's Miriam Linna.

- *The Sonics Boom* (Norton; NW 905) This is the complete original 1966 album—with classics like "Cinderella," "He's Waitin'," "Louie Louie," and "Shot Down"—plus the bonus tracks of an alternate 1964 take of "The Witch," the 45-only "The Hustler," and both "The Witch" and "Psycho" from the 1972 reunion gig. Tougher than ever—and with fun notes by Norton's Miriam Linna.

- *Maintaining My Cool* (Jerden; JRCD 7001) This is essentially the current form of the band's third album, Jerden's *Introducing the Sonics* from 1966. Highlights include: "High Time" and "You've Got Your Head On Backwards." Cover design by Art Chantry, notes by Peter Blecha.

Don and the Goodtimes

- *Don and the Goodtimes* (Jerden; JRCD 7016) This is the finest collection of Don and the Goodtimes tunes one could hope for. All of the band's best stuff is included: the early radio hits ("Money," "Sweets for My Sweets," and "Little Sally Tease"), the Northwest teen-dance standards ("Louie Louie," "Tall Cool One," Dave Lewis' "Lip Service," the Kingsmen's "Jolly Green Giant"), and the latter-day Top 40 national pop hits ("You Were Just a Child" and "I Could Be So Good to You.") Cool graphics, notes by Neal Skok.

Heart

- *Greatest Hits* (Capitol; 53376-2) Each of the two dozen albums that Heart released over the past three decades contained some exceptional music, but 1998's seventeen-track *Greatest Hits* compendium provides a good overview of the band's finest work from 1975 through 1983.

Alice in Chains

- *The Essential . . .* (Sony; 760649-2) Among the three "best of" compilations that Sony has released in recent years—1999's *Nothing Safe*, 2001's *Greatest Hits*, and 2006's *The Essential . . .*—none are perfectly satisfactory. Programming flaws (like tacking on demo versions or remixes rather than original hits, shoehorning in previously unreleased oddities, and issuing one disc with a miserly ten tunes) considered, this two-disc set seems preferable. The best solution though, is to simply scoop up these original discs: 1990's *Facelift*, 1992's *Dirt*, 1994's *Jar of Flies*, 1995's *Alice in Chains*, and 1996's *MTV Unplugged*.

Soundgarden

- *A-SIDES* (A&M Records; 31454 0833 2) While several of Soundgarden's original discs—like 1991's *Badmotorfinger*, 1994's *Superunknown*, and 1996's *Down on the Upside*—can be considered essential listening on their own, this 1997 release offers up a nice concise look back at many of the band's best tunes from both the Sub Pop and later A&M eras.

Screaming Trees

- *Clairvoyance* (Hall of Records; HOR1112) The band's debut release from 1986 is the one that blew away many of us original fans—some of whom believe that they never quite topped its exciting and original sounds. So it was a glorious day in 2005 when this long-awaited CD finally hit the market.

- *Ocean of Confusion: Songs of Screaming Trees 1989–1996* (Sony; EK 92852) In 2005 the band's singer compiled what he believed to their finest work from the Sony years, and this nineteen-song set (which includes two previously unissued bonus tracks) probably represents them better than any single one of their dozen other albums.

Mudhoney

- *Superfuzz Bigmuff* (Sub Pop; SPCD 773) While any of the eight-plus albums by Mudhoney will rock you, this 2008 reissue of the band's grungy Sub Pop debut EP from 1988 includes many bonuses. The label's promotional text tells one everything you need to know about the now lengthy two-disc, thirty-two-track, set: "This is the deluxe, re-mastered edition of *Superfuzz Bigmuff*, containing the original EP in its correct running order, singles, demos, and two blistering live recordings from 1988, all re-mastered, or in some cases, mastered for the first time."

Pearl Jam

- *rearviewmirror: greatest hits 1991–2003* (Epic; E2K 93535) This two-disc, thirty-three-song set is a good encapsulation of the band's career. And although the 2004 set includes a couple of remixes of early hits, its offerings do seem to include the prime creations of Pearl Jam—and it *might* even save one from having to shell out the bucks to acquire copies of their eight studio albums, not to mention their unquantifiable (okay: 258-plus at last count) ongoing series of "official bootleg" live discs issued since 2000.

Mad Season

- *Above* (Columbia; CK 67057) Although this sole album by the short-lived "supergroup" (comprised of members of Pearl Jam, Alice in Chains, and the Screaming Trees) yielded only two charting hits in 1995—"River of Deceit" (No. 2) and "I Don't Know Anything" (No. 20)—*any* of the starkly beautiful songs on this half-million-selling classic could have done well on the radio.

Nirvana

- *Bleach* (Sub Pop; SP34b) In the months following the June 15, 1989, release of this LP, Nirvana was still a little secret that a mere thirty thousand of us initial buyers shared. But, Nirvana's talents were too great to hide from the world, and in the wake of 1991's *Nevermind* breakthrough, *Bleach* hit the *Billboard* charts in 1992 and went on to enjoy sales surpassing the one-million mark.
- *Nevermind* (DGC; DGCD-24425) *What?!* You don't *already* have this multi-platinum-selling masterpiece on your iPod? Sorry, then, I just don't think anyone can help you.

COMPILATION DISCS

- *Love That Louie* (Ace Records; ADCHD 844) A remarkable disc featuring twenty-four tracks—each of them "Louie Louie"–related. From songs that may have inspired Richard Berry to pen the original, to just about every worthwhile rock 'n' roll version of the tune, many of the Northwest's "Louie" knockoffs, and more! A beautiful booklet, with great graphics and detailed notes by Alec Palao.
- *Northwest Killers: Vols. 1, 2, 3* (Norton; NW 906 / NW 907 / NW 908) A compilation series with the sequential titles of *Stomp!*, *Shout!*, and *Work It On Out!*—these three discs represent some of the finest (mostly previously unreleased) tunes dug out from the vaults of Kearney Barton's

Audio Recording studios. Timeless Northwest '60s garage rock—including the Legends' "Louie Come Back" and the Nomads' "Louie Louie"—with fun radio spots for Audio as bonus tracks.

- *The Grunge Years* (Sub Pop; 112b) This thirteen-track set from 1991 highlights the early days of Sub Pop and the then-emerging sound of grunge. Memorable tunes include Nirvana's "Dive," TAD's "Stumblin' Man," the Screaming Trees' "Changing Man," and Mudhoney's "Come to Mind."

- *Wild and Wooly: The Northwest Rock Collection* (Experience Music Project; EMPCD001) The most ambitious and expansive overview compilation set ever: forty-seven tracks ranging from Seattle's first-ever rock 45 (Joe Boot and the Fabulous Winds' 1958 milestone, "Rock and Roll Radio"), through the "Louie Louie" days, the psychedelic '60s, '70s punk, '80s new wave and heavy metal, '90s grunge and Riot Grrls era, and beyond. Clayton Watson and the Silhouettes, the Frantics, the Wailers, the Ventures, the Dynamics, the Viceroys, the Kingsmen, the Counts, the Raiders, Merrilee Rush, the Sonics, Heart, the U-Men, the Wipers, Queensrÿche, Green River, the Screaming Trees, the Fastbacks, Soundgarden, Mudhoney, the Mono Men, Nirvana, Pond, Pearl Jam, the Presidents, Sleater-Kinney, Modest Mouse, and more—they're *all* here. Deluxe booklet, tons of photos, notes by Peter Blecha.

INDEX